viva la repartee

Also by Dr. Mardy Grothe

★ ★ ★ ★ ★ ★ ★ ★ ★ ★ ★

Oxymoronica

Never Let a Fool Kiss You or a Kiss Fool You

viva la repartee

Clever Comebacks and Witty Retorts
from History's Great Wits & Wordsmiths

Dr. Mardy Grothe

Collins

An Imprint of HarperCollinsPublishers

* * * * * * * * * * *

HarperCollins books may be purchased for educational, business, or
sales promotional use. For information, please write: Special Markets Department,
HarperCollins Publishers, 10 East 53rd Street, New York, NY 10022.

FIRST EDITION

Designed by Lorie Pagnozzi

Library of Congress Cataloging-in-Publication Data

Grothe, Mardy.
    Viva la repartee: clever comebacks and witty retorts from history's great wits &
wordsmiths/Mardy Grothe.—1st ed.
        p.   cm.
    ISBN-10: 0-06-078948-4
    ISBN-13: 978-0-06-078948-0
    1. Quotations, English.   2. Wit and humor.   3. Invective—Humor.   I. Title.

PN6084.H8G76   2005
082'.02'07—dc22   2005045586

09 WBC/RRD 10 9

TO RUTH BELT ROBINSON,
tireless advocate and inspiring role model

* * * * * *

contents

introduction

Since the beginning of civilization, people have been regaling one another with tales of clever comebacks and witty replies. The stories—almost always told with a tone of admiration—pay homage to great wit, especially when that wit is exhibited under pressure. Two classic yarns feature Winston Churchill.

The first involves Nancy Astor, an American socialite who married into an English branch of the wealthy Astor family (she holds the distinction of being the first woman elected to Parliament). At a 1912 dinner party in Blenheim Palace—the Churchill family estate—Lady Astor became annoyed at an inebriated Churchill, who was pontificating on some topic. Unable to take any more, she finally blurted out, "Winston, if you were my husband, I'd put poison in your coffee." Without missing a beat, Churchill replied:

Nancy, if you were my wife, I'd drink it.

The second story also involves a London party and a female member of Parliament (M.P.), and once again a slightly inebriated Churchill. This time, it was Bessie Braddock, a socialist M.P. from Liverpool, who finally had enough. She reproached Churchill by charging, "Winston, you're drunk!" The Grand Old Man may have had one too many drinks, but he still had his wits about him, replying:

You're right, Bessie. And you're ugly.
But tomorrow morning, I'll be sober.

Most people couldn't come up with better comebacks if they had a month to think about it. But Churchill was able to compose *and* deliver his words almost instantaneously. A truly great reply that defeats—or deflates—an opponent is called a *retort*, which the *Oxford English Dictionary* (*OED*) defines this way:

> *A sharp or incisive reply, especially one by which the first speaker's statement or argument is in some way turned against himself.*

The word *retort*, which first appears in English in 1557, derives from the Latin word *retortus*, meaning "to turn back." And this, of course, is exactly what a perfectly executed retort does: it turns back a personal attack, transforming a momentary threat into a personal triumph.

Retorts do not occur in a vacuum, but in social interaction, and usually in response to some kind of critical remark. In a pressure-filled situation like this, some exceptional individuals are able to remain calm. But even more important, they're somehow able to use their wit and their verbal skills to formulate a reply that turns the tables on the aggressor. When most of us regular people are thrust into a similar situation, we don't perform nearly so well. Many of us crumble, or become tongue-tied. Or we just blurt out some expletive or other unsatisfying remark. Yes, we may eventually come up with a great reply, but it usually comes to our mind far too late, well after it was needed. The all-too-common phenomenon is captured by a wonderful French expression: *l'esprit de l'escalier* ("the wit of the staircase").

The concept of *staircase wit*, authored by the French writer Denis Diderot, refers to those devastatingly clever remarks that we're unable to produce when they're needed, but come to mind with perfect clarity moments later, as we're walking down the staircase and heading out the door. There is no similar expression in English, but the Germans have long had their own word for it: *Treppenwitz* (also "staircase wit"). The writer Heywood Broun certainly had this phenomenon in mind when he wrote: "Repartee is what you wish you'd said."

While most of history's great retorts are spread by admiring fans, some are told by the authors themselves, eager to share their moments of brilliance. Truman Capote was fond of regaling people with an anecdote about one of his finer moments. At the height of his popularity, he was drinking one evening with friends in a crowded Key West bar. Nearby sat a couple, both inebriated. The woman recognized Capote, walked over to his table, and gushingly asked him to autograph a paper napkin. The woman's husband, angry at his wife's display of interest in another man, staggered over to Capote's table and assumed an intimidating position directly in front of the diminutive writer. He then proceeded to unzip his trousers and, in Capote's own words, "hauled out his equipment." As he did this, he bellowed in a drunken slur, "Since you're autographing things, why don't you autograph this?" It was a tense moment, and a hush fell over the room. The silence was a blessing, for it allowed all those within earshot to hear Capote's soft, high-pitched voice deliver the perfect emasculating reply:

**I don't know if I can autograph it,
but perhaps I can initial it.**

A retort is a verbal counterpunch against someone who's taken the first shot. No matter how knee-buckling the first blow, an exceptional retort can turn a match around, and even knock out an opponent. Perhaps *the* classic example in the history of wit is the story of a famous exchange between two eighteenth-century political rivals, John Montagu, also known as the Fourth Earl of Sandwich, and the reformist politician, John Wilkes. During a heated argument, Montagu scowled at Wilkes and said derisively, "Upon my soul, Wilkes, I don't know whether you'll die upon the gallows, or of syphilis" (some versions of the story say "a vile disease" and others "the pox"). Unfazed, Wilkes came back with what many people regard as the greatest retort of all time:

**That will depend, my Lord, on whether
I embrace your principles, or your mistress.**

It's almost impossible to think about the word *retort* without thinking of another word we've borrowed from the French: *repartee*. The *OED* defines it this way:

1. *A ready, witty, or smart reply; a quick and clever retort.*

2. *Sharpness or wit in sudden reply; such replies collectively; the practice or faculty of uttering them.*

Repartee derives from a seventeenth-century French word *repartie*, meaning "an answering blow or thrust." Originally a fencing term, *repartie* itself comes from another French word meaning "to reply promptly." By the 1700s, when the word began to become popular in English, the preferred pronunciation was reh-par-TEE, but over the years more and more English speakers began to say reh-par-TAY (probably influenced by other French borrowings like *fiancée* and *negligee*). While both pronunciations are considered acceptable, I prefer the "TAY" version.

The word *repartee* often conjures up an interaction marked by the quick exchange of sharp and witty remarks. And when it comes to repartee, nobody did it better than the members of that legendary collection of wits known as the Algonquin Round Table (more on them in a later chapter). For many decades, a delightful story has been told about one member of the group, playwright Marc Connelly. One evening, Connelly was dining with friends when another member of the group snuck up from behind, placed his hands on top of Connelly's bald head, and said to the amusement of the other guests, "Marc, your head feels as smooth as my wife's ass." Connelly instantly raised his hands to his head, began rubbing his own scalp, and with a wry smile, said:

So it does, so it does.

While the word *retort* suggests the notion of putting adversaries and opponents in their place, *repartee* is a broader term that refers to clever or witty remarks in almost any social situation. Repartee stories have been around for centuries.

In the first century A.D., the Greek writer Plutarch wrote *Parallel Lives,* a book recounting the heroic deeds and exemplary characters of major figures in Greek and Roman history. While most of the stories celebrated the exploits of ancient heroes, Plutarch also provided revealing little anecdotes about their private lives. One charming story involved a Greek nobleman named Antigonus. Informed by a messenger that his adult son Demetrius was ill, Antigonus decided to pay him a visit. Arriving at the front door of his son's house, the concerned father ran head-on into a beautiful young woman, who brushed quickly by as she was leaving. Slightly puzzled, Antigonus went straight to the bedroom and began ministering to his son. As he placed his hand on his son's forehead, he asked, "How are you feeling?" The son looked up weakly and said in a soft voice, "The fever has just left me, I think." Antigonus replied knowingly:

Yes, I know.
I met it going out the door.

As centuries passed, stories of great replies were passed on by many writers. In the sixteenth century, the French writer Michel Eyquem de Montaigne gave birth to a whole new literary form, the essay. In one of his famous pieces, he wrote admiringly:

Diogenes was asked what wine he liked best;
and he answered as I would have:
Somebody else's.

In the mid-1700s, Voltaire was invited by friends to attend an orgy in Paris. Having never participated in such an event, but always open to new experiences, he eagerly accepted the invitation. The next day, as the group rehashed the previous night's activities, the intellectually curious philosopher reported that he had learned many new things and had greatly enjoyed the experience. Happy to learn that they might have converted the great philosopher to their hedonistic ways, the group invited him to join them again later that evening. Voltaire graciously declined by offering a bon mot that only served to enhance his reputation as a great wit and wordsmith:

**Ah no, my good friends,
once a philosopher,
twice a pervert.**

Bon mot (pronounced bohn-MOH, with the first syllable short and clipped) is yet another locution we have borrowed from the French. The *OED* defines it this way: "A clever or witty saying; a witticism; repartee." Literally meaning "good saying," the term has been used in English since the early 1700s to describe a clever reply or witty remark. The members of the Algonquin Round Table, who often used the expression to describe their witticisms, were largely responsible for popularizing the term in America. The plural is bon mots (bohn-MOHZ).

It's almost impossible to have a conversation about retort and repartee without hearing anecdotes involving some of the most familiar names in the history of wit: Winston Churchill, W. C. Fields, Groucho Marx, Dorothy Parker, George Bernard Shaw, Mark Twain, Mae West, and, of course, Oscar Wilde. But it would be a mistake to assume that great wits are the only people who've authored truly great replies. Indeed, some of history's most clever rejoinders have come from people not normally associated with great wit.

The thirtieth U.S. president, Calvin Coolidge, was well known as a man of few words, but he also cultivated a somewhat dour persona (he once said, "I think the American public wants a solemn ass as a president and I think I'll go along with them"). One evening during the Coolidge administration, a noted opera singer was invited to the White House for an after-dinner recital. These "command performances" can be daunting, and this particular evening things did not go well. The singer got a case of the nerves and gave a perfectly dreadful recital. The guests did their best to conceal their true reactions, giving the diva a polite round of applause at the end. During the performance, however, one of the guests leaned over and whispered in President Coolidge's ear, "What do you think of the singer's execution?" He whispered back:

I'm all for it.

Another figure rarely associated with witticisms is Mohandas Gandhi. In the decades prior to World War II, the Mahatma led a massive campaign of civil disobedience designed to help colonial India win its independence from the British Empire. In 1931, shortly after being named *Time* magazine's "Man of the Year," Gandhi traveled to London to meet with British authorities. The entire nation was curious to learn more about this "little brown man," as many called him. Constantly swarmed by press and photographers, Gandhi was peppered with questions wherever he went. One day a reporter yelled out, "What do you think of Western civilization?" It was a defining moment, and Gandhi's reply instantly transformed him from an object of curiosity into a celebrity. In his heavy Indian accent, he answered:

I think it would be a good idea.

Happily, clever and creative replies aren't a thing of the past, and great new ones are constantly being added to this wonderful oral tradition. One of my favorites was authored by the talented Dolly Parton, whose many assets include a marvelous sense of humor and a very quick mind. A few years ago, her answer to an interviewer's question was so widely circulated it became a part of pop culture. When asked, "How long does it take to have your hair done?" she replied:

I don't know.
I'm not there when my hair is done.

Parton and her associates were so pleased with the remark that it eventually found its way into one of the "talking" exhibits in her Dollywood theme park.

Another example comes from the singer and actress Jennifer Lopez, another entertainer with a sharp mind and a quick wit. Several years ago, when asked what she got on her SATs, she cleverly dodged the question by answering:

Nail polish.

One further recent example occurred in 1997, a couple of years after Christopher Reeve's devastating equestrian accident in 1995. Appearing before an adoring audience on Bravo TV's *Inside the Actors Studio*, Reeve was asked by host James Lipton what it was like to have acted with Katharine Hepburn. He delighted the audience with his answer:

People say I acted with Katharine Hepburn.
The truth is I acted *near* Katharine Hepburn.

While repartee is often viewed as a method of putting people down, Reeve's reply proves that great replies can also honor people. Such examples of what I've been calling *uplifting repartee* combine cleverness with warmheartedness and generosity of spirit—and we end up feeling a little better for having heard them. I can still remember the tingle I felt when I first heard Thomas Jefferson's famous remark after being named America's second ambassador to France.

Benjamin Franklin was America's first ambassador to France. Even though he was in his seventies, he quickly learned the language and, with his colorful personality and engaging manner, took the country by storm (French women began to adopt a hairstyle imitating his beaver caps and the press often referred to him as *l'ambassadeur électrique*). Arriving in Paris in 1785, Jefferson formally presented his papers to the country's foreign minister. When the French official said, "So you are to replace Dr. Franklin?" Jefferson replied:

I succeed Dr. Franklin. No one can replace him.

Jefferson's reply illustrates another fascinating aspect of great replies—the very best become deeply embedded in our collective consciousness. These days, at retirement ceremonies all around the globe, it's now commonplace for new replacements to cite Jefferson's remark when making comments about the people who are stepping down.

Witty repartee is not the sole province of great wits, celebrities, or historical figures. Indeed, some of the most impressive contributions come from anonymous sources. An exceptional example occurred on an Eastern Airlines flight Muhammad Ali was taking back in the 1970s. As the flight attendant made her final check of the passengers, she noticed that Ali's seat belt was not fastened. When the Champ was asked to buckle up, the ever-playful boxing legend brought a smile to the faces of his fellow travelers by boasting, "Superman don't need no seat belt." The day was won by the quick-thinking flight attendant, however, who got a hearty round of applause when she shot back:

Superman don't need no airplane either.

The most celebrated replies in history tend to be short and pithy. Indeed, as you shall see in Chapter Three, "Laconic Repartee," some of the very best contain only one or two words. Every now and then, though, a great long-winded reply comes along. And one of the all-time greats comes from another member of the Algonquin Round Table: the writer and wit George S. Kaufman.

In the early 1950s, Kaufman was a guest panelist on the CBS television show *This Is Show Business*. The format of the show called for host Clifton Fadiman to introduce and briefly interview a celebrity guest. As the show progressed, the guest would reveal a problem and seek "advice" from a celebrity panel. One evening, the guest was Eddie Fisher, a handsome young "bobby sox" idol who was exploding on the music scene (in a few years he would go on to marry Debbie Reynolds, become a major film star, have a daughter named Carrie Fisher, and leave Reynolds for Elizabeth Taylor). Fisher's "problem" that evening was that a beautiful chorus girl was rebuffing his advances on the grounds that he was too young for her. When it came time for the panelists to offer advice, Kaufman said, "Mr. Fisher, on Mount Wilson there is a telescope that can magnify the most distant stars up to twenty-four times the magnification of any previous telescope. This remarkable instrument was unsurpassed in the world of astronomy until the development and construction of the Mount Palomar telescope—an even more remarkable instrument of magnification. Owing to advances and improvements in optical technology, it is capable of magnifying the stars to four times the magnification and resolution of the Mount Wilson telescope." At this point, Kaufman paused and the camera panned to the puzzled faces of the guest and the other panelists. Looks of puzzlement turned to gales of laughter when Kaufman concluded:

**Mr. Fisher, if you could somehow put
the Mount Wilson telescope *inside* the Mount Palomar telescope,
you still wouldn't be able to detect my interest in your problem.**

Even though I've been fascinated by clever comebacks and witty replies for many decades, I was surprised to discover that a comprehensive collection of these verbal gems has never been published. While there have been dozens of books on put-downs, insults, barbs, and zingers, these books have only occasionally included retorts and rejoinders. And while there have been a number of smaller books along the theme of "I Wish I'd Said That," no major publisher has ever brought forth a book that does justice to this extremely interesting subject.

Viva la Repartee is my attempt to fill that void. *Viva* is a venerable Italian and Spanish expression of acclaim, generally translated as "long live" (the related French word is *vive*). Both *viva* and *vive* have been successfully adopted into our language, but English speakers generally find that *viva* rolls off the tongue a bit easier than the French equivalent. So, by performing a cross-cultural marriage of *viva* with the lovely French word *repartee*, this book is my attempt to celebrate the most impressive retorts, ripostes, rejoinders, comebacks, quips, ad-libs, off-the-cuff comments, wisecracks, bon mots, and other clever remarks to come out of the mouths—and the brains—of people throughout history.

In this Introduction, I've tried to introduce the concept and whet your interest. The rest of the book will be organized into chapters like "Literary Repartee," "Political Repartee," "Sports Repartee," and, for you readers interested in the saucier side of things, a final chapter on "Risqué Repartee." In each chapter, I'll write a few introductory words and then present several dozen anecdotes that fit within the theme of that chapter. The entries in each chapter are presented alphabetically by author. You will also find an index of names at the end of the book, which will identify the authors *and* the recipients of the replies to be found in these pages.

In the remainder of the book, you'll undoubtedly find some of your favorite quips and comebacks, but you can also expect to discover many new ones—some of which appear in print here for the first time. While every bon mot may be considered a *quotation*, this is not a book of quotations. This is an anthology of *anecdotes*, each one chronicling a memorable reply.

With quotations, great care is generally taken to ensure the accuracy of the quote. With anecdotes, however, this can often be difficult. Anecdotes, after all, are *stories*. And as we know from the long oral tradition of storytelling, two observers to the same event will often tell wildly varying stories about it.

Another thing we know about anecdotes is that many are clearly fabricated. The inventors of these stories have usually dreamed up a great reply on their own and then concocted a story—often one involving a famous figure—to give their creation an air of *verisimilitude* (meaning "an appearance of being true"). An example is a story involving the famous American lexicographer, Noah Webster. According to the tale, Webster was once engaged in some hanky-panky with the chambermaid when his wife opened the door to his study and found the couple in a compromising position. "Noah! I'm surprised!" she exclaimed. Webster, a stickler for the proper use of words, was said to have replied:

No, my dear. I am surprised. You are astonished.

The humorous point of the story, of course, is that Webster chose a rather inappropriate moment to quibble about usage and the precise definitions of the words *surprise* and *astonish*.

Over the centuries, people have invented thousands of similar stories, and then attributed them to the famous people of their era (a version of the Webster story was being told about Dr. Samuel Johnson a century earlier). The term for stories like this is *apocryphal* (uh-POCK-ruh-fuhl), a word that derives from the world of biblical scholarship. Specifically, the *Apocrypha* refers to a number of documents written around the same time as many other Old Testament books, but which are not generally accepted as divinely inspired. In popular usage, *apocryphal* means "of dubious or questionable authenticity; invented." Many of the anecdotes found in these pages could be described in this way.

As you delve into the book, you will find that almost every entry consists of a "setup" portion, in which the author of the reply is identified and some other background or contextual information is provided. Advance readers have said that their reading experience was greatly enhanced when they kept the replies hidden from view and tried to imagine what they might have said in a similar situation. Go ahead and give it a try with the entry below:

> John F. Kennedy was far more likely to be the author than the recipient of a clever comeback, but he was once bested by a White House visitor. In 1961, JFK wrote an open letter to the CEOs of twelve major American steel companies, warning them of inflationary trends in the economy and pleading with them to postpone price increases. In early 1962, however, many of the companies announced plans to increase prices. An angry JFK responded, "My father always told me all businessmen are sons-of-bitches, but I never believed it until now." In retaliation, Kennedy threatened an antitrust investigation of the steel industry, causing the companies to back down. After the confrontation, JFK's stature in the business community plummeted, as many complained that he was hostile to business interests. Hoping to improve relations, the president invited a group of business leaders to the White House. At the meeting, Kennedy tried to demonstrate that he was bullish on the American economy, saying, "Things look great. Why, if I weren't president, I'd buy stock myself." One outspoken—and witty—executive replied:

"_____."

Think about how you might have responded. And remember, you have the luxury of time to formulate a reply, while the executive responded immediately. The business leader's actual reply was: "If you weren't president, so would I."

As you journey through the book, occasionally try formulating your own reply before looking at what was actually said. If you do, I predict that you will often struggle to come up with a clever reply. I'm also certain it will heighten your admiration for the remarks that were actually delivered.

As I was doing the research for the entries in this book, I came across a wealth of incidental information that I found fascinating. It happened so often that, even though I was ostensibly doing a book on the subject of repartee, the extent of my general knowledge—not to mention my knowledge of trivia—was skyrocketing. I couldn't resist including some of that material for your enjoyment as well.

The replies to be celebrated in these pages have come from innumerable sources: biographies and autobiographies, books of anecdotes, quotation anthologies, newspaper and magazine articles, movies, television programs, and of course, Web sites. Many of the most popular replies have been described scores of times, some have been documented only once or twice (often in quite obscure sources), and some appear here for the first time. The whole subject brings to mind an anecdote that includes—what else?—a great reply.

Before he became president of Columbia University in 1901—a post he held for 44 years—Nicholas Murray Butler was a young professional trying to establish a name for himself by the writing of books. One day he was talking with friend—and fellow writer—James Brander Matthews about original writing versus borrowing from others. It was a subject Matthews had thought much about and he offered his views on the subject: "In the case of the first man to use an anecdote, there is originality; in the case of the second, there is plagiarism; with the third, it is lack of originality; and with the fourth, it is drawing from a common stock. . . ." Before Matthews could get any further, Butler interrupted:

Yes, and in the case of the fifth, it is research.

With a tip of the hat to Dr. Butler, it is fair to say that most of the entries in this book come from my own reading and research. But a few years back I also began routinely asking people to tell me about their favorite comebacks and retorts. Almost every person I've met has a favorite story, and many people have more than one. (I can't tell you how many times I've heard the two Churchill stories mentioned at the beginning of this Introduction). I've also been assisted by scores of members of my informal Repartee Research Group, all of whom are subscribers to a weekly newsletter (*Dr. Mardy's Quotes of the Week*) that I send out via e-mail every Sunday morning to subscribers all around the globe. My heartfelt thanks to all those who have helped.

While I've been aided by the efforts of many people, I take sole responsibility for any errors or mistakes to be found in these pages. If you discover any, or if you simply want to offer some feedback, you can contact me at: DrMGrothe@aol.com

Also feel free to pass along any examples of repartee that are not included here. I've also launched a Web site where you can delve a bit more deeply into the subject: www.vivalarepartee.com. Come up and visit sometime.

Viva la repartee!

classic retorts,
ripostes, & rejoinders

After the opening performance of *Arms and the Man* in London in 1894, playwright George Bernard Shaw joined the actors on stage to acknowledge a rousing, appreciative ovation. Amidst the sustained applause, a solitary voice cried out: "Boo! Boo!" Shaw looked in the direction of the voice and said:

> **I quite agree with you, my friend,**
> **but what can we two do against**
> **a whole houseful of the opposite opinion?**

Shaw's reply enthralled the audience and helped cement his reputation as a great wit. One of the most talented playwrights of all time, he proved in that moment that he was as skilled in the art of extemporaneous repartee as he was at the craft of witty dialogue for the characters in his plays.

A similar story is told about the reception Oscar Wilde received after one of his plays. After an extended period of warm applause, during which the author was presented with a number of floral bouquets from admiring fans, one disgruntled person in the audience threw a rotten cabbage at the playwright. Wilde simply leaned over, picked up the foul-smelling vegetable, and coolly replied:

Thank you, my dear fellow.
Every time I smell it,
I shall be reminded of you.

Both stories illustrate a familiar phenomenon. Someone hurls an insult or makes a critical remark. In that moment, the recipient of the attack is placed in what sociologists call a "one-down" position. Onlookers to such an interaction often describe a slight feeling of apprehension, as they try to imagine how the drama will unfold. Sometimes, the person being attacked descends to the level of the aggressor, goes on a counterattack, and everything goes downhill. Every now and then, though, the targets are able to come up with a few clever words that turn the tables on their opponents. Replies like this are called *retorts*, as we saw that term defined in the Introduction:

> *A sharp or incisive reply, especially one by which the first speaker's statement or argument is in some way turned against himself.*

In the language of repartee, though, the Shaw and Wilde comebacks could also be described by two other words: *riposte* and *rejoinder*.

The *OED* defines *riposte* (pronounced ruh-POST) this way: "To reply or to retaliate; to answer." The word comes from the Italian *risposta*, meaning "to answer, reply." The term was originally used in the sport of fencing, where it described a quick retaliatory thrust that is given after parrying an opponent's lunge. In the mid-1800s, the word was extended to the arena of human interaction, where it began to be used to describe an effective verbal reply. Today *riposte* is virtually synonymous with *retort*, both words describing a quick and sharp response to an insult or attack. Historically used mainly as a noun, in recent years it has also begun to be used as a verb, "to deliver a riposte" (as in "He riposted.").

Rejoinder is another term that has become virtually synonymous with *retort* and *riposte*. The best current definition appears in the *Oxford American Dictionary* (OAD), which says, "Something said in answer or retort." The word comes from a fifteenth-century French legal term, *rejoindre*, meaning "to answer to a legal charge." A few centuries ago, the word became a part of popular usage when it began to be used to describe a sharp and quick reply. While *rejoinder* is a commonly used noun, the verb *rejoin* (meaning "to say in reply") is rarely used. When people deliver a rejoinder, though, it is technically correct to say that they *rejoined*, and not that they *rejoindered*.

Admiring stories about great retorts have been told from the very beginning of civilization. In the fifth century B.C., the aging Greek leader Pericles was engaged in a heated debate with his nephew Alcibiades over how Athens should be governed. The frustrated Pericles finally played the Age Card. "When I was your age, Alcibiades," he charged condescendingly, "I talked just the way you are now talking." Alcibiades' reply stands as a model for all young people who've been similarly put down by a smug elder:

**If only I had known you, Pericles,
when you were at your best.**

While the ability to forge clever replies has always been useful in dealing with adversaries and opponents, it has proved invaluable in dealing with *friends*—especially when friends engage in the time-honored tradition of expressing their affection in a form of ritualized insult behavior. There are many words for this phenomenon: banter, razzing, kidding, jesting, ribbing, raillery, roasting, busting chops, and, of course, busting balls. Another word to describe this intriguing form of human interaction is *badinage* (BAD-uh-nazh), which the *OED* defines as "light trifling raillery or humorous banter."

The word derives from the French *badin,* meaning "joker," and the phenomenon shows up mainly in the good-natured teasing and playful banter that people—especially men—engage in with one another. The word, which first appeared in English in 1658, shows up in an intriguing passage in Benjamin Disraeli's 1880 novel *Endymion*: "Men destined to the highest places should beware of badinage."

While *badinage* is not a particularly well-known word, the phenomenon is very common. We saw an example in the previous chapter when Marc Connelly's friend ribbed him about his bald head. I also recall an episode of

Frasier in 1997 in which Niles, with his pet parrot on his shoulder, greets his brother at the door. When Frasier says, "Good evening, Niles. Or should I say, 'Avast ye, matey!'" Niles brushes aside the remark by saying, "I don't have time for your badinage." Surprised at hearing the word used in a TV sitcom, I recall saying to my wife, Katherine, "Honey, there are twenty million people watching this program tonight and maybe only a handful of people know what he just said."

A classic badinage anecdote has been told for more than a century about Hermann Adler, the chief rabbi of London, and Herbert Vaughan, the Roman Catholic cardinal and archbishop of Westminster. At an official luncheon one day, Vaughan looked over at his Jewish colleague and said, "Dr. Adler, when may I have the pleasure of helping you to a slice of this most excellent ham?" Guests at the luncheon, aware of the Jewish prohibition about eating pork, were startled at what seemed like a lapse of sensitivity. Adler knew exactly what his colleague was up to, however, and brought gales of laughter to the relieved guests when he replied:

How about at Your Eminence's wedding?

Another wonderful example showed up at a Manhattan party in the 1930s, attended by George Gershwin, Oscar Levant, and a number of musicians and show business personalities. Levant and Gershwin, good friends as well as musical colleagues, often engaged in friendly banter with one another. This particular evening, Levant said, "George, if you had to do it all over, would you fall in love with yourself again?" Even though everybody knew Levant was teasing, they waited eagerly to see how Gershwin would respond. The great songwriter ignored the remark and rejoined with a playful insult of his own:

Oscar, why don't you play us a medley of your hit?

Whether they come from friends or enemies, insults and barbs have always been best dealt with by witty replies. And some of the best replies have achieved a kind of exalted, or classic, status. Let's examine more replies that may be so designated.

⚹ ⚹ ⚹ ⚹ ⚹ ⚹ ⚹ ⚹ ⚹ ⚹ ⚹

After the death of England's Protestant King Charles II in 1685, his Roman Catholic brother James II assumed the throne. Charles II's son was James Scott, the Duke of Monmouth, who soon led an unsuccessful rebellion (called "Monmouth's Rebellion") against James II. The insurrection was short-lived and the rebels were quickly brought to trial before Chief Justice George Jeffreys, so notorious for his cruelty he was called "Hanging Judge Jeffreys." At the trial, the judge stuck his cane in the chest of one of the rebels, charging, "There is a rogue at the end of my cane!" The insolent defendant, even though facing death on the gallows, still had his wits about him, replying:

At which end, my Lord?

⚹ ⚹ ⚹ ⚹ ⚹ ⚹ ⚹ ⚹ ⚹ ⚹ ⚹

In the late 1700s, the beautiful Sophie Arnould was lighting up the French stage, both as an actress and as an opera singer. A free spirit, Arnould frequented the salons of Paris, where she often stole the hearts of male admirers, many of whom became her lovers. The winds of revolution were beginning to blow in France as well as in America, and French authorities often found it hard to distinguish between political intrigue and amorous activities. One evening, Arnould was visited by a suspicious police lieutenant, who demanded the names of several high-ranking dinner guests she had entertained earlier that evening. The discreet Arnould said, "I'm sorry, lieutenant, but I can remember none of their names." The incredulous police officer sneered, "But a woman like you ought to remember things like that." Arnould replied:

Of course, lieutenant, but with a man like you, I am not a woman like me.

★ ★ ★ ★ ★ ★ ★ ★ ★ ★

Lady Margot Asquith, the wife of English prime minister Herbert Asquith, was no demure politician's wife. A vivacious and witty woman, she authored some of the most delicious barbs in English history, saying of David Lloyd George, "He could not see a belt without hitting below it," and of English barrister, F. E. Smith (also known as Lord Birkenhead), "Lord Birkenhead is very clever but sometimes his brains go to his head." She was also the recipient of a famous zinger, when Dorothy Parker said of her autobiography, "The affair between Margot Asquith and Margot Asquith will live as one of the prettiest love stories in all literature." When Lady Asquith was introduced to Jean Harlow, the brassy American actress persisted in mispronouncing her first name as MAR-gut, as if it rhymed with "harlot." It was a not-so-subtle put-down, and Lady Asquith could easily have taken offense. Instead, she crafted one of history's most famous ripostes, sweetly replying:

My dear, the *t* is silent, as in Harlow.

★ ★ ★ ★ ★ ★ ★ ★ ★ ★

In the years before the Civil War, Brooklyn preacher Henry Ward Beecher was an outspoken abolitionist. As the war got under way, he logged many miles speaking in favor of the Emancipation Proclamation and against the Confederacy. He even made a famous trip to England to drum up British support for the Union cause. While speaking in Manchester, however, he encountered a hostile crowd of Englishmen, many of whom supported the South. One heckler yelled out, "Why didn't you whip the Confederates in sixty days, as you said you would?" Beecher, who knew the Revolutionary War was still a sensitive topic for many Britishers, hesitated only briefly before replying:

**Because we found
we had Americans to fight this time,
not Englishmen.**

✳ ✳ ✳ ✳ ✳ ✳ ✳ ✳ ✳ ✳ ✳ ✳

Lilian Braithwaite was a Shakespearean actress who also made many films in the early days of cinema. One day, she ran into drama critic James Agate at London's Savoy Grill. Agate, who had once said he considered Braithwaite the wittiest woman in London, said upon meeting her, "My dear Lilian, I have long wanted to tell you that, in my opinion, you are the second most beautiful woman in London." Agate was undoubtedly trying to lure the actress into an inquiry about whom he considered the most beautiful, for which he had almost certainly prepared a witty reply. But Braithwaite refused to take the bait. Instead, she proved she was indeed one of the wittiest women in London when she sweetly replied:

**Thank you so much, James.
I shall always cherish that,
coming from our second-best dramatic critic.**

✳ ✳ ✳ ✳ ✳ ✳ ✳ ✳ ✳ ✳ ✳ ✳

While she eventually became known as the Divine Sarah, the early stage efforts of the legendary actress Sarah Bernhardt were nothing special. However, the owner of the Odeon Theater, Felix Duquesnel, saw great potential in the young actress and decided to offer her a contract. There was one hitch, however. She had to be interviewed by his partner before the deal could be done. During the interview, Bernhardt did her best to impress, but she was turned off by the man's imperious and condescending style. Near the end of the interview, he sighed dismissively, "If I were alone in this, I wouldn't give you a contract." Bernhardt retorted:

**If you were alone in this, monsieur,
I wouldn't sign.**

✳ ✳ ✳ ✳ ✳ ✳ ✳ ✳ ✳ ✳ ✳ ✳

In the mid-1600s, Richard Busby was emerging as a giant figure in English society. A bookish man of very slight stature, he headed London's famed Westminster School, a training ground for the children of England's elite. One day, Busby was seated in a crowded London coffeehouse. An Irish nobleman of enormous girth and questionable manners entered the establishment and tried to get past the diminutive Busby, saying in a mocking tone, "May I pass to my seat, oh giant?" Busby rose from his chair, allowing the man through, and replied in turn, "Certainly, oh pygmy." When the Irishman noticed that the man he had mocked was the highly regarded Busby, he attempted a half-hearted apology. "My expression alluded to the size of your intellect," he offered lamely. Busby's reply has been celebrated for centuries:

And my expression to the size of yours.

✳ ✳ ✳ ✳ ✳ ✳ ✳ ✳ ✳ ✳ ✳

Although not especially well remembered today, Ilka Chase was a familiar name in the 1930s and '40s. A writer, actress, and radio celebrity, she starred in Broadway plays and Hollywood films, wrote numerous books, and hosted a number of popular radio shows. Soon after the publication of her 1942 autobiography *Past Imperfect*, she ran into an actor (some accounts say it was Humphrey Bogart) at a party. The actor congratulated Chase and said, "I thought your book was wonderful. I can't tell you how much I enjoyed it. By the way, who wrote it for you?" Chase delivered the perfect riposte:

I'm so glad you liked it.
By the way, who read it to you?

✳ ✳ ✳ ✳ ✳ ✳ ✳ ✳ ✳ ✳ ✳

While serving in Parliament early in his career, Winston Churchill dozed off as another member of the House of Commons delivered a long and rambling speech. Upset at the sight of a colleague sleeping during his speech, the enraged M.P.

interrupted his speech to say in a booming voice, "Mr. Churchill, must you fall asleep while I'm speaking?" Churchill, hardly moving a muscle, replied with his eyes still closed:

No, it's purely voluntary.

★ ★ ★ ★ ★ ★ ★ ★ ★ ★ ★

At a White House luncheon in 1943, Winston Churchill was challenged by Helen Reid, the sister of the anti-British owner of the *Chicago Tribune*. Referring to England's colonization of India, she attacked him and the British for their treatment of the Indians. It was a tense moment, but Churchill coolly responded:

Before we proceed further, let us get one thing clear.
Are we talking about the brown Indians of India,
who have multiplied . . . under benevolent English rule?
Or are we speaking of the red Indians in America who,
I understand, are almost extinct?

★ ★ ★ ★ ★ ★ ★ ★ ★ ★ ★

While serving in Congress in the early years of the nineteenth century, Henry Clay of Kentucky and John Randolph of Virginia became mortal enemies (they even fought a famous duel in 1826). One day the two men ran head-on into one another on a narrow Washington sidewalk. Randolph scowled at Clay and snapped, "I never sidestep skunks." Clay stepped aside and calmly replied:

I always do.

★ ★ ★ ★ ★ ★ ★ ★ ★ ★ ★

Noël Coward was one of the most versatile figures in show business history. A respected actor, dramatist, screenwriter, producer, director, and composer, he added novelist and poet to his resume in his later years. A witty and literate man, he wrote two extremely engaging autobiographies, *Present Indicative* in 1937 and *Future Indefinite* in 1954. In 1928, Coward delivered a sparkling performance in S. N. Behrman's play *The Second Man.* After the second night's show, Coward was in his dressing room when the *Daily Express* drama critic Hannen Swaffer barged into the room without knocking. Swaffer, who could be insufferable at times, inappropriately used Coward's nickname as he said in a mocking cockney accent, "Nowley, I've always said you could act better than you write." The actor Raymond Massey, who witnessed the interaction, chronicled the story and helped to immortalize Coward's retort:

And I've always said the same about you.

✶ ✶ ✶ ✶ ✶ ✶ ✶ ✶ ✶ ✶ ✶

Edna Ferber worked for a number of years as a news reporter in the Midwest before moving to New York City in 1912. After her novel *So Big* won the Pulitzer Prize in 1926, she quickly followed up with the hit play *Show Boat* (so successful and financially remunerative, she called it her "oil well"). Ferber was fond of wearing tailored suits well before they became fashionable. One day, she arrived at the Algonquin Hotel wearing a suit that was very similar to one that the English actor Noël Coward was wearing. Ferber and Coward were friends (she once described him as her favorite theater companion) and Coward saw an opportunity to engage in a bit of playful badinage with one of his favorite people. Carefully looking her over, he observed, "Edna, you look almost like a man." Ferber looked Coward over in a similar manner and came back with a classic riposte:

So do you.

✶ ✶ ✶ ✶ ✶ ✶ ✶ ✶ ✶ ✶ ✶

Margaret Fuller was one of America's first great female voices, a cofounder of *The Dial* with Ralph Waldo Emerson and a pioneer in the suffragist movement. In

1845, she joined the staff of Horace Greeley's *New York Tribune*, becoming America's first female newspaper correspondent and literary critic. Greeley's wife, Mary, was a woman of strongly held views—some of them quite strange—and for a time was actively involved in the era's equivalent of today's "animal rights" movement. Running into Fuller on a New York street one day, Mrs. Greeley noticed that Fuller was wearing kid gloves. In an indignant tone, she sneered, "Skin of a beast!" Maintaining her composure, Fuller calmly asked, "What gloves do you wear?" When Mrs. Greeley replied smugly, "Silk," Fuller observed with a tone of mock disgust:

Entrails of a worm!

✷ ✷ ✷ ✷ ✷ ✷ ✷ ✷ ✷ ✷ ✷

After serving in the Ambulance Service in World War I, Robert Hutchins returned home to earn a bachelor's and a law degree from Yale University. In 1929, in news that rocked the academic world, he was named president of the University of Chicago at only thirty years of age. He headed up the university until 1951, arousing controversy for many of his reforms (such as abandoning intercollegiate football and using comprehensive exams rather than classroom time to measure academic progress). During the McCarthy era, he aroused the ire of many conservatives by opposing loyalty oaths and vigorously defending academic freedom. At a news conference just after his retirement in 1951, a right-wing journalist asked with clear disdain, "Is Communism still being taught at the university?" Hutchins, who was used to loaded questions, was not about to be suckered into an answer that might be misconstrued. He replied calmly:

Yes, and cancer at the medical school.

✷ ✷ ✷ ✷ ✷ ✷ ✷ ✷ ✷ ✷ ✷

At a 1963 press conference, a reporter known for his conservative leanings said in a slightly confrontational style to John F. Kennedy, "The Republican National

Committee recently adopted a resolution saying you were pretty much of a failure. How do you feel about that?" Not about to be thrown off by the question, JFK simply smiled, shrugged, and to the delight of the rest of the press corps, said:

I assume it passed unanimously.

⋆ ⋆ ⋆ ⋆ ⋆ ⋆ ⋆ ⋆ ⋆ ⋆

Chef and restaurateur Peter Langan was a colorful figure in an industry known for larger-than-life characters. In 1979, he partnered with actor Michael Caine to open Langan's Brasserie in London. During the 1980s, it became "the" place to dine and to see celebrities (it's still going strong a quarter of a century later). Langan's eccentric behavior—often fueled by alcohol—attracted some customers and repelled others. Even Langan's detractors had to admit that he was responsible for some special moments. One night, he was confronted by an irate patron who, loudly and angrily, pointed at a cockroach in her food. It was a tense moment, and the eyes of all the customers were on the owner, wondering how he'd respond. He didn't disappoint, declaring:

Madam, it must have come from next door.
That cockroach is dead. All ours are alive.

Langan then added to his legend by grabbing the cockroach, throwing it in his mouth, and washing it down with a bottle of champagne that had been sitting on the table.

⋆ ⋆ ⋆ ⋆ ⋆ ⋆ ⋆ ⋆ ⋆ ⋆

Abraham Lincoln may have been one of the most unattractive presidents in American history, but there was still something special about his face. Walt Whitman once wrote of him: "He has a face like a Hoosier Michael Angelo, so awful ugly it becomes beautiful, with its strange mouth, its deep-cut, criss-cross lines, and its doughnut complexion." During a debate, Lincoln was once accused by perennial adversary Stephen Douglas of being two-faced. A master of self-deprecating humor, he turned to the audience and said:

**If I had two faces,
do you think I'd be wearing this one?**

✳ ✳ ✳ ✳ ✳ ✳ ✳ ✳ ✳ ✳

In the 1920s, Dorothy Parker was establishing a reputation as a witty woman with a sharp tongue (the actress Mrs. Patrick Campbell [stage name of actress Beatrice Campbell] called her "My pretty, pretty cobra"). At the same time, Clare Booth Luce was becoming a respected journalist and well-known playwright. While both women were highly talented, their numerous political, philosophical, and personal differences resulted in a strained relationship. One day, Parker was about to step through a doorway when she came face to face with Luce. As the story goes, Mrs. Luce stepped aside, extended the palm of her hand, and said coyly, "Age before beauty." Parker glided through the door, saying ever so sweetly:

Pearls before swine.

✳ ✳ ✳ ✳ ✳ ✳ ✳ ✳ ✳ ✳

Pablo Picasso, who continued to live in Paris during the German occupation of the city in World War II, was regarded as a Communist sympathizer and routinely harassed by Nazi authorities. One day, during an inspection of Picasso's Paris apartment, a Nazi officer paused to look at a photograph of Picasso's *Guernica*. Considered one of history's most passionate antiwar paintings, *Guernica* is a huge mural (over 25 feet in width) that depicts the complete destruction of the Spanish town of Guernica by German planes in 1937. Pointing at the photograph, the Nazi officer said brusquely, "Did you do that?" Picasso paused for only a second before replying:

No, you did.

★ ★ ★ ★ ★ ★ ★ ★ ★ ★

In the fourth century B.C., the Greek philosopher Diogenes was the leading proponent of a philosophical movement that advocated an almost total rejection of luxury. As he entered the home of Plato one day, Diogenes was disgusted by the sight of the opulence around him. With a smug air of superiority, he wiped his shoes on the costly carpet and said contemptuously, "Thus do I trample on the pride of Plato." Plato's rebuke was done mildly, but it couldn't have been more effective. He simply said:

With greater pride.

★ ★ ★ ★ ★ ★ ★ ★ ★ ★

The Renaissance artist known as Raphael (his full Italian name was Raffaello Sanzio) studied under both Leonardo da Vinci and Michelangelo, and was himself known as a master painter by his early twenties. In 1508, he was summoned by Pope Julius II to help decorate the Vatican. Over the next twelve years (until his premature death in 1520 at age thirty-seven), he painted some of the world's great masterpieces. The Renaissance may have been a high point in the history of civilization, but it was not a dazzling time in Vatican history, as the church became headed by some pretty disreputable characters (Julius himself fathered three illegitimate children before becoming pope and was informally called "Julius the Terrible" for his bad temper and propensity to whack subordinates with a cane). One day, while working on a fresco, Raphael was the recipient of some unsolicited—and ill-informed—criticism from a band of cardinals. When one complained, "The face of the apostle Paul is far too red," the painter showed both courage and wit by replying:

He blushes to see into whose hand the church has fallen.

★ ★ ★ ★ ★ ★ ★ ★ ★ ★ ★

In 1910, former president Theodore Roosevelt was asked by President William Howard Taft to interrupt his big-game hunting trip to Africa to represent America at the funeral of the recently deceased English king, Edward VII. While in London, Roosevelt ran into the German emperor, Wilhelm II. A year earlier, the two men had both been heads of state. In an attempt to be gracious, the German kaiser invited Roosevelt to call on him the next day, but he stressed, "Be there at two o'clock sharp, for I can only give you forty-five minutes." Roosevelt may have been a former president, but he wasn't about to let the German emperor pull rank on him. Equally graciously, he replied:

**I will be there at two o'clock sharp,
but unfortunately I have just twenty minutes to give you.**

★ ★ ★ ★ ★ ★ ★ ★ ★ ★ ★

The author of some of the most influential plays in literary history, including *The School for Scandal* and *The Rivals*, Richard Brinsley Sheridan also served for a number of years in the House of Commons. A liberal member of that body, Sheridan was a thorn in the side of many conservatives in the English aristocracy. Strolling through Piccadilly Square one day, Sheridan was overtaken by two English lords, who each took a position beside him. As they continued walking, one of the men said, "I say, Sherry, we were just discussing whether you were a rogue or a fool." Sheridan immediately took each man by the arm and turned the tables on both:

Why, I do believe I am between both.

★ ★ ★ ★ ★ ★ ★ ★ ★ ★ ★

Horace Dutton Taft, the brother of U.S. president William Howard Taft, was a noted educator and the founder of the exclusive Taft School in Connecticut. As headmaster of the school, he ran a tight ship and put up with little nonsense from his young charges. One day, an outraged father barged into Taft's office to protest the recent expulsion of his son. Banging his fist on the desk and pointing his finger in Taft's face, he exclaimed, "You think you can run this school any damn way you please, don't you?" Taft remained calm under the onslaught and simply replied:

Your manner is crude and your language vulgar, but you have somehow got the point.

✶ ✶ ✶ ✶ ✶ ✶ ✶ ✶ ✶ ✶

In the history of nations, an uneasy relationship has often existed between military and civilian leaders. Such was the case during Napoleon's reign. One day, the emperor was meeting with a top military adviser and his trusted foreign minister, Charles Maurice de Talleyrand. During the meeting, the general kept using the expression "weaklings" to describe the citizenry. When Talleyrand politely asked for a clarification of the offensive term, the arrogant general said smugly, "We call weakling anybody who is not military." Talleyrand, one of history's most quick-witted politicians, retorted:

Ah yes, as we call military all those who are not civil.

✶ ✶ ✶ ✶ ✶ ✶ ✶ ✶ ✶ ✶

While living in London in 1897, Mark Twain decided to visit the American-born artist James McNeill Whistler. Whistler, who often came across as vain and conceited, was not exactly Twain's favorite type of person, but Twain thought it appropriate to pay his respects to a fellow American living overseas. Entering the studio, and before removing his hat and gloves, Twain began closely examining some of Whistler's recent work. Whistler cried out, "For the love of God! Be careful, Clemens! Apparently you don't realize that the paint is still fresh." Twain, who was rarely at a loss for words, put the pompous painter in his place with one of his most inspired rejoinders:

No need to be concerned, I have my gloves on.

★ ★ ★ ★ ★ ★ ★ ★ ★ ★ ★

In 1878, James McNeill Whistler filed a libel suit against English critic John Ruskin, who a year earlier had written that Whistler asked "two hundred guineas for flinging a pot of paint in the public's face." Although Whistler won the suit, he was awarded only a single farthing, the least valuable coin at the time. Whistler's legal expenses left him nearly penniless, forcing the proud painter to declare bankruptcy. Whistler did, however, have one wonderful moment during the trial. When Ruskin's lawyer asked him how long it had taken to paint a certain portrait, he told him two days. Ruskin's lawyer taunted him, "The labor of two days? Is that for which you ask two hundred guineas?" News reports show that courtroom visitors burst into spontaneous applause when Whistler declared:

No. I ask it for the knowledge of a lifetime.

★ ★ ★ ★ ★ ★ ★ ★ ★ ★ ★

At a London dinner party in the early 1900s, the noted Jewish writer Israel Zangwill was unable to stifle a yawn. A woman seated across the table suddenly revealed her anti-Semitism when she said disdainfully, "Mind your Jewish manners! I thought you were going to swallow me." Just as quickly, Zangwill put the bigot in her place by replying:

**Have no fear, madam,
my religion prohibits my doing that.**

classic quips, ad-libs, & off-the-cuff remarks

In the previous chapter, we examined classic retorts, ripostes, and rejoinders. Every reply in that chapter came in response to some kind of insult or personal attack. But not all examples of repartee come under duress or in response to a threat. Many are exceedingly clever remarks that have been stimulated by the events and circumstances of everyday life.

A perfect example occurred on a busy London street in the late 1800s. The noted actor and theatrical producer Herbert Beerbohm Tree spotted a man with a huge grandfather clock strapped to his back. The man was hunched over and appeared to be struggling mightily under the weight of the clock. Tree fell in step with the man and, after a few moments, leaned over and asked sympathetically:

My good man, why not carry a watch?

History has failed to record the workman's reaction, but Tree's clever query has been admired for more than a century by fans of repartee. His words might best be described as a *quip*, which the *American Heritage Dictionary* (*AHD*) defines this way:

1. *A clever, witty remark often prompted by the occasion.*

2. *A clever, often sarcastic remark; a gibe.*

The key words in this definition are "prompted by the occasion." Quips are little verbal gems that spontaneously emerge in a conversation or are stimulated by some event or occurrence. The origin of the word is uncertain, but quip has been used in English for centuries. As the definition suggests, some quips include a trace of sarcasm.

At a London party just after World War I, the English actress Mrs. Patrick Campbell found herself in a boring conversation with an elderly scientist who droned on and on about the social organization of ants. At one point in his monologue he asserted, "Ants even have their own police force and their own army." Mrs. Campbell—whose great beauty and sparkling wit made her a special friend of George Bernard Shaw—sweetly interjected:

No navy, I suppose?

In another example, the English military leader Bernard Law Montgomery—best known to Americans as Field Marshall Montgomery from his World War II days—hopped into a London cab one day en route to Waterloo Station. "Where you headed, mate?" said the taxi driver. Montgomery simply said, "Waterloo." When the cabbie looked back and said "Station?" Montgomery, who was known for being sarcastic on occasion, rolled his eyes, looked at his watch, and quipped:

Certainly. We're a bit late for the battle.

Quips have an offhand quality about them, meaning they appear without previous thought or preparation. Another term for such remarks is *off-the-cuff*, which the *AHD* defines as "without preparation; impromptu." *Off-the-cuff* is an American colloquial expression that first appeared in the late 1930s. Since the early days of men's wear, *cuff* has been the term for the folded-over trim at the end of a shirtsleeve, much like we see in fancy dress shirts today. The *off-the-cuff* expression comes from the world of formal affairs in the 1930s, when tuxedo-clad dinner guests would jot brief notes on the cuffs of their sleeves during the meal in order to give the impression of speaking spontaneously later on when they were called upon to deliver a few after-dinner remarks. Such remarks were clearly not spontaneous, but as years passed the expression took on the meaning it has today.

With quips and off-the-cuff remarks, the authors are simply presented with a stimulus—usually a quite unexpected stimulus—and they provide the response. Some classic examples have come in response to questions.

In 1882, the twenty-eight-year-old Oscar Wilde embarked on a yearlong lecture tour of America. During that much heralded trip, he traveled to more than seventy cities and towns across the U.S. and Canada, lecturing on art and the aesthetic movement to intellectuals in Boston, farmers in Nebraska, and miners in Colorado. With his velvet coat, frilly silk shirts, and patent leather shoes, Wilde looked every inch the English dandy. He also shocked people with his open displays of sensuality (when he met Walt Whitman in New Jersey, the two men greeted each other with a kiss on the lips). Wilde's tour started with a bang on January 2, 1882, when he arrived at New York Harbor. Asked by a U.S. Customs official if he had anything to declare, he famously replied:

I have nothing to declare but my genius.

A decade earlier, when the teenage Wilde was a student at Trinity College in Dublin, the provost of the school was a larger-than-life figure named John Pentland Mahaffy. An ancient history scholar, Mahaffy was an extraordinarily clever fellow whose witty replies were legendary. In one popular story, he was engaged in a heated debate with a women's rights advocate when the woman charged, "What *is* the difference between man and woman?" In an instant, Mahaffy answered:

Madam, I can't conceive.

Mahaffy's brilliant reply—simultaneously blending the two separate meanings of the word *conceive*—has been celebrated by language lovers ever since.

Another term that is commonly used for clever quips and off-the-cuff comments is *ad-lib*, which is defined as "to improvise and deliver extemporaneously." *Ad-lib* is a shortened version of the Latin expression *ad libitum* (ADD LIB-uh-tum), meaning "at the discretion of the performer." Throughout history, *ad libitum* has been used in the theater and on the concert stage as a direction to performers to use their discretion to alter or even omit a part of what was planned. In the Jazz Age, the full expression was shortened to *ad-lib* to indicate an improvisation on the part of a musician or an impromptu line delivered by an actor. In recent years, the meaning of ad-lib has been extended to include almost any kind of spontaneous remark, especially a clever and witty one.

One of the most famous ad-libs in theatrical history came from the great Czechoslovakian tenor Leo Slezak. A century ago, Slezak was one of the biggest names in the world of opera. One night, while playing the title role in Wagner's opera *Lohengrin*, he ran into an unexpected problem. At the end of the opera, a swan appears at the back of the stage, drawing a boat that is to return Lohengrin to his place with the Knights of the Holy Grail. This particular night, however, a stagehand erred and sent the swan boat off prematurely. It was the end of the opera, but there stood Slezak, watching the swan boat sail off without him. It was an awkward moment for the performers on stage and members of the audience, who were familiar with the opera's famous ending. As people began to fidget in their seats, Slezak brought the house down when he turned to a singer next to him and ad-libbed:

What time is the next swan?

Slezak, by the way, was the father of the well-known American character actor Walter Slezak, who appeared in scores of plays and films in the middle of the twentieth century. When Walter published his autobiography in 1962, he honored the memory of his father by titling it *What Time Is the Next Swan?*

Whether they're called *quips*, *off-the-cuff remarks*, or *ad-libs*, there is no doubt that clever remarks that have been "prompted by the occasion" have delighted people for centuries. You'll find more classic examples below.

✶ ✶ ✶ ✶ ✶ ✶ ✶ ✶ ✶ ✶ ✶

The English comedian Tony Allen decided to catch the act of an American comedian performing at a London club. The visiting comic's routine began with his asking questions of people in the audience, and saying clever things in response. This particular night, however, things weren't going very well. Finally, the visiting comedian came to Allen, and said, "And what do you do?" Allen got off the best line of the evening, replying:

**I'm a comedian.
What do you do?**

✶ ✶ ✶ ✶ ✶ ✶ ✶ ✶ ✶ ✶ ✶

A great philosopher, an eminent statesman, and a masterful writer, Sir Francis Bacon also served for a time as Lord Chancellor of England (1618–1621). While sitting on the bench one day, Bacon looked down at a defendant named Hogg, who had been charged with murder. When asked by the judge if he had anything to say in his defense, the man made a feeble attempt at humor, saying: "Your honor should let me go. We're kin. My name is Hogg, and Hogg is kin to Bacon." The defendant's strategy was unsuccessful, but it did inspire the witty Judge Bacon to reply:

Not until it's hung.

✶ ✶ ✶ ✶ ✶ ✶ ✶ ✶ ✶ ✶ ✶

The American stage and screen star Ethel Barrymore once invited a young actress to a dinner party at her Manhattan town house. The young woman neither showed up nor apologized later for not calling. Several days later, the insensitive young woman unexpectedly ran into Miss Barrymore on a New York street. She said lamely, "I believe I was invited to your house for dinner last week." Barrymore had the perfect response to the young woman's social slight. She simply asked:

And did you come?

⋆ ⋆ ⋆ ⋆ ⋆ ⋆ ⋆ ⋆ ⋆ ⋆ ⋆

The English conductor Thomas Beecham, known for his razor-sharp wit, was sitting in the nonsmoking compartment of a Great Western Railway train when a well-dressed woman entered and took a seat directly across from him. Almost immediately, the woman took a cigarette out of a jeweled case and said to Beecham, "I hope you won't object to my smoking." Beecham wisecracked:

Certainly not, if you won't object to my getting sick.

The woman became irate, informing Beecham haughtily, "I'll have you know that I am one of the director's wives." The quick-thinking Beecham replied:

Madam, if you were the director's only wife, I should still be sick.

⋆ ⋆ ⋆ ⋆ ⋆ ⋆ ⋆ ⋆ ⋆ ⋆ ⋆

The English writer and caricaturist Max Beerbohm was an English dandy with a great wit (dubbed the Incomparable Max by George Bernard Shaw). A *Saturday Review* drama critic for many years, Beerbohm once unexpectedly ran into the prominent English actor John Drew. Even though Drew had recently shaved his trademark mustache for a stage role, Beerbohm immediately recognized the actor. Drew, however, could not place Beerbohm, and apologized for any slight that might be taken. Beerbohm lived up to his famous nickname, coming to Drew's rescue in a most creative way:

**That's okay.
You probably didn't recognize me without your mustache.**

⋆ ⋆ ⋆ ⋆ ⋆ ⋆ ⋆ ⋆ ⋆ ⋆

During his three decades as host of *The Tonight Show*, Johnny Carson delivered some of the funniest lines in the history of show business. While many of his best lines were undoubtedly written by his stable of talented comedy writers, one of Carson's funniest—and most famous—remarks was a spontaneous quip he made on a 1965 show. The guest that night was Ed Ames, formerly of the popular singing group The Ames Brothers and at the time appearing on the *Daniel Boone* television series in the role of Mingo, a Harvard-educated, tomahawk-throwing Indian. When Ames said he had taken tomahawk-throwing lessons, Carson asked for a demonstration. Within seconds, a curtain opened, revealing the chalked outline of a standing human figure on a huge wooden log. As Ames hurled the tomahawk at the target, he said, "This is how you take care of an enemy." To everyone's shock, the blade of the tomahawk landed squarely in the crotch of the human figure, with the handle pointing up and out, looking almost like an erect penis. There was a moment of stunned silence, which was immediately followed by Carson's quip:

**Gee, Ed, I didn't even know you were Jewish.
A frontier bris!**

A bris, of course, is the Jewish circumcision ritual. After Carson's remark, the audience erupted into one of the longest laughs in television history. As the laughter died down, Ames said to Carson, "Would you like to give it a try?" Carson declined, and got one last laugh as he said, "I can't hurt him any more than you did."

⋆ ⋆ ⋆ ⋆ ⋆ ⋆ ⋆ ⋆ ⋆ ⋆

During a rehearsal session one day, the actress and singer Elaine Stritch sang a song titled "When the Tower of Babel Fell." She pronounced the name of the biblical city in the usual way, rhyming it with "scrabble." Sitting in on the session that day was Stritch's old friend Noël Coward, a notorious tease. Sensing an opportunity to pull the leg of a friend, Coward interrupted and said in his most erudite tone, "I believe the correct pronunciation is BAY-buhl." Stritch was not buying it, however, and countered, "Everyone pronounces it the way I do. It means mixed-up language. Gibberish. It's where we get the word 'babble' from." Coward instantly replied:

No, that's a fabble.

✳ ✳ ✳ ✳ ✳ ✳ ✳ ✳ ✳ ✳ ✳

Clarence Darrow attended law school for only one year before being admitted to the Ohio bar in 1878. In the course of his long and distinguished career, he earned a place in American legal history for his work in high-profile criminal trials (defending Leopold and Loeb, Eugene Debs, and John T. Scopes in the famous Scopes "Monkey Trial"). While his most famous cases highlighted controversial social issues, Darrow wasn't simply motivated by principle. One time, a relieved client shook his hand after a "Not Guilty" verdict, saying, "How can I ever show my appreciation?" He answered:

Ever since the Phoenicians invented money, there has been only one answer to that question.

✳ ✳ ✳ ✳ ✳ ✳ ✳ ✳ ✳ ✳ ✳

Benjamin Disraeli and William Gladstone were the two great English politicians of the nineteenth century. Gladstone was an establishment figure, with powerful family connections, an Oxford education, and a serious, even "preachy" style. Disraeli was eccentric and unorthodox, with Jewish roots, no university education, and a witty, flamboyant manner. In a famous encounter between the two,

Gladstone charged that Disraeli had a reputation for being cynical and making a joke out of any subject. Disraeli acknowledged that there might be some truth to the reputation. Hoping to score a point, Gladstone quickly challenged his adversary, "Then make a joke about Queen Victoria." Disraeli's instantaneous reply is a classic:

The Queen is not a subject.

★ ★ ★ ★ ★ ★ ★ ★ ★ ★ ★

During the 1890s, Georges Feydeau was one of France's most popular playwrights, authoring numerous bedroom farces that titillated Parisian audiences. He was also known for living the high life, and even had a table permanently reserved for him at Maxim's, the famous Paris restaurant. Dining at the restaurant one night, he ordered lobster, but was not pleased when the crustacean delivered to his table had only one claw. When the waiter was summoned, he offered Feydeau a most creative explanation: "The lobster must have lost his claw in a fight with one of the other lobsters in the tank." Feydeau immediately instructed the waiter:

**Then I want you to take this one back,
and bring me the winner.**

★ ★ ★ ★ ★ ★ ★ ★ ★ ★ ★

While the initials in W. C. Fields's name stood for William Claude, they could have meant "wisecrack." On one occasion, the president of a local garden club asked Fields if he would give an after-dinner speech at the group's annual meeting. When Fields declined, the woman pleaded with him, "But surely you believe in clubs for women?" Fields considered the woman's plea and replied:

**Certainly, but only if
all other means of persuasion fail.**

★ ★ ★ ★ ★ ★ ★ ★ ★ ★ ★

W. C. Fields died at age sixty-seven on December 25, 1946, his life cut short by his notorious alcohol consumption (by some accounts, he drank as much as two quarts of gin a day). Some wags thought it was a fitting irony that Fields died on Christmas, the one holiday he despised the most. As he lay in his hospital bed shortly before his death, Fields was visited by the actor Thomas Mitchell, a good friend. When Mitchell entered the hospital room, he was shocked to find the irreligious Fields paging through a Bible. Fields was a lifelong agnostic, and fervently antireligious (he once said that he had skimmed the Bible while looking for movie plots, but found only "a pack of wild lies"). "What are you doing reading a Bible?" asked the astonished Mitchell. A wiseacre to the end, Fields replied:

I'm looking for loopholes.

✶ ✶ ✶ ✶ ✶ ✶ ✶ ✶ ✶ ✶ ✶

As "gotcha" journalism became more and more popular in the 1980s, reporters would routinely surprise politicians and other celebrities with questions about drug use, extramarital affairs, and other tawdry topics. Some politicians got angry (like Gus Savage, the Illinois politician who shot back at a reporter, "Have you stopped wearing your wife's lingerie? Have you stopped messing around with little boys?"). Others dodged such questions (like presidential candidate George W. Bush, whose stock answer was, "When I was young and crazy, I was young and crazy."). But nobody can rival the ingenuity of Wyche Fowler Jr., the Georgia politician who served in Congress during the 1970s and '80s. In the middle of a senatorial campaign, Fowler was asked if he had smoked marijuana in the 1960s. The clever candidate replied with tongue in cheek:

Only when committing adultery.

✶ ✶ ✶ ✶ ✶ ✶ ✶ ✶ ✶ ✶ ✶

After a brief attempt at a legal career in the 1860s, W. S. Gilbert was drawn to parody and humorous verse, eventually teaming up with composer Arthur

Sullivan to produce some of the most inspired comic operas in history. Gilbert was at a party one evening, just after the death of an aging English composer. News of the composer's death had not yet been formally reported, however, and a man who was unaware of the development asked Gilbert what the composer was up to these days. Trying to be discreet, Gilbert said, "He is doing nothing." The man persisted, saying, "Surely he is composing?" Gilbert added to his reputation as one of the wittiest men in London when he quipped:

On the contrary, he is decomposing.

★ ★ ★ ★ ★ ★ ★ ★ ★ ★ ★

In 1938, NBC launched the quiz show *Information Please*. Hosted by Clifton Fadiman, at the time an editor at *The New Yorker*, the show went on to become one of the most popular shows in radio history, running until 1952. The program included regular panelists, like Franklin Pierce Adams of Algonquin Round Table fame, and guest panelists, who were chosen as much for their wit as the extent of their knowledge. When the widely traveled John Gunther—the author of the popular *Inside* series of travel books—appeared on the show, he was asked, "Who is Reza Pahlavi?" He thought for a moment and, with a slight hesitation in his voice, correctly answered, "The ruler of Persia." Pahlavi, of course, was also known as the shah of Iran, and Fadiman seized the opportunity to punningly ask Gunther, "Are you shah?" Gunther matched Fadiman's punning abilities and went one step further by instantly answering:

Sultanly!

★ ★ ★ ★ ★ ★ ★ ★ ★ ★

Oscar Levant was a wonderful pianist and composer, and the leading Gershwin interpreter after Gershwin's premature death in 1937. He also had a remarkable sense of humor that he incorporated into his concerts, his appearances on television talk shows, and cleverly written books like *Memoirs of an Amnesiac* and *The*

Unimportance of Being Oscar. In the last few decades of his life, his reputation as a humorist rivaled his reputation as a musician. During World War II, the forty-something Levant appeared before a draft-board examiner, who asked, "Do you think you can kill?" Levant took a moment to think about the question, and then replied:

> ### I don't know about strangers,
> ### but friends, yes.

✶ ✶ ✶ ✶ ✶ ✶ ✶ ✶ ✶ ✶

Born in England, Oliver Herford lived most of his adult life in New York City. In the early decades of the twentieth century he became one of the most versatile talents in the city—a writer, illustrator, cartoonist, comedian, and poet. He was also a master at crafting humorous definitions, such as "Manuscript: something submitted in haste and returned at leisure" and "Diplomacy: lying in state." While lunching at his club one day, he was approached by another member of the club—a notorious bore—who said to him, "I just heard somebody in the lobby say he'd offer me fifty dollars to resign my membership. What should I do?" Herford pondered the man's dilemma for a moment before advising:

> ### Hold out for a hundred.

✶ ✶ ✶ ✶ ✶ ✶ ✶ ✶ ✶ ✶

From 1950 to 1961, Groucho Marx's *You Bet Your Life* was one of the most popular shows on television. In addition to being a perfect vehicle for Groucho's quick wit, the show featured several gimmicks that became part of television history (a little bird that appeared whenever a contestant uttered "the magic word" and the question "Who is buried in Grant's tomb?"). On stage in front of a live audience, Groucho would typically interview contestants for a short while before moving on to the quiz portion of the show. However, so many of Groucho's quips were off-color or risqué, it generally took up to two hours to produce enough suitable material for a half-hour show. One night, a contestant revealed that he was the father of ten children. When Groucho asked, "Why so many children?" the man answered, "Well, Groucho, I love my wife." Marx hesitated for a moment, glanced briefly at the audience in his inimitable manner, and then delivered one of the most famous lines never to be actually broadcast on the show:

> **I love my cigar,**
> **but I take it out of my mouth once in a while.**

✳ ✳ ✳ ✳ ✳ ✳ ✳ ✳ ✳ ✳

Despite his great wealth, Groucho Marx enjoyed working in his own yard, tending to the shrubbery and sometimes even mowing his lawn. Attired in his work clothes one day, Marx was hard at work when a well-dressed woman in a Mercedes brought her car to a stop in front of his house. Surveying the beautifully manicured grounds, she hoped she could convince the talented landscaper to work for her. "Gardener," she hollered out as she rolled down her window, "how much does the lady of the house pay you?" Marx grabbed a handkerchief from his back pocket, wiped the sweat off his brow, and replied:

> **I don't get paid in dollars.**
> **The lady of the house just lets me sleep with her.**

✳ ✳ ✳ ✳ ✳ ✳ ✳ ✳ ✳ ✳

A professor at Columbia University for nearly fifty years, Sidney Morgenbesser was called the Kibitzing Philosopher for the whimsical give-and-take dialogue he used in his classroom with generations of students. Famed for his intellectual playfulness, Morgenbesser believed that witticisms and jokes were a perfect platform for launching into serious philosophical discussions. One of his quips has achieved almost reverential status in the academic world. One day in the 1950s, the noted British philosopher J. L. Austin delivered a guest lecture on the analysis of language to Columbia staff and students. At one point, Austin asserted that two negatives can sometimes make a positive, but it had never been demonstrated that two positives could make a negative. In his best Lower East Side accent, Morgenbesser refuted the assertion by saying:

Yeah! Yeah!

★ ★ ★ ★ ★ ★ ★ ★ ★ ★

While serving as Great Britain's ambassador to Germany in the mid-1930s, Sir Eric Phipps often had to hold his nose—and his tongue—as he saw brutal figures in the Nazi party assume power and adopt a veneer of sophistication and class. One day, Phipps had an appointment with Hermann Goering, one of the chief architects of the developing police state in Germany. Long past the time the meeting was scheduled to begin, there was no sign of the Nazi leader, and Phipps was becoming increasingly annoyed. Finally, Goering arrived and issued a feeble apology, saying he was delayed at a shooting party. Phipps could hold his tongue no longer. He quipped:

Animals, I hope.

★ ★ ★ ★ ★ ★ ★ ★ ★ ★

Albert Einstein learned to play the violin as a child, and the instrument became a kind of companion to him his entire life (he once said that playing the violin was his favorite form of relaxation). By adulthood, he was a talented amateur violinist and, as his fame grew, he occasionally played with some of the world's great musicians. While visiting the acclaimed cellist Gregor Piatigorsky one day, Einstein gave a short demonstration of his skill. When Einstein finished playing, he asked with anticipation, "Did I play well?" It was a rare opportunity for Piatigorsky—also a raconteur and a wordsmith—and he took full advantage of it, replying:

You played *relatively* well.

⋆ ⋆ ⋆ ⋆ ⋆ ⋆ ⋆ ⋆ ⋆ ⋆

In 1948, the American playwright and screenwriter Irwin Shaw published his first novel, *The Young Lions*, based on his experiences in the recent war. The novel was a great success, and three years later, Shaw moved to Europe, where he lived for the next twenty-five years. Almost all of his subsequent works, including *Rich Man, Poor Man*, were written in Europe. While dining out one evening in Paris, Shaw and his companions were promptly seated at their table, but they waited for an interminably long time before anybody paid any attention to them. Finally, the maître d' arrived at the table. When he announced that snails were the specialty of the house, Shaw quickly rejoined:

I know, and you have them dressed as waiters.

⋆ ⋆ ⋆ ⋆ ⋆ ⋆ ⋆ ⋆ ⋆ ⋆

One of the wittiest lawyers in history, English attorney F. E. Smith became famous for verbally demolishing rival attorneys—and a few judges—in courtroom skirmishes. He also occasionally demonstrated great wit outside the courtroom. He once attended a London social engagement in honor of the visiting U.S. president Woodrow Wilson. Wilson, the president of Princeton University before turning to politics, was still deeply interested in higher education. At one point, he asked Smith, "What, in your opinion, is the trend of the modern English undergraduate?" It was a perfect setup for the wisecracking Smith, who said:

Steadily toward drink and women, Mr. President.

⋆ ⋆ ⋆ ⋆ ⋆ ⋆ ⋆ ⋆ ⋆ ⋆

Even though the first successful appendectomy was said to have been performed by a British army surgeon in 1735, it wasn't until the 1880s that the procedure was described in medical journals and taught in medical schools. It was a welcome solution to an age-old malady and, by the turn of the century, was becoming so popular it was almost a staple in the arsenal of many surgeons in Europe and America. Shortly before he died in 1902, the German physician-turned-politician Rudolf Virchow was asked, "Is it true that a human being can survive without an appendix?" Even though he had not practiced medicine for many years, Virchow stayed in touch with developments in the field. Aware of the increasing popularity of the procedure, he wryly quipped:

Human beings, yes, but not surgeons.

★ ★ ★ ★ ★ ★ ★ ★ ★ ★ ★

James McNeill Whistler was born in Lowell, Massachusetts, in 1834. He dropped out of West Point Military Academy to pursue an art career, moving to Paris in 1855. After mastering the modern French painting methods, he formally settled in London in 1863, where he developed a reputation as a great painter and a great wit. A world traveler, his paintings showed influences from all parts of the globe, including the Far East and South America. One day, Whistler was asked how such a cosmopolitan figure could have been born in such an unfashionable place as Lowell, Massachusetts. He replied:

The explanation is quite simple.
I wished to be near my mother.

★ ★ ★ ★ ★ ★ ★ ★ ★ ★ ★

In 1899, things were not going well for the English in the Boer War in South Africa. Despite vastly superior numbers, the British military was routinely embarrassed by Boer troops. During one particularly bad week—dubbed "Black Week" in the press—the English suffered three successive setbacks, and faith in the formidable English military machine began to sink to record lows. In one press report, British commander R. H. Buller tried to put a positive spin on things, saying about one battle that English forces had retreated without losing a man, a flag, or a cannon. When artist and wit James McNeill Whistler read the report, he wisecracked to a friend:

Or a minute.

★ ★ ★ ★ ★ ★ ★ ★ ★ ★

Oscar Wilde once wrote about Whistler, "That he is indeed one of the very great masters of painting, is my opinion. And I may add that in this opinion Mr. Whistler himself entirely concurs." Whistler was one of the world's great egotists, but he tooted his own horn in such a clever way that it usually entertained rather than offended people. When a female fan once gushed to him, "I only know of two painters in the world, yourself and Velásquez," he replied:

Why drag in Velásquez?

★ ★ ★ ★ ★ ★ ★ ★ ★ ★

Once the toast of the town in London society, and celebrated the world over as the leader of the Aesthetic Movement, Oscar Wilde was never the same after losing a controversial libel case he had brought against the Marquess of Queensbury, the father of his lover, Lord Alfred Douglas. After the Marquess accused Wilde of being a sodomite, Wilde (urged on by Douglas) sued for criminal libel. Wilde not only lost the case, but was later prosecuted in a second trial for homosexuality. Even though he testified brilliantly, he was found guilty and, incredibly, sentenced in 1895 to two years at hard labor. While waiting to be transported to Reading Gaol, the once proud Wilde stood handcuffed on a dreary railway platform, soaked to the bone by a driving rain. Somehow, Wilde was able to call upon his legendary wit during this most difficult time, commenting to the guard who was accompanying him:

If this is the way Queen Victoria treats her prisoners, she doesn't deserve to have any.

✶ ✶ ✶ ✶ ✶ ✶ ✶ ✶ ✶ ✶ ✶

P. G. Wodehouse was one of the most prolific writers of the twentieth century, churning out more than 120 books and plays in his lifetime (most famously his captivating stories of Bertie Wooster and his butler, Jeeves). Wodehouse had a grand, offbeat sense of humor that showed up as much in his life as in his books. He dedicated his *Heart of a Goof* book to his daughter, writing, "To Lenore, without whose never-failing sympathy and encouragement, this book would have been finished in half the time." Wodehouse left England for America after World War II, becoming a U.S. citizen in 1955. At a cocktail party during the height of the Cold War, he and a friend found themselves in the presence of a serious young man who was consumed with the notion that a nuclear war would soon destroy the entire human race. When the man mentioned the impending nuclear threat for the umpteenth time, the frustrated Wodehouse whispered to his companion:

I can't wait.

laconic repartee

If you know what the word *spartan* means—to be rigorously self-disciplined and economical—then you might also know what the word *laconic* means. If you don't, I think you'll find the explanation interesting.

Spartan derives from the ancient Greek city-state of Sparta. Technically, the word is a *toponym*—in plain English, a place name—meaning it was inspired by a geographical place. The etymology of the word is fascinating. After a massive internal revolt around 600 B.C., the rulers of Sparta transformed their domain from a place of great learning and culture to an aggressive military state, constantly at war with its neighbors. Unlike the open society of Athens, the other great city-state of the time, Sparta had more in common with modern-day totalitarian states. All government decisions were made in secrecy. At birth, infants judged too weak and sickly were taken from their parents and left to die of exposure. At age seven, the fittest children were forcibly removed from their homes and conscripted into the military, many of them serving for the rest of their lives. Since the entire society was organized to support the military regime, the soldiers as well as the citizens lived lives of austerity and rigorous self-discipline. Today, the word *spartan* literally means to live like the Spartans—an austere existence with no luxuries and only the basic necessities.

Laconic (pronounced luh-KAHN-ick) is also derived from a place name, coming from Laconia, a geographical region in southern Greece. Sparta was the capital of Laconia. *Laconic* means to be economical in speech—that is, to use very few words—in the same way that *spartan* means to be economical in goods and possessions. In the ancient world, the Laconians were known for their extreme brevity of speech. Their terseness is captured in stories that go back more than 2,000 years.

In the fourth century B.C., after Spartan troops won the Battle of Thebes, the victorious general sent a message back to his superiors saying, "Thebes is taken." Laconians prided themselves on never using two or three words when one would do, so this three-word message was judged too wordy for the commanders back in Sparta. They sent the general a reprimand that said:

Taken would have been sufficient.

Later in the same century, Sparta was at war with Macedonia, which was ruled at the time by Philip II, father of Alexander the Great. As Philip and his army gathered on the outskirts of the city, he sent a message to Spartan leaders: "You are advised to submit immediately. If I enter Laconia, I shall raze Sparta to the ground." The Spartans defiantly sent one of history's greatest one-word replies:

If.

If brevity is the soul of wit, as William Shakespeare observed in *Hamlet*, this classic reply from the Spartans is a perfect example. But brief as it is, it is twice as long as the most concise reply in history, authored by the great French writer Victor Hugo. Shortly after *Les Misérables* was published in 1862, Parisians were scooping up all available copies, and the buzz surrounding the book resulted in speedy translations into English, German, and other languages. One day, Hugo sent a telegram to his publisher inquiring about sales of the book. The message on the telegram couldn't have been briefer. It simply said: "?" The publisher's reply, sent by return telegram, matched Hugo's brevity and exceeded his cleverness:

!

Today we use the word *laconic* to describe people who use very few words when they speak. The term often has been used to describe Calvin Coolidge, the 30th U.S. president. In a profession noted for windbags, Coolidge was a politician of very few words, well deserving the nickname Silent Cal (he once said, "I've never been hurt by something I didn't say"). Coolidge's taciturn style frustrated the many people around him who felt a man of his stature should be more talkative. At a White House dinner one evening, a female guest sidled up to the president and whispered in his ear, "You must talk to me, Mr. President. I made a bet today that I could get more than two words out of you." Coolidge whispered back:

You lose.

In the rest of the chapter, let's take a look at more comebacks and rejoinders that contain only one or two words—what might be called *laconic repartee.*

✶ ✶ ✶ ✶ ✶ ✶ ✶ ✶ ✶ ✶ ✶

The winner of a 1959 Pulitzer Prize for *Fiorello!* and six Tony awards for such musicals as *Pal Joey*, *The Pajama Game*, and *Damn Yankees!* George Abbott was a demanding, no-nonsense director who could be tough on actors. He was also no fan of the Method school of acting, which trained actors to find motivation for their acting in life experience. One day, when a method actor asked Abbott, "What's my motivation?" he snapped back:

Your job!

✶ ✶ ✶ ✶ ✶ ✶ ✶ ✶ ✶ ✶ ✶

One of the original members of Sigmund Freud's inner circle, Alfred Adler broke ranks with Freud in 1911, and the two men never talked again. In his distinguished career, Adler offered numerous psychological insights, including the now well-accepted notion that people who feel inferior often overcompensate and become egocentric, aggressive, and power hungry. One day, while strolling through Central Park, a friend told Adler that a mutual acquaintance, an aggressive type who fit the model of a typical overcompensator, had fallen in love. Adler thought for a moment and asked:

Against whom?

⋆ ⋆ ⋆ ⋆ ⋆ ⋆ ⋆ ⋆ ⋆ ⋆ ⋆

For many years, a Franciscan priest by the name of Andrew Agnellus served as an adviser to the British Broadcasting Company (BBC) on religious affairs. One day, a BBC producer sent a memo to Father Agnellus asking how he might ascertain the official Catholic view of heaven and hell. The witty priest's return memo said simply:

Die.

⋆ ⋆ ⋆ ⋆ ⋆ ⋆ ⋆ ⋆ ⋆ ⋆ ⋆

On a graffiti-covered wall of the New York City subway system in the late 1960s, someone had scrawled the words "Question Authority." Just below, in different handwriting, another graffiti artist penned the perfect one-word riposte:

Why?

⋆ ⋆ ⋆ ⋆ ⋆ ⋆ ⋆ ⋆ ⋆ ⋆ ⋆

In the early years of the twentieth century, a female temperance speaker concluded her diatribe on the dangers of alcohol by saying, "I would rather commit adultery than take a glass of beer." A voice from the predominantly male crowd shouted out:

Who wouldn't?

✶ ✶ ✶ ✶ ✶ ✶ ✶ ✶ ✶ ✶

In 1957, the magnificent Mann Auditorium was dedicated in Tel Aviv, giving the Israel Philharmonic Orchestra a beautiful new home. A short while later, a visiting West German government official was given a tour of the city by a representative of the Israeli government. It was a time of rapprochement between the two countries, and old suspicions were gradually being replaced with trust and cooperation. As the two men walked by the auditorium, the German turned to his guide and said, "How wonderful it is that the relationship between our two countries has improved to such a point that an auditorium has been dedicated in the name of the great German writer, Thomas Mann." The Israeli replied, "I'm afraid you are mistaken. The auditorium is not named after Thomas Mann, but after Frederic Mann." "Frederic Mann?" the man replied. "What did he write?" The Israeli guide smiled and said:

The check.

✶ ✶ ✶ ✶ ✶ ✶ ✶ ✶ ✶ ✶

In the fourth century B.C., Archelaus was the son of the ruler of Macedonia, but he was not eligible to be in the line of succession because his mother was a slave. He took matters into his own hands by arranging for the murder of his uncle and half-brother before seizing power in 413 B.C. The Greek historian Plutarch tells a great story about the time Archelaus paid a visit to the royal barber. After seating himself in the barber's chair, the ruler became annoyed as the talkative barber began to prattle on and on about events of the day. When the barber finally stopped babbling and asked the king, "How would you like your hair trimmed, Your Highness?" Archelaus replied:

In silence.

★ ★ ★ ★ ★ ★ ★ ★ ★ ★ ★

Many writers have jealously guarded their privacy, but few prized it as much as the introverted James M. Barrie, especially when he was focused on a new project. After the spectacular success of his 1904 play *Peter Pan*, he was much sought after by fans and journalists. While writing in his study one day, Barrie heard the doorbell ring. Slightly annoyed at the interruption, he walked to the front door only to discover a reporter, who said, "Sir James Barrie, I presume?" As he slammed the door, Sir James said:

You do!

★ ★ ★ ★ ★ ★ ★ ★ ★ ★ ★

The Bohemian poet and writer Maxwell Bodenheim was one of the most colorful figures in Greenwich Village from 1915 until his tragic death in 1954, when he and his wife were murdered in their apartment by a former mental patient. In 1917, Bodenheim and playwright Ben Hecht participated in a debate with a curious and provocative resolution: "That people who attend literary debates are imbeciles." Hecht went first, speaking in favor of the resolution. Arguing cogently from the lectern, he spoke with great eloquence. After a rousing performance, he stated with a flourish, "The affirmative rests." Hecht sat down and Bodenheim walked up to the lectern. He scrutinized the audience for several moments without saying a word. He then looked over at Hecht and said:

You win.

★ ★ ★ ★ ★ ★ ★ ★ ★ ★ ★

One of the few people in history to win Oscar, Emmy, Grammy, and Tony awards, Mel Brooks began his career as a stand-up comic in the Catskills and a writer on Sid Caesar's *Your Show of Shows* before going on to produce such classic films as *Blazing Saddles*, *Young Frankenstein*, and *The Producers*. In 2000, he adapted *The Producers* to the stage, producing a staggeringly successful Broadway musical. Brooks's occasional use of scatological humor has appealed to many people, but offended some others. In a *Playboy* interview in 1975, the interviewer observed, "You've been accused of vulgarity." Instantly, Brooks shot back:

Bullshit!

✶ ✶ ✶ ✶ ✶ ✶ ✶ ✶ ✶ ✶ ✶

In December 1999, William F. Buckley Jr. taped his final *Firing Line* interview. For thirty-three years, the founder of modern-day conservatism had engaged in spirited intellectual discourse with guests of every political persuasion on this long-running television program. Later that evening, Ted Koppel interviewed Buckley on ABC's popular *Nightline* show. As the show drew to a close, Koppel said to his famous guest, "Mr. Buckley, we have only a few moments left. Could you sum up in ten seconds?" The loquacious Buckley startled Koppel but endeared himself to viewers when he replied:

No.

✶ ✶ ✶ ✶ ✶ ✶ ✶ ✶ ✶ ✶ ✶

At a London social gathering in the 1930s, Winston Churchill and a number of friends were embroiled in a lively discussion about the roles of men and women. At one point, an outspoken woman blurted out, "By the year 2100, women will rule the world." Churchill thought for a moment and, to the delight of the assembled guests, said:

Still?

✲ ✲ ✲ ✲ ✲ ✲ ✲ ✲ ✲ ✲ ✲

One cold and rainy London day, a horde of journalists gathered around Noël Coward to query him about his latest project. A reporter from the newspaper the *Sun* hollered out, "Mr. Coward, have you anything to say to the *Sun*?" Coward replied pleasantly:

Shine.

✲ ✲ ✲ ✲ ✲ ✲ ✲ ✲ ✲ ✲ ✲

Shortly after becoming the fortieth U.S. president following Richard Nixon's resignation, Gerald Ford made the most controversial decision of his presidency by pardoning Nixon. The action set off a firestorm and haunted Ford in his 1976 presidential campaign against Jimmy Carter. On the stump, Ford's strategy was to talk as little as possible about Nixon and the pardon. At one point, CBS reporter Fred Barnes took notice of the strategy, saying: "Mr. President, two or three times today you talked about your 'predecessor,' and once you referred to 'Lyndon Johnson's successor.' Are you trying to avoid saying the name of Richard M. Nixon?" It was a tense moment and the press corps waited expectantly for a reply. Nobody expected Ford's candid answer:

Yes.

✲ ✲ ✲ ✲ ✲ ✲ ✲ ✲ ✲ ✲ ✲

Passing through French customs early in his career, Alfred Hitchcock was questioned by a suspicious inspector who looked quizzically at the occupation stated on the passport: "Producer." The customs official asked, "What do you produce?" Hitchcock answered:

Gooseflesh.

✷ ✷ ✷ ✷ ✷ ✷ ✷ ✷ ✷ ✷

In the mid-1800s, Douglas Jerrold was a successful playwright and one of England's best-known humorists. Believed to be in an unhappy marriage, he often took long walks to get away from home. During a walk one day, he ran into a man with a reputation for being a nonstop talker and a colossal bore. The man bounded up to Jerrold and said, "Well, well, Jerrold, what's going on?" As Jerrold bolted off, he said:

I am.

✷ ✷ ✷ ✷ ✷ ✷ ✷ ✷ ✷ ✷

A pontiff with a rare and rich sense of humor, Pope John XXIII once reported to an interviewer that important problems would frequently come to mind in the middle of the night, disturbing his sleep. Half awake, he'd make a mental note: "I must speak to the pope about that." "Then," he confessed, "I would be wide awake and remember—I am the pope!" Once asked by a journalist, "How many people work in the Vatican?" the pontiff pondered the question, giving the impression that he was trying to come up with an accurate estimate. Then, with a straight face, he answered:

About half.

✷ ✷ ✷ ✷ ✷ ✷ ✷ ✷ ✷ ✷

During his major league baseball career, Alex Johnson developed a reputation as a talented ballplayer with an attitude problem. Regarded by managers and coaches as surly and uncooperative, he ended up playing for eight separate teams in his thirteen-year career. An aggressive contact hitter who rarely struck out, he was never much of a home run threat. In 1969, while playing with the Cincinnati Reds, he hit a career-high seventeen home runs, fifteen more than the previous year. A few months into the season, reporters began to take notice of the newfound punch in his bat. One day, an interviewer said, "Alex, you hit only two homers all of last year and this season you already have seven. What's the difference?" Proving he could be just as challenging with reporters as with managers, the ballplayer with a chip on his shoulder said:

Five.

★ ★ ★ ★ ★ ★ ★ ★ ★ ★ ★

Even when members of the Algonquin Round Table pondered some of life's most serious questions, one or another of the witty group would somehow find a way to lighten the conversation. During a discussion of suicide one day, George S. Kaufman was asked by another member of the group, "So, how would you kill yourself?" Kaufman considered the question thoughtfully for several moments before replying:

With kindness.

★ ★ ★ ★ ★ ★ ★ ★ ★ ★ ★

While serving as a drama critic at the *New York Times* in the 1920s, the witty George S. Kaufman was often approached by publicity-seeking promoters and agents. One day, he was asked by an agent, "So, how do I get our leading lady's name in the *Times*?" Kaufman's advice was immediate:

Shoot her.

★ ★ ★ ★ ★ ★ ★ ★ ★ ★ ★

During the 1960 presidential race, John F. Kennedy's youth and modest political experience were considered major obstacles to winning the election. At a Seattle press conference during the height of the campaign, a reporter asked Kennedy: "Senator, do you feel that strong personalities, such as President Eisenhower and

Governor Rockefeller, campaigning against you will be perhaps a severe handicap in your campaign?" The confident candidate replied:

No.

★ ★ ★ ★ ★ ★ ★ ★ ★ ★ ★

At a dinner party, the musician and wit Oscar Levant was seated next to an attractive—and very talkative—young lady. It was a classic "captive audience" situation, and Levant feigned interest as best he could. In the middle of one of her monologues, the woman noticed Levant trying to stifle a yawn. "Am I keeping you up?" she asked with a tone of mock indignation. Her mild annoyance disappeared completely when he replied:

I wish.

★ ★ ★ ★ ★ ★ ★ ★ ★ ★ ★

The critic John Mason Brown said of Algonquin Round Table wit Dorothy Parker, "To those she did not like, she was a stiletto made of sugar." One day, Parker and a friend were discussing a prominent actress, noted for her brash manner and tendency to say whatever was on her mind. When the friend said, "She's so outspoken," Parker asked:

By whom?

★ ★ ★ ★ ★ ★ ★ ★ ★ ★ ★

In 1842, British commander Charles James Napier led vastly outnumbered British forces to victory over Indian troops, allowing England to annex the Province of Sindh (in modern-day Pakistan) and make an important advance in their colonization efforts. In one of the most popular stories in the annals of military history, Napier immediately sent a dispatch to Lord Ellenborough, the British governor of India at the time. He sent a simple one-word message:

Peccavi.

Peccavi is Latin for "I have sinned," making Napier's message also one of history's most famous puns.

✶ ✶ ✶ ✶ ✶ ✶ ✶ ✶ ✶ ✶ ✶

At a press conference announcing the completion of his massive twelve-volume *A Study of History*, the English historian Arnold Toynbee was asked by a reporter, "What purpose has impelled you to devote thirty-five years of your life to this single great work?" Toynbee answered:

Curiosity.

✶ ✶ ✶ ✶ ✶ ✶ ✶ ✶ ✶ ✶ ✶

Appearing in more than eighty films in his career, Spencer Tracy won two Best Actor Oscars (he was nominated for seven others) and starred in such classic films as *Boys Town*, *Father of the Bride*, *Bad Day at Black Rock*, and *Inherit the Wind*. When a reporter once asked, "What do you look for in a script?" he replied with a twinkle:

Days off.

✶ ✶ ✶ ✶ ✶ ✶ ✶ ✶ ✶ ✶ ✶

The English poet Lewis Morris hoped to be named poet laureate of England after Alfred, Lord Tennyson's death in 1892, but his name was scarcely mentioned. His constant complaints about the situation quickly grew tiresome to his friends. In a conversation with Oscar Wilde, he surfaced the subject once again, saying, "It's a conspiracy of silence, I tell you, a conspiracy of silence! Oscar, what do you think I should do?" Wilde's recommendation was immediate:

Join it.

* * * * * * * * * * *

Clever people are always looking for opportunities to strut their stuff, and the greatest wits are exceptionally good at seizing opportunities that are not apparent to regular folks. When Oscar Wilde was asked one day, "What are you working at these days?" he replied:

At intervals.

* * * * * * * * * * *

The director of such classic films as *Double Indemnity*, *The Lost Weekend*, *Stalag 17*, and *Some Like It Hot*, the aging Billy Wilder was one of a number of Hollywood veterans who began to struggle as a new breed of studio executives—called "movie brats" by old-timers—began to take over the film industry. Near the end of his career, Wilder was invited by a studio head to discuss a potential collaboration. The young CEO began the meeting by saying, "It's great to meet you at last, Billy. Before we start talking about future possibilities, though, please tell me, what have you done?" The three-time Oscar winner considered the question for a moment and then replied graciously:

After you.

* * * * * * * * * * *

After five years with the British band Take That, Robbie Williams embarked on a solo career in 1995. He struggled at first—his drinking, drugging, and skirt-chasing certainly didn't help—but returned to stardom with a number of hit singles and top-selling albums. When once asked by an interviewer, "What's the weirdest thing you've ever received from a fan?" he replied:

Herpes.

* * * * * * * * * * *

As the twelfth century came to an end, a Jewish physician and writer from Spain named Joseph ben Me'ir ibn Zabara produced a wonderful little book called *The Book of Delight*. Like Aesop's fables and Geoffrey Chaucer's tales, Zabara's book of folk tales contained numerous moral sayings ("If you conceal your vices, conceal your virtues.") and pithy epigrams ("He who rushes is often late."). In a story much repeated over the centuries, he told of a man whose brother had recently died. When the man was asked by a family friend, "What was the cause of his death?" he replied:

Life.

stage & screen repartee

As the theatrical world began to morph into the film world in the early part of the twentieth century, witty and wisecracking dialogue moved from the stage to the cinema, where it could be enjoyed, not by a few thousand people, but by millions. A classic example comes from a stage *and* screen legend.

In 1926, after spending a few decades paying her dues and developing her provocative stage persona, Mae West began writing, producing, and starring in her own Broadway shows. In her first play, titled *Sex*, she challenged social convention by playing a prostitute. The show was an immediate success, and West achieved national fame when she was jailed for eight days for "corrupting the morals of youth." In 1928, she followed up with her next hit play, *Diamond Lil*, in which she more fully displayed the sultry, wisecracking style that would become her trademark. In one scene, a woman gazes at West's jewelry and says with admiration, "Goodness! What beautiful diamonds." West replies:

Goodness had nothing to do with it, dearie.

West was so proud of that piece of dialogue that she reprised it a few years later in her 1932 Hollywood film debut, *Night After Night*. As years went by, the line became a cinema classic, so indelibly associated with West that she titled her 1959 autobiography, *Goodness Had Nothing to Do with It*.

In the 1939 film *My Little Chickadee,* West was joined by W. C. Fields, another entertainer known for his way with repartee. In that comedy classic, Fields plays gambler Cuthbert J. Twillie, and West plays shady lady Flower Belle Lee. The two pretend to be married as they plan to fleece the inhabitants of an unsuspecting town. In one scene, when a man at a card table asks Cuthbert, "Is this a game of chance?" he quips:

Not the way I play it.

In another scene, Flower Belle appears before a judge who is not pleased with her courtroom demeanor. When the judge says, "Are you showing contempt for this court?" she wisecracks:

I'm doing my best to hide it.

Blond sex symbols with a saucy side have been a Hollywood staple since the beginning of the film industry. The mold was not set by Mae West, however, but by cultural icon Jean Harlow. Before she died at age twenty-six in 1937, Harlow made thirty-six films. In her 1932 film *Red-Headed Woman,* she dropped her trademark platinum blond hair to play Lil Andrews, a conniving girl from the wrong side of the tracks who is attempting to sleep her way to the top. Made before the Hays Production Code was established, the movie has themes that are "adult" even by today's standards. In one scene, as she tries on a dress, Lil asks the sales assistant, "Can you see through this dress?" When the clerk replies, "I'm afraid you can, miss," Harlow announces:

I'll wear it!

Hollywood comedies are a rich source of clever banter and witty repartee. Bud Abbott and Lou Costello, who are best remembered these days for their classic "Who's on First?" routine, made some enormously successful films in the 1940s and '50s. In their 1942 film *Rio Rita,* the boys get fired from their jobs in a pet shop and end up as hotel detectives in a Texas resort teeming with Nazi agents. They still find time for one of their favorite pastimes: girl-watching. In one scene, as Costello is drooling over a beautiful girl, Abbott observes, "Beauty is only skin deep." Still captivated, Costello comes back with:

That's deep enough for me.

From 1940 to 1962, Bob Hope and Bing Crosby made seven light and breezy "road" movies, all characterized by great on-screen chemistry and cleverly written dialogue. In the 1942 film *Road to Morocco*, the cash-strapped pair find themselves shipwrecked off the coast of Morocco. Crosby's character sells Hope's character into slavery to Princess Shalimar (Dorothy Lamour), but soon regrets the decision. As the plot unfolds, both men desire her, but discover a formidable foe in the form of an Arab mullah (Anthony Quinn). In one scene, when heroic action is required, Crosby says, "We must storm the palace." Hope, whose road characters were always long on talk and short on courage, says:

You storm. I'll stay here and drizzle.

In their final road picture, 1962's *Road to Hong Kong*, the two aging buddies play a couple of con artists who become enmeshed in Cold War tensions when one of them accidentally memorizes the only copy of a secret formula for rocket fuel. Hope, whose film characters never had much success with women, seems as if he's making some headway with a stunning agent named Diane (Joan Collins). When she says, "I could love you body and soul," he quips:

They're available—in that order.

When it comes to Hollywood repartee, however, nobody did it more famously than the Marx Brothers. After beginning their career on vaudeville and the Broadway stage, the group launched a spectacular film career in the 1920s. With a skillful blend of slapstick physical comedy and witty—often zany—dialogue, they made some of the most popular comedies in screen history. In *Horse Feathers*, their 1932 parody of college life, Groucho plays Professor Quincy Adams Wagstaff, the president of Huxley College. In one scene, Chico, in the role of a local misfit turned football player, informs Wagstaff, "There's a man outside with a big black mustache." Groucho wisecracks:

Tell him I've got one.

In 1933's *Duck Soup*, Groucho plays Rufus T. Firefly, a wacky character who becomes dictator of the financially strapped country of Freedonia (he enlists Chico and Harpo as spies). On the day of Firefly's inauguration, his wealthy financial backer, Gloria Teasdale (Margaret Dumont), says, "Notables from every country are gathered here in your honor. This is a gala day for you." He replies:

Well, a gal a day is enough for me.
I don't think I could handle any more.

In the 1946 film *A Night in Casablanca*, Groucho plays the new manager of a hotel in Casablanca (previous managers have all been murdered), and the brothers do their madcap best to ferret out Nazi agents. At one point, a woman says to Groucho's character, "Oh, Monsieur Kornblow!" When he says, "Call me Montgomery," she says, "Is that your real name?" He replies to her in the same way he replied in true life when people asked him if Groucho were his real name:

No, I'm just breaking it in for a friend.

While Groucho usually delivered the punch lines, writers occasionally reserved some special ones for Chico. In the 1935 film *A Night at the Opera*, the boys take on the pretensions of grand opera and the hypocrisy of high society. At one point in the film, Groucho, as Otis B. Driftwood, tries to give

Chico, in the role of Fiorello, a lesson in contract law. When Groucho says, "That's in every contract. It's what they call a sanity clause," Chico responds with a look of suspicion, saying:

You can't fool me.
There ain't no Sanity Clause.

Some of Hollywood's most deliciously charming repartee has occurred off screen. During the casting of the 1942 film *Woman of the Year*, Katharine Hepburn was selected to play opposite screen veteran Spencer Tracy, thus beginning a professional and personal relationship that would last for twenty-five years (they did eight additional films together and had a legendary—and technically illicit—romantic relationship). When the regal Hepburn met the short and stocky Tracy for the first time, she said in her distinctive patrician manner, "I'm afraid I'm a little tall for you, Mr. Tracy." A commanding figure, Hepburn did not often meet men who could stand up to her, so her respect for Tracy shot up when he replied:

Not to worry, Miss Hepburn,
I'll soon cut you down to size.

Other off-screen examples are maliciously charming. When Harry Cohn, the pathological head of Columbia Pictures, died in 1958, a huge throng showed up for his funeral. Cohn may have been a genius at recognizing and promoting talent, but his dictatorial ways and notoriously bad treatment of people made him an object of loathing throughout Hollywood. When somebody commented to comedian Red Skelton that he was surprised by the large number of people who turned out for Cohn's funeral, Skelton replied:

It just goes to show you,
if you give the people what they want,
they'll show up.

And some could have happened in no other place in the world except a movie set. All the action in Alfred Hitchcock's 1944 film *Lifeboat* takes place in a single boat, occupied by eight survivors of a freighter sunk by a German U-boat. Shooting in such a small, confined space presented unique—and quite unexpected—problems for cinematographer Glen MacWilliams. One day, he noticed that the notorious Tallulah Bankhead was not wearing any panties. By necessity, the cameras had to be placed extremely low in the boat, and MacWilliams could see much more than he expected as he was shooting up at the actors. Approaching the director, he laid out the problem: "She has nothing on underneath. I can see everything, and it's there on the film. What am I going to do?" Hitchcock briefly considered the situation before observing:

**I don't know whether this is a problem
for wardrobe, makeup, or hairdressing.**

Some of the most interesting replies in theatrical history don't come from actors and directors, but from people sitting in the seats out front. In the mid-1900s, a young playwright asked the aging Carl Sandburg if he would be willing to preview his new play. Sandburg had a longstanding interest in the theater, so he was happy to comply. Attending a rehearsal several days later, the elderly poet fell asleep in the middle of the play. When the news reached the playwright, he was upset, and a little angry. "How could you fall asleep when you knew I wanted your opinion?" he groused to Sandburg. The distinguished poet replied:

Young man, sleep *is* an opinion.

While boring plays merely put people to sleep, bad ones can be a painful ordeal. One night, drama critic Robert Benchley and some colleagues attended the premiere of a dreadful play. Benchley struggled through the first act, but just barely. As the second act began, the rising curtain revealed an unoccupied living room, furnished with a couch, end table, lamp, and telephone. All of a sudden, the silence on stage was broken by the ringing of the telephone. Benchley rose from his seat and, heading for the aisle, whispered to his associates:

I think that's for me!

Clever quips and witty ripostes have shown up in every arena of human activity, but nowhere has it appeared with more panache and style than in the theatrical world. More examples of *stage and screen repartee* follow.

✻ ✻ ✻ ✻ ✻ ✻ ✻ ✻ ✻ ✻

Devastating remarks about Broadway plays have been made for a century, and they continue to be made up to the present day. A few years ago, Woody Allen was asked by a reporter, "Without naming any names, is there anyone in the theater who has hurt you so much that you want revenge?" Allen reflected for a moment and replied:

Revenge is putting it mildly.
A lady from Queens sitting next to me at *Cats*
woke me before it was over.

✻ ✻ ✻ ✻ ✻ ✻ ✻ ✻ ✻ ✻

In the 1946 adaptation of the Raymond Chandler mystery *The Big Sleep*, Humphrey Bogart plays private eye Philip Marlowe, who is hired by wealthy socialite Vivian Sternwood Rutledge (Lauren Bacall) to keep an eye on her wild young sister. The film was criticized for being overly complicated, but fans and critics alike praised the smart—and sometimes suggestive—dialogue between Bogie and Bacall. At one point, as the pair describe how they judge racehorses, the conversation turns to how they might evaluate each other. After her analysis of him, Marlowe says, "You don't like to be rated yourself," to which she replies, "I haven't met anyone yet that can do it. Any suggestions?" He then offers his analysis, saying, "Well, I can't tell till I've seen you over distance of ground. You've got a touch of class, but I don't know how far you can go." It's a great snippet of double-entendre dialogue, capped off by her famous reply:

A lot depends on who's in the saddle.

⋆　⋆　⋆　⋆　⋆　⋆　⋆　⋆　⋆　⋆

While performing in a matinee in New York City early in his career, John Barrymore was told that Jane Cowl, a prominent actress at the time, would be in the audience. During the performance, Miss Cowl chatted loudly with her companions, to the consternation of Barrymore, his fellow actors, and the audience. At the end of the play, an appreciative audience brought Barrymore back for a curtain call. He won the audience over for a second time when he bowed deeply in the direction of the disruptive actress and said:

I'd like to take this opportunity to thank Miss Cowl for the privilege of costarring with her this afternoon.

⋆　⋆　⋆　⋆　⋆　⋆　⋆　⋆　⋆　⋆

In the 1932 film *A Bill of Divorcement*, veteran actor John Barrymore teamed up with the twenty-five-year-old Katharine Hepburn in her first screen role. Barrymore wasn't used to working with such a headstrong, outspoken, and unconventional actress. And Hepburn was probably a little turned off by an actor who was so full of himself (he once said, "My only regret in the theater is that I could never sit out front and watch myself"). As filming ended, Hepburn sighed with relief and said to her costar, "Thank goodness I don't have to act with you anymore." Barrymore riposted:

I didn't know you ever had, darling.

✳ ✳ ✳ ✳ ✳ ✳ ✳ ✳ ✳ ✳ ✳

In the 1930s, the acclaimed English conductor Sir Thomas Beecham was taking the orchestra at London's Covent Garden Opera through a dress rehearsal for a full-scale production of *Aida*. Originally composed by Giuseppe Verdi for the opening of Cairo's new opera house in 1871, *Aida* is a famously lavish production, calling for horses and, if available, even elephants. When a horse was brought on stage for the rehearsal, it almost immediately began to do what stage managers fear an animal will do in such a situation. Beecham, noted as much for his great wit as his musical abilities, found the whole episode quite amusing. He stopped the orchestra and observed to the players:

> **You see, gentleman,**
> **not only a great performer, but a critic, too!**

✳ ✳ ✳ ✳ ✳ ✳ ✳ ✳ ✳ ✳ ✳

Sarah Bernhardt starred in a number of Oscar Wilde's plays (in 1893, *Salomé* was written—in French—especially for her). While the pair had great respect for one another and enjoyed a close relationship for more than twenty years, they sometimes clashed over how she was interpreting a role. While in rehearsal for *Salomé* just before the 1894 Paris opening, the two strong-willed personalities got into a brief but heated dispute. After the flare-up, a now calm Wilde pulled out a cigarette, and said, "Do you mind if I smoke?" The Divine Sarah, still miffed, replied coldly:

> **I don't care if you burn.**

✳ ✳ ✳ ✳ ✳ ✳ ✳ ✳ ✳ ✳ ✳

One of Denmark's most popular pianists, Victor Borge fled to the United States in 1940. Even though he spoke very little English, he soon began to win over American audiences with his unique blend of musicianship and humorous patter.

He once played to a very sparse crowd at a theater in Flint, Michigan. The sight of so many empty seats might have dampened the spirits of the average performer. But not the irrepressible Borge, who looked out into the audience and said:

**Flint must be an extremely wealthy town.
I see that each of you bought two or three seats.**

★　★　★　★　★　★　★　★　★　★　★

In the 2002 film *The Man from Elysian Fields*, Andy Garcia plays an impoverished writer who becomes an "escort" for a beautiful client whose husband (played by James Coburn) is a famous writer who is ailing and near death. On the first night that Garcia's character is sleeping with his client, the woman's husband walks in on them. Unaffected, she casually introduces her husband to the startled escort, who is hiding beneath the sheets. Rattled, but in awe at meeting a writer he greatly admires, Garcia's character nervously says, "It's a pleasure to meet you, sir." The husband replies:

**I'd like to say the pleasure is all mine,
but that would be foolish, wouldn't it?**

★　★　★　★　★　★　★　★　★　★　★

When Prince Albert ascended to the English throne in 1936, he chose the name George VI, honoring Queen Victoria's wishes that no future monarch should be named Albert. Shortly after the inauguration, he and his wife, the Duchess of York, attended a London production of *Tonight at 8:30* starring Noël Coward and Gertrude Lawrence. As the regal couple stepped into the royal box just before the opening act, the entire audience rose to their feet. Observing from off stage, Lawrence said to Coward, "What an entrance!" Coward, rarely at a loss for words, added his own reaction:

What a part!

★ ★ ★ ★ ★ ★ ★ ★ ★ ★

The director of such classic films as *The Philadelphia Story*, *A Star Is Born*, and *My Fair Lady*, George Cukor in 1952 was directing *It Should Happen to You*, a film starring Judy Holliday and a newcomer named Jack Lemmon. A little too eager to impress, Lemmon found himself overacting a number of scenes. Each time he did, Cukor would shout, "Less! Less!" This happened again and again. Finally, Lemmon said in frustration, "Mr. Cukor, don't you want me to act at all?" Cukor replied with a smile:

Dear boy, you're finally beginning to understand.

★ ★ ★ ★ ★ ★ ★ ★ ★ ★

The screenwriter Julius Epstein was working for Warner Brothers when Jack Warner instituted a policy that required writers to punch a time clock and be at work all day, from nine o'clock to six. When the writers protested, the movie mogul defended his policy by saying, "If executives can come in at nine, railroad presidents can come in at nine, bank presidents can come in at nine, why can't writers come in at nine?" The writers caved in and struggled under the new regimen. Several months later, a film with a script cowritten by Epstein was panned by critics. At a staff meeting, Warner angrily blamed the writers, charging, "This is absolutely the worst crap you have ever written." To the delight of his peers, Epstein sweetly replied:

I can't understand it.
We came in every morning at nine.

★ ★ ★ ★ ★ ★ ★ ★ ★ ★

In the 1934 comedy *It's a Gift*, W. C. Fields plays grocery clerk Harold Bissonette, who moves his family to California to take over an orange grove (which turns out to be a shack and one scrawny tree). Shortly after his arrival, Bissonette is approached by a land developer, who learns the land is destined to become the site of an athletic stadium. He makes a few ridiculously low offers, but Bissonette, whose resolve has been bolstered by generous swigs from his flask of gin, stands firm. When the frustrated developer finally exclaims, "You're drunk!" Bissonette replies in a way that would have made Winston Churchill proud:

> **Yeah, and you're crazy.**
> **I'll be sober tomorrow,**
> **but you'll be crazy the rest of your life.**

✳ ✳ ✳ ✳ ✳ ✳ ✳ ✳ ✳ ✳ ✳

Born and raised in Omaha, Nebraska, the teenage Henry Fonda was introduced to acting by Marlon Brando's mother, the founder of a local community theater. From his debut role in the 1934 Broadway play *The Farmer Takes a Wife* to his final role in the 1981 film *On Golden Pond* (for which he won an Oscar for Best Actor), Fonda created some of the most memorable characters in stage and screen history. Late in his career, he was approached by a young actor, who asked with deference, "What is the most important thing a young actor has to know?" The aging actor smiled and said:

> **How to become an old actor.**

✳ ✳ ✳ ✳ ✳ ✳ ✳ ✳ ✳ ✳ ✳

Hollywood feuds are carried out with a bit more flair than feuds in other industries. In 1997, NBC's West Coast president Don Ohlmeyer suspected that Michael Ovitz, then president of the Walt Disney Company, was working behind the scenes to fuel a sexual harassment charge against him. In an interview, Ohlmeyer described Ovitz as "The Antichrist." When fellow media mogul David Geffen was told of Ohlmeyer's characterization of Ovitz, he replied:

> **Apparently, Don Ohlmeyer thinks**
> **more highly of Mike Ovitz than I do.**

✳ ✳ ✳ ✳ ✳ ✳ ✳ ✳ ✳ ✳ ✳

For years, when Hollywood producer Samuel Goldwyn would run into Groucho Marx, the first words out of Goldwyn's mouth were always, "How's Harpo?" While Groucho initially accepted this as a mild eccentricity, it began to bother him after a time. Finally, when it happened once again, Marx erupted, "Goddamn it, Sam, every time we meet, you ask 'How's Harpo?' and that's it. You never ask how I am, and you never ask about anything else. To be honest with you, I'm getting sick and tired of it." Goldwyn got a contrite look on his face and said, "I'm sorry, Groucho. How are you?" Feeling better, Groucho said, "I'm fine, Sam. Thanks for asking." Goldwyn then said:

And how's Harpo?

✳ ✳ ✳ ✳ ✳ ✳ ✳ ✳ ✳ ✳ ✳

Best known for the comic operas he wrote in collaboration with Arthur Sullivan, W. S. Gilbert was a brilliant librettist and lyricist. He could also be perfectionistic and demanding, qualities that caused the relationship between the two men to deteriorate over time. Gilbert could also be dictatorial with actors. During a rehearsal one day, he laced into an actor and wouldn't let up. Finally, the proud actor took a stand, saying, "See here, sir, I will not be bullied. I know my lines." Gilbert shot back:

Possibly, but you don't know mine.

✳ ✳ ✳ ✳ ✳ ✳ ✳ ✳ ✳ ✳ ✳

While W. S. Gilbert was often difficult with actors, he could occasionally be quite charming and engaging. One day, he was searching the playhouse for an actress, eager to speak with her about her recent performance. When he asked the men on the stage crew if they had seen her, one of the stagehands replied,

"She's round behind." Gilbert got a great laugh from the entire crew when he quipped:

Yes, I know that, but where is she?

⋆ ⋆ ⋆ ⋆ ⋆ ⋆ ⋆ ⋆ ⋆ ⋆

After a decade of foundation-laying roles on the New York stage and in occasional films, John Goodman in 1988 landed the role of Dan Conner in the hit TV sitcom *Roseanne*. A big man with an engaging personality, he went on to establish himself as a respected character and comedic actor. In 1994, shortly after the release of *The Flintstones*, he appeared on *The Tonight Show with Jay Leno*. When Leno asked Goodman what playing the role of Fred Flintstone was likely to do for his career, he answered:

I can pretty much kiss those Ibsen festivals good-bye.

⋆ ⋆ ⋆ ⋆ ⋆ ⋆ ⋆ ⋆ ⋆ ⋆

Rex Harrison's most famous role began in 1956 when he played Professor Henry Higgins (opposite Julie Andrews as Eliza Doolittle) in *My Fair Lady*, Lerner and Loewe's adaptation of Shaw's famous *Pygmalion* story. The musical was a spectacular success, running for over six years. Harrison also starred in the 1964 film version (this time with Audrey Hepburn as Eliza), winning an Oscar for his performance. In the film, the snobbish and misogynistic Higgins takes a bet from Colonel Hugh Pickering (played by Wilfrid Hyde-White) that he can't transform a Cockney flower girl into a high-class lady. At one point, Pickering asks Higgins, "Are you a man of good character where women are concerned?" Higgins responds with a question of his own:

**Have you ever met a man of good character
where women are concerned?**

★ ★ ★ ★ ★ ★ ★ ★ ★ ★ ★

The leading man in Cecil B. DeMille's first feature film, 1914's *The Squaw Man*, Dustin Farnum became America's first matinee idol, earning more than $10,000 per week. While walking down a Manhattan street one day, he ran into the humorist Oliver Herford. Born in England, Herford's writings and cartoons were done in the style of the English humor magazine *Punch*, and often lampooned politicians and celebrities. When Herford asked Farnum, "How are things going?" the vain actor said, "I've never been better! My new play is a smash hit. Why, only yesterday, I had the audience glued to their seats." Herford dryly replied:

How clever of you to think of it.

★ ★ ★ ★ ★ ★ ★ ★ ★ ★ ★

Alfred Hitchcock's 1944 film *Lifeboat*, a drama about eight survivors of a freighter sunk by a German U-boat, was one of the most popular films of the year (it was also nominated for three Academy Awards). While posing for publicity photographs for the film, actress Mary Anderson approached the director and asked, "What is my best side, Mr. Hitchcock?" His reply was soon being circulated all around Hollywood:

My dear, you're sitting on it.

★ ★ ★ ★ ★ ★ ★ ★ ★ ★ ★

George S. Kaufman and Morrie Ryskind cowrote the script for the Marx Brothers 1928 Broadway production of *Animal Crackers* (later made into the classic 1930 film). During rehearsal for the play, Groucho and the rest of the brothers took so many liberties with their lines that the play was beginning to bear little relationship to the original script. It was upsetting to the writers, but given the ad-libbing nature of the artists on stage, there was little they could do about it. During a rehearsal one day, Kaufman and Ryskind were observing from the back of the theater when Kaufman suddenly jumped to his feet and exclaimed in a voice loud enough for the players on stage to hear:

> ### Excuse me, Morrie,
> ### but I think I just heard one of the original lines!

✳ ✳ ✳ ✳ ✳ ✳ ✳ ✳ ✳ ✳ ✳

One day in the 1930s, actress Ruth Gordon and George S. Kaufman were discussing Gordon's latest play, an avant-garde production that featured the actress on an empty stage, with no scenery or props. Excited about a play that would fully display her acting talent, Gordon gushed: "In the first scene, I'm on the left side of the stage, and the audience has to imagine I'm eating dinner in a crowded restaurant. Then in scene two, I run over to the right side of the stage and the audience imagines I'm in my own drawing room." Kaufman, who didn't share Gordon's enthusiasm for the play, interrupted to say:

> ### And the second night, you have to imagine
> ### there's an audience out front.

✳ ✳ ✳ ✳ ✳ ✳ ✳ ✳ ✳ ✳ ✳

Working at Columbia Pictures during studio head Harry Cohn's tyrannical reign, the young Herman J. Mankiewicz attended a meeting in which Cohn launched into an attack on a film he'd seen the previous night in his private screening room. When somebody suggested Cohn might have had a different reaction if he'd viewed the film in a crowded theater, he scoffed at the idea, saying, "When I'm alone in a projection room, I have a foolproof device for judging whether a picture is good or bad. If my fanny squirms, it's bad. If my fanny doesn't squirm, it's good. It's as simple as that." The image was too much for the irreverent Mankiewicz, who lost his job at Columbia when he quipped:

> ### Imagine, the whole world wired to Harry Cohn's ass!

✳ ✳ ✳ ✳ ✳ ✳ ✳ ✳ ✳ ✳

In the 1966 movie *The Professionals*, Lee Marvin and Burt Lancaster head up a group of world-weary adventurers who are hired by rich Texan J. W. Grant (Ralph Bellamy) to rescue his young and beautiful wife, Maria (Claudia Cardinale), from her Mexican kidnappers. They ultimately discover that Maria hasn't been kidnapped at all, but has escaped from her physically abusive husband and run off with her Mexican lover. They "rescue" her anyway and head back to Texas to complete the contract and collect the reward money. At the very last minute, Marvin's character realizes that returning Maria to her husband would be wrong, and he sets her free. Grant is livid, and lashes out by saying, "You bastard!" In the final line of the film, Marvin delivers the perfect retort:

Yes sir. In my case, an accident of birth.
But you, you're a self-made man.

✳ ✳ ✳ ✳ ✳ ✳ ✳ ✳ ✳ ✳

A staple ingredient of all James Bond films was the relationship between Bond and M's secretary, Miss Moneypenny. When Agent 007 would show up for a meeting with M, he and Moneypenny could always be counted on to engage in a bit of provocative dialogue. In the 1962 film *Dr. No*, Sean Connery's Bond arrives at M's office and says to Moneypenny (played by Lois Maxwell), "What gives?" She replies provocatively:

Me—given an ounce of encouragement.

✳ ✳ ✳ ✳ ✳ ✳ ✳ ✳ ✳ ✳

In the 1997 film *As Good As It Gets*, Jack Nicholson plays the role of romance novelist Melvin Udall, a highly successful writer with a major chip on his shoulder and a serious obsessive-compulsive disorder. Nicholson's performance earned him his third Oscar for Best Actor, and the film was popular with moviegoers, in large part because of the smart dialogue. In one scene, an adoring female fan gushes at Melvin, saying, "How do you write women so well?" The bad-tempered writer offers one of the great—albeit one of the most insensitive—replies in film history:

> **I think of a man,**
> **and then take away reason and accountability.**

★ ★ ★ ★ ★ ★ ★ ★ ★ ★ ★

Hosting the forty-sixth annual Academy Awards ceremonies in 1974, David Niven was about to introduce Elizabeth Taylor when a thirty-three-year-old Californian named Robert Opal shocked a national television audience by "streaking" across the stage and flashing a peace sign to the much-amused celebrities in the auditorium. As security guards escorted the nude man from the stage, Niven looked into the camera and observed:

> **Probably the only laugh that man will ever get**
> **is for stripping and showing his shortcomings.**

★ ★ ★ ★ ★ ★ ★ ★ ★ ★ ★

On the day he showed up to shoot the famous torture scene in the 1976 film *Marathon Man*, with Laurence Olivier in the role of the evil Nazi dentist, Dustin Hoffman looked like death warmed over. Film buffs have long believed that Hoffman stayed up for three nights to prepare for the scene, but he recently revealed the truth: "My first marriage was breaking up, Studio 54 was all in vogue, and (there was) the excuse not to sleep for a week for your art so you could party big time. Love, sex, drugs, rock 'n roll. I did that for my art and showed up to shoot on location. I had the rawness of voice, it looked like the character hadn't slept, it was the greatest preparation I've ever done." When Hoffman arrived on the set and explained how he had "prepared" for the scene, Olivier simply replied:

> **Dear boy, why not try *acting*?**

★ ★ ★ ★ ★ ★ ★ ★ ★ ★

The Nobel Prize–winning playwright Eugene O'Neill was born in a Times Square hotel room in 1888, not far from where his actor father was starring in a Broadway play. James O'Neill was a popular nineteenth-century actor who often dragged his family with him on national tours. The first two decades of O'Neill's early life were unhappy and trouble-filled. His mother was a morphine addict, he was kicked out of Princeton, he was married and divorced within three years, he lived in drunken squalor in New York City flophouses, and he contracted tuberculosis. While recovering from TB in his midtwenties, he engaged in a period of voracious reading, which enhanced his recovery and inspired him to become a playwright. When he informed his father of his decision to work in this aspect of the theatrical world, he attempted to establish a connection between himself and his father by saying, "A chip off the old block, eh?" The elder O'Neill responded with what he thought was a more appropriate metaphor:

Say, rather, a slice off the old ham.

★ ★ ★ ★ ★ ★ ★ ★ ★ ★

Making her first musical appearance at age ten on a television variety show, Dolly Parton moved to Nashville after high school and was soon writing and singing chart-topping songs. An extraordinary singer-songwriter, her Oscar-nominated role in the 1980 movie *Nine to Five* extended her talents to the film world as well. Also a successful entrepreneur, in 1986 she opened Dollywood, a popular theme park in the Smoky Mountains. When once asked if she resented "dumb blonde" jokes, she demonstrated wit to match her many other skills:

Not at all.
In the first place, I know I'm not dumb.
And in the second, I know I'm not blonde.

✶ ✶ ✶ ✶ ✶ ✶ ✶ ✶ ✶ ✶ ✶

Growing up in the early 1900s in New York City's Hell's Kitchen turned out to be excellent preparation for the many "tough-guy" roles that actor George Raft would play in his long Hollywood career. Raft added to his "heavy" mystique by spending much of his life hanging around with Bugsy Siegel and other real-life gangsters. A lifelong gambler and a profligate spender, he was reputed to have gone through $10 million during his career. When once asked where all his movie earnings went, he said:

> **Part of the loot went for gambling,**
> **part for horses, and part for women.**
> **The rest I spent foolishly.**

✶ ✶ ✶ ✶ ✶ ✶ ✶ ✶ ✶ ✶ ✶

In 1960, Otto Preminger brought Leon Uris's epic novel *Exodus* to the screen with an all-star cast, headed by Paul Newman. The film, which dramatized the emergence of Israel as an independent nation in 1947, ended up being a very lengthy 212 minutes long. At an early screening of the film, Preminger invited a number of friends from the entertainment industry, including comedian Mort Sahl. After about three hours, when Sahl began to notice people squirming in their seats, he brought a little comic relief to their discomfort when he stood up and hollered:

> **Otto, let my people go!**

✶ ✶ ✶ ✶ ✶ ✶ ✶ ✶ ✶ ✶ ✶

Steven Spielberg wanted the American composer and conductor John Williams to write the score for his film *Schindler's List*. Williams had already composed scores for a number of Spielberg films, so he seemed a natural choice to do this one as well. However, when Spielberg showed the composer an unscored version of the film, Williams was so moved that he felt inadequate to the task. "You need a better composer than I am to score this film," Williams said. Spielberg replied:

Yes, I know, but they're all dead.

✴ ✴ ✴ ✴ ✴ ✴ ✴ ✴ ✴ ✴

The 1992 thriller *Basic Instinct* contains one of the most notorious scenes in movie history. Sharon Stone plays the role of a sultry bisexual murder suspect. As she is being grilled in a police interrogation room by burned-out detective Michael Douglas and several other cops, she seductively uncrosses her legs, revealing that she is wearing no panties. As the sensuous suspect displays her wares to the leering detectives, she slowly lights a cigarette. Informed by a detective that smoking is not allowed, she replies provocatively:

What are you going to do, charge me with smoking?

✴ ✴ ✴ ✴ ✴ ✴ ✴ ✴ ✴ ✴

In the late 1960s, Tom Stoppard's *Rosencrantz & Guildenstern Are Dead* was hugely successful, with long runs in London, New York, and Tokyo. Stoppard was not terribly surprised, however, having been confident about the play's chances from the beginning. After the 1967 premiere, a friend who didn't understand the play approached Stoppard and asked, "Tom, what's it about?" The cocksure playwright replied:

It's about to make me a rich man.

✶ ✶ ✶ ✶ ✶ ✶ ✶ ✶ ✶ ✶ ✶

Beginning with the 1942 film *Woman of the Year* and ending with *Guess Who's Coming to Dinner* in 1967, Spencer Tracy starred in nine films with lifelong love Katharine Hepburn. In every film, Tracy got top billing. One day, the playwright-turned-director Garson Kanin questioned Tracy for insisting that his name always appear first on marquees and billboards. "Why not?" asked the testy Tracy. When Kanin countered with, "How about ladies first?" Tracy answered firmly:

This is a movie, not a lifeboat.

✶ ✶ ✶ ✶ ✶ ✶ ✶ ✶ ✶ ✶ ✶

One of a number of top movie studio executives who enjoyed a brief nap in the early afternoon, Jack Warner gave his secretary strict orders not to be disturbed at such times. One day, however, Bette Davis—extremely angry over a script change—stormed past the secretary and into Warner's office. Even though Warner was reclining on the couch with his eyes closed, Davis was so upset she ranted and raved for several minutes. As she finally began to calm down, Warner—with his eyes still closed—reached for the phone and said something to his secretary that caused Davis to buckle over with laughter (and, it is said, that instantly resolved the crisis):

**Come in and wake me up.
I'm having a nightmare.**

✶ ✶ ✶ ✶ ✶ ✶ ✶ ✶ ✶ ✶ ✶

Thirty-nine-year-old Mae West made her film debut in the 1932 film *Night After Night*. While she didn't have a starring role, she was such a force on screen that George Raft, the film's headliner said, "She stole everything but the camera." During the shooting of the film, however, West was concerned that the seasoned

English actress Alison Skipworth was stealing some of her scenes. When the sixty-nine-year-old Skipworth heard West complaining to the director, she approached the buxom new star and said, "You forget, I've been an actress for forty years." West replied sweetly:

Don't worry, dear. I'll keep your secret.

✴ ✴ ✴ ✴ ✴ ✴ ✴ ✴ ✴ ✴

In the 1934 film *Belle of the Nineties*, Mae West plays Ruby Carter, a nightclub entertainer who moves from St. Louis to New Orleans so that her boxer boyfriend can concentrate on winning the championship title. She soon becomes the toast of the town and the central figure in a series of entanglements. When a preacher named Brother Eben (Sam McDaniel) asks Ruby, "Are you in town for good?" she replies in a classic double-entendre:

I expect to be here, but not for good.

✴ ✴ ✴ ✴ ✴ ✴ ✴ ✴ ✴ ✴

Born in a small town in Austria, Billy Wilder began his career as a scriptwriter in 1920s Germany. The rise of Hitler forced the Jewish Wilder to flee his homeland, first to France and then to America, where he became one of Hollywood's most famous directors. During World War II, he served as a colonel in the U.S. Army. In 1945, after hostilities ended, he stayed on in Germany to screen film footage coming out of the concentration camps and to audition performers for postwar plays to be presented to German audiences. One day, while casting for an upcoming Passion play, he auditioned the German actor Anton Lang. Lang, who had been a member of Hitler's SS during the war, told Wilder that he had played the role of Christ in some prewar Passion plays, and would dearly love to play the role once again. Wilder replied coolly:

On one condition; use real nails.

✳ ✳ ✳ ✳ ✳ ✳ ✳ ✳ ✳ ✳

In addition to being one of the world's most gifted poets, William Butler Yeats was also a prolific playwright, authoring twenty-six plays in his lifetime. Yeats loved the energy of the theater, and was often seen in the empty seats during rehearsals of his plays. In 1908, the acclaimed English actress Mrs. Patrick Campbell was starring in the title role of his play *Deirdre*. During one problematic scene, the volatile actress threw one of her typical temper tantrums. In the middle of the eruption, she noticed Yeats at the back of the theater. Thinking she might have found an ally, she regained her composure and yelled out from the stage, "Mr. Yeats, I'd give anything to know what you're thinking." Yeats thought for a moment, and then replied:

I'm thinking of the master of a wayside Indian railway station, who sent a message to his company's headquarters saying, "Tigress on the loose: wire instructions."

literary repartee

The plays of George Bernard Shaw are characterized by some of the wittiest dialogue of all time, and occasionally some snappy and provocative comebacks. As it turns out, Shaw's interest in repartee would also stand him in good stead in his personal affairs. A tall, stick-thin vegetarian, Shaw's eating habits and physique were the object of much interest. While comments were rarely made directly to him, an exception occurred one day when Shaw ran into the portly writer G. K. Chesterton (some versions of the story say it was the equally portly newspaper magnate, Lord Northcliffe). Chesterton looked Shaw over and said, "Looking at you, Shaw, one would think there was a famine in the land." Shaw examined the oversized body of his adversary and said:

**Looking at you,
one would think you caused it.**

Shortly afterward, according to literary legend, the two authors met again, allowing Chesterton to exact a measure of revenge. As the story goes, after Shaw said to his rotund rival, "If I were as fat as you, I'd hang myself," Chesterton rejoined, "And if I had it in mind to hang myself, I'd use you as the rope!" While both of these stories are surely apocryphal, they've been told and retold by fans of both writers for more than eighty years.

While reading Dan Brown's *The Da Vinci Code* recently, I came across a wonderful little story that not only brought a chuckle, but made me wonder if Brown might not have been inspired by the first Shaw anecdote. At one point in the book, the protagonist Robert Langdon runs into his old friend Sir Leigh Teabing after a long absence. Looking at Langdon, Teabing says, "It looks like you lost some weight." Langdon looks at Teabing and replies:

It looks like you found some!

When it comes to the literary life, there is *real life* repartee, there is *fictional* repartee, and I've even discovered a spectacular example of what might be called *hypothetical* repartee. It involves the poets Carl Sandburg and T. S. Eliot, who for many years shared the same publisher and the same editor, Robert Giroux at Harcourt Brace. One day many years ago, both men were scheduled to meet with Giroux on the same day. Knowing Sandburg and Eliot didn't have the greatest fondness for one another, Giroux instructed his staff to make sure the two men didn't run into each other. When he returned to his office after lunch, however, Giroux was aghast to discover both men in his office, sitting as far from one another as possible. Entering the room, Giroux sensed a definite chill in the air as he heard Sandburg say to Eliot, "Your face has deep lines." Because of Giroux's arrival, the interaction was interrupted and Eliot had no chance to respond. Later, Giroux related the story to his friend, the poet and lawyer Melvin Cane. If he had been in Eliot's shoes, Cane said, he would have replied:

I can't say the same for your poetry.

Whether they appear in the actual lives of writers or in their literary creations, clever quips and witty replies are one of the most fascinating aspects of the literary life. Let's examine more *literary repartee* in the remainder of the chapter.

⋆ ⋆ ⋆ ⋆ ⋆ ⋆ ⋆ ⋆ ⋆ ⋆ ⋆

Best known as the author of the spectacularly successful 1904 play *Peter Pan*, the Scottish writer James M. Barrie wrote many other novels and plays, including a popular 1902 satire, *The Admirable Crichton*, and the highly regarded *What Every Woman Knows* in 1908. In an interview at the height of his career, a journalist said, "Sir James, I suppose some of your plays do better than others. They're not all successes, are they?" Barrie, who may have been waiting for a moment like this for years, smiled and said:

> **No, some peter out**
> **and some pan out.**

✳ ✳ ✳ ✳ ✳ ✳ ✳ ✳ ✳ ✳ ✳

The American writer Jay McInerney once recalled a story from his college days at Syracuse University when he was in a class taught by short story writer Raymond Carver. Carver's struggles with alcoholism in the 1970s had nearly ruined his life, but after a successful rehabilitation in the '70s, he taught for several years before re-embarking on a full-time writing career. During one class, a student complained, "This class is called 'Form and Theory of the Short Story,' but all we do is sit around and talk about the books. Where's the form and the theory?" Carver was not a professional educator; he was a writer who was teaching on the side. After a long pause, he replied:

> **Well, that's a good question.**
> **I guess I'd say the point here**
> **is that we read good books and discuss them.**
> **And then you form your own theory.**

✳ ✳ ✳ ✳ ✳ ✳ ✳ ✳ ✳ ✳ ✳

G. K. Chesterton was a prolific and wide-ranging author, respected and admired for his literary criticism, essays, volumes of poetry, biographies, novels, and Father Brown mystery stories. A corpulent man who often made jokes about his

size, he once remarked, "Just the other day in the Underground I enjoyed the pleasure of offering my seat to three ladies." In an interview, he was once asked the
classic question, "What book would you most like to have with you on a desert
island?" He replied:

Thomas's Guide to Practical Shipbuilding.

★ ★ ★ ★ ★ ★ ★ ★ ★ ★

In 1904, Kentucky-born Irvin S. Cobb moved to New York City, where he became
a staff writer at the *World* newspaper. He went on to become an extremely popular
columnist and a well-known writer, with more than sixty books to his credit. Like
many other employees at the paper, he struggled under the dictatorial style of
editor Charles Chapin. Arriving at work one day, Cobb was told that Chapin was
sick at home. He remarked:

Nothing trivial, I presume.

★ ★ ★ ★ ★ ★ ★ ★ ★ ★

Irvin S. Cobb was walking down a Manhattan street one day when he ran into
Fannie Hurst, another popular writer in the early part of the century. Hurst had
recently put on some significant weight, so Cobb passed by without saying
anything. Hurst teased Cobb by saying, "Irvin, aren't you going to say hello?"
Doing a double take, Cobb said, "Don't tell me it's Fannie Hurst?" She replied,
"Yes, the same Fannie Hurst." Cobb, a man of ample girth himself, stepped back
and quipped:

The same Hurst, I will concede,
but definitely not the same *fanny*.

★ ★ ★ ★ ★ ★ ★ ★ ★ ★

The English statesman Benjamin Disraeli was also a prolific writer, cranking out scores of novels in his career, many of them written to help pay off debts accumulated as a result of his costly political campaigns and extravagant lifestyle. One day, an unknown author sent him a first draft of his novel, asking for feedback. Disraeli sent a note saying:

Thank you for the manuscript.
I shall lose no time in reading it.

Disraeli loved the line so much that he used it for the remainder of his career when he received unsolicited manuscripts.

★ ★ ★ ★ ★ ★ ★ ★ ★ ★ ★

In the latter part of the eighteenth century, Antoine de Rivarol was famous in his own country of France and well known throughout Europe for his clever epigrams and aphorisms. He also achieved notoriety for *The Little Almanac of Our Great Men*, a 1788 satire that lampooned the famous figures of his day. De Rivarol was approached one day by a minor French poet who requested some feedback about a little two-line poem he had recently written. The witty aphorist examined the poem for a moment and replied:

Very nice, although there are dull stretches.

★ ★ ★ ★ ★ ★ ★ ★ ★ ★ ★

In 1946, two years before he was to win the Nobel Prize in literature, T. S. Eliot met newly named editor Robert Giroux at the Ritz-Carlton in Manhattan. Giroux was understandably nervous about meeting such a towering figure, but Eliot immediately put the young editor at ease by asking him, as one editor to another, if he had ever had any author trouble. Later in the conversation, Giroux asked Eliot if he agreed with the widely held notion that most editors are failed writers. Eliot replied:

Perhaps, but so are most writers.

✶ ✶ ✶ ✶ ✶ ✶ ✶ ✶ ✶ ✶ ✶

Book editor Maxwell Perkins had a gift for recognizing and developing literary talent. In the early decades of the twentieth century, he played a major role in the success of F. Scott Fitzgerald, Ernest Hemingway, Thomas Wolfe, and many other writers. In 1928, Wolfe sent Perkins a rambling and massive (1,114 pages) first draft of a fictionalized autobiography he was planning to title *Look Homeward Angel*. Opening the manuscript, Perkins was touched to discover that Wolfe had dedicated the book to him. As he dug into the book, however, he found it tough going. Recognizing that he had a major editing job on his hands, he sent a copy to old friend F. Scott Fitzgerald and asked for his reactions. A few weeks later, Perkins received a note from Fitzgerald that read:

Dear Max, I liked the dedication,
but after that I thought it fell off a bit.

✶ ✶ ✶ ✶ ✶ ✶ ✶ ✶ ✶ ✶ ✶

The author of more than forty books of fiction, biography, poetry, and essays, Hamlin Garland was best known for his autobiographical novels about farm life in the Midwest. He befriended some of the most famous people of the time—like Mark Twain, Theodore Roosevelt, and Walt Whitman—and kept up a voluminous correspondence with them. At the height of his career, he attended a Boston dinner party at which the hostess served a dish of mushrooms. Hesitating before the dish, the hostess assured him the mushrooms were not poisonous. A short while later, noticing he still hadn't touched the dish, she said, "Are you still afraid of the mushrooms?" Garland good-naturedly replied:

No, I was just thinking of the effect
on American letters should you be wrong.

★ ★ ★ ★ ★ ★ ★ ★ ★ ★

When Elinor Glyn died in 1943, she was one of England's best-known celebrities, the author of many racy (for the time) novels that several decades earlier had scandalized Edwardian England. Glyn's notoriety inspired one of my favorite poems, the one I always recall when I try to remember the correct pronunciation of the word "err":

> *Would you like to sin*
> *With Elinor Glyn*
> *On a tiger skin?*
> *Or would you prefer*
> *To err*
> *With her*
> *On some other fur?*

In 1899, Glyn sent a manuscript of her first novel, *The Visits of Elizabeth*, to a London publisher. Hoping to put some pressure on the publisher, the little-known writer appended a note that read, "Would you please publish the enclosed manuscript or return it without delay, as I have other irons in the fire." The publisher, likely turned off by some of the racier passages in the manuscript, returned it with a rejection slip that read:

Put this with your other irons.

★ ★ ★ ★ ★ ★ ★ ★ ★ ★

Beginning with his *Inside Europe* book in 1936, the widely traveled John Gunther became something of a cottage industry, producing many other similarly titled books over the decades. After *Inside U.S.A.* was published in 1947, Sinclair Lewis said that it was "the richest treasure-house of facts about America that has ever been published, and probably the most spirited and interesting." After the publication of *Inside South America* in 1967, Gunther revealed in an interview with Clifton Fadiman that he was busy working on his next book, *Inside Australia*. When Fadiman asked, "What will you do when you run out of continents?" Gunther, now past sixty-five and not in the best of health, smiled and said:

Try incontinence.

Sadly, Gunther died of liver cancer in 1970 and would never finish the Australia project. (It was taken over by another writer and published in 1972.)

★ ★ ★ ★ ★ ★ ★ ★ ★ ★

Dr. Samuel Johnson's ten-volume *Lives of the English Poets*, which surveyed all the major English poets up to the late 1700s, established Johnson as the leading authority on English poetry. One day, Johnson's colleague Maurice Mann asked Johnson about the relative merits of two current English poets, saying, "Pray Sir, do you reckon Derrick or Smart the best poet?" Both men were considered quite inferior by Johnson, and he almost seemed offended that he was asked to judge them. In disgust, he answered:

Sir, there is no settling the point of precedency between a louse and a flea.

★ ★ ★ ★ ★ ★ ★ ★ ★ ★

In 1922, James Joyce's novel *Ulysses* was published in Paris (English publishers had shunned the book, and it would not appear in America until 1936). Joyce's stream-of-consciousness story of a day in the life of three Dubliners provoked immediate and intense reaction, some critics viewing it as impenetrable trash, others hailing it as a classic. Several years after the book was published, a fan approached Joyce on a Zurich street and gushed, "May I kiss the hand that wrote *Ulysses?*" Joyce demurred, saying:

No, it did lots of other things too.

★ ★ ★ ★ ★ ★ ★ ★ ★ ★

Joseph Heller's 1961 debut novel *Catch-22* was originally titled *Catch-18*, but the title was so similar to Leon Uris's *Mila 18* that it was changed at the last minute. The book got off to an extremely slow start, and seemed in danger of being lost to obscurity. But that all changed one day when a reporter asked the writer S. J. Perelman if he had read any good books lately, and he replied *"Catch-22."* Within months, the book was being critically praised (many hailing it "a modern masterpiece") and well on the way to becoming one of the best-selling books of all time. It took Heller thirteen years to finish his next novel, *Something Happened*, but it quickly became a best-seller as well. In 1987, Heller was asked by a reporter to comment on reports that he had recently signed a contract for $4 million for his next two novels. He replied:

> **I will only confirm that I got less than I asked for and more than I deserve.**

★ ★ ★ ★ ★ ★ ★ ★ ★ ★

John Pentland Mahaffy was an Irish scholar who was regarded as one of the world's experts on Greek and Roman history. A man of great wit as well as erudition, he once went hunting with some friends when another member of the party accidentally shot a bullet through the top of his hat, inches above his skull. The unflappable Mahaffy pulled the hat off his head and observed to his distraught colleague:

> **Two inches lower and you would have shot away ninety percent of the Greek in Ireland.**

★ ★ ★ ★ ★ ★ ★ ★ ★ ★

Born in New York City, Frank McCourt was raised in poverty in Limerick, Ireland. He returned to New York City at age nineteen, went to college on the

GI bill, fell in love with literature, and eventually ended up teaching high school English in New York City for more than two decades. In 1996, *Angela's Ashes*, McCourt's memoir about his Irish youth, shot to the top of the *New York Times* best-seller list. The book remained on the best-seller list for 117 weeks, ultimately selling more than five million copies worldwide. It also won McCourt a Pulitzer Prize and the National Book Award. When asked, at age sixty-seven, how his life had changed as a result of his newfound fame, McCourt replied:

> **Supermodels with legs up to their shoulders**
> **kept coming up and praising me.**
> **I said to my wife, "If this had happened 30 years ago,**
> **I'd be dead of whiskey and fornication."**

★ ★ ★ ★ ★ ★ ★ ★ ★ ★

After winning the Nobel Prize in literature in 1978, Isaac Bashevis Singer suffered the fate of many previous winners—people who previously paid little attention to him now showed great interest. In one interview, a journalist discovered something the writer's fans had long known, that he was a strict vegetarian. When the reporter asked, "Are you a vegetarian for religious reasons or out of concern for your health?" Singer answered:

> **I do it out of consideration for the chicken.**

★ ★ ★ ★ ★ ★ ★ ★ ★ ★

Born in Paris in 1671, Jean-Baptiste Rousseau (no relation to Jean-Jacques Rousseau), was a lyric poet and writer of sacred songs and odes. He died in poverty, but his odes went on to become popular with French composers throughout the eighteenth and nineteenth centuries. After writing *Ode to Posterity*, he sent a copy to Voltaire, seeking the opinion of the most respected literary figure of his time. After reading it, Voltaire looked at the title one last time before delivering his devastating verdict:

I do not think this poem will reach its destination.

★ ★ ★ ★ ★ ★ ★ ★ ★ ★ ★

In a famous 1849 essay, Henry David Thoreau became history's first great proponent of the concept of "civil disobedience." Protesting a government that legally permitted the practice of slavery, he refused to pay the Massachusetts poll tax, an act that resulted in his arrest in 1846. While he spent only one night in jail (his aunt Maria paid the tax without his permission, making him furious), the experience set the stage for one of his most famous replies. When Ralph Waldo Emerson heard that Thoreau had been arrested, he rushed over to the Concord jail. Seeing his colleague and dear friend behind bars, he said with concern, "Henry, why are you here?" Thoreau, hoping to appeal to Emerson's conscience, answered the question with a question:

Waldo, why are you *not* here?

★ ★ ★ ★ ★ ★ ★ ★ ★ ★ ★

In 1927, thirty-three-year-old Ohio native James Thurber was hired by Harold Ross as managing editor and staff writer for the recently launched *New Yorker* magazine. Almost immediately, Thurber's short stories, humorous essays, and cartoons helped set the cosmopolitan and urbane tone of the publication. In the early 1930s, Hollywood mogul Samuel Goldwyn was luring many writers out to Hollywood, and he did his best to entice Thurber, once offering him $500 a week. Thurber, who had no desire to leave his adopted home of New York City, declined the offer with the fictitious but plausible reply, "I'm sorry, but Mr. Ross has met the increase." Undaunted, Goldwyn offered $1,000, but was again rejected, again with Thurber saying that Mr. Ross had met the increase. He then offered $1,500. Again, the same result. He eventually raised his offer to $2,500, but Thurber kept declining in the same manner. After several months elapsed, Thurber was again contacted by Goldwyn, this time with an offer of $1,500 per week. Goldwyn had either forgotten his previous offer or had reconsidered it. How would Thurber reply this time? As it turns out, with his characteristic whimsy:

I'm sorry, but Mr. Ross has met the decrease.

★ ★ ★ ★ ★ ★ ★ ★ ★ ★

James Thurber's short stories, humorous sketches, and modern fables were widely translated, and he developed an international following. One day, a bilingual friend told Thurber that he had just read the French edition of *My Life and Hard Times,* a 1933 collection of autobiographical pieces. When the friend said, "You know, the book is even better in French," Thurber replied:

Yes, my work tends to lose something in the original.

★ ★ ★ ★ ★ ★ ★ ★ ★ ★

A masterful storyteller, Russian-born Sholem Aleichem created such unforgettable characters as Tevye the milkman, the eventual protagonist of the musical play *Fiddler on the Roof.* In the early 1900s, when Aleichem and Mark Twain were both living in New York City, legend has it that the two men were introduced to one another at a party. In that famous first meeting, Aleichem said that he too was a writer, adding, "Many people call me the Yiddish Mark Twain." Twain was a great admirer of Jewish people, once describing them as "a marvelous race . . . by long odds, the most marvelous the world has produced." A voracious reader, he was also familiar with Aleichem's writings. One can only imagine how Aleichem must have felt when Twain replied:

Yes, and many call me the American Sholem Aleichem.

★ ★ ★ ★ ★ ★ ★ ★ ★ ★

During a lecture tour in Utah, Mark Twain found himself in a discussion of polygamy with a Salt Lake City man who had several wives. After some time, neither man was able to make much headway with the other. Finally, the Mormon man charged, "Can you cite a single passage of scripture which forbids polygamy?" Twain fired back:

Certainly. "No man can serve two masters."

★ ★ ★ ★ ★ ★ ★ ★ ★ ★ ★

For many years, the outspoken Gore Vidal was famous for saying things that many people think but would never admit (like "Every time one of my friends succeeds, I die a little"). A popular guest on television talk shows, he could always be counted on for his candor and his wit, if not for his sensitivity. He had a long-term feud with Truman Capote, and when told of Capote's death in 1984, was said to have quipped:

Good career move.

★ ★ ★ ★ ★ ★ ★ ★ ★ ★ ★

In the 1760s, the aging French philosopher Voltaire was visited in his Swiss home by the legendary Giacomo Casanova, who had recently fled his creditors in Italy to seek greener pastures elsewhere. As the two men chatted, Voltaire learned that Casanova had just come from a visit with the Swiss poet and physiologist Albrecht von Haller. Voltaire praised von Haller's poetry and said he once had a most enjoyable visit with him. "Your praise for him is ill-returned," said Casanova, "for he has spoken disparagingly of you and your work." Voltaire took it all in before thoughtfully concluding:

Perhaps we are both mistaken.

★ ★ ★ ★ ★ ★ ★ ★ ★ ★ ★

Like many great satirical writers, Evelyn Waugh had a sharp and vicious tongue, a weapon he even used occasionally on his friends. One day, Randolph Churchill, son of the famous British statesman, went to an English hospital to have a lung removed. When Waugh was told the next day that the removed lung was not cancerous, he commented to a friend:

A typical triumph of modern science to find the only part of Randolph that was not malignant and remove it.

★ ★ ★ ★ ★ ★ ★ ★ ★ ★ ★

In his early years, Evelyn Waugh was brash and irreverent, much in the tradition of Oscar Wilde and George Bernard Shaw. After converting to Roman Catholicism in 1930, he mellowed some, but remnants of his earlier personality remained. Attending a dinner party at the Paris home of writer Nancy Mitford, Waugh treated a young French writer with great rudeness. Appalled by his behavior, Mitford asked Waugh how he could be so cruel and still consider himself a practicing Roman Catholic. He replied:

You have no idea how much nastier I would be if I was not a Catholic.

★ ★ ★ ★ ★ ★ ★ ★ ★ ★ ★

Primarily remembered today for his paintings, James McNeill Whistler also became a successful author with the publication of his 1890 book *The Gentle Art of Making Enemies*. An exceedingly witty man, he was one of the few people who could hold his own with the incomparable Oscar Wilde. In one legendary exchange, after Whistler had offered a particularly clever observation, Wilde said admiringly, "I wish I had said that." Whistler seized the moment, replying:

You will, Oscar, you will.

★ ★ ★ ★ ★ ★ ★ ★ ★ ★

Oscar Wilde was already a celebrated figure when the young George Bernard Shaw began to establish his reputation. One evening, the men met at the home of a mutual friend. Shaw, eager to impress Wilde, went to great length to describe his future plans, including his plan to publish his own magazine. Humoring his younger colleague, Wilde listened patiently and finally asked what the magazine would be called. Shaw said, "I'd want to impress my own personality on the public." And then, banging his fist on the table, he added, "I'd call it *Shaw's* magazine. Shaw! Shaw! Shaw!" Wilde calmly asked:

And how would you spell it?

Wilde was punning the name of Shaw with the epithet "pshaw" (now often pronounced "puh-SHAW" but in Wilde's day pronounced simply "shaw"). The word is rarely used these days, but for centuries has been an expression of contempt or disgust. At the time, according to an observer who was present, Wilde's question so impressed Shaw that he laughed heartily at the joke made against him.

6

political repartee

In 1798, a shocking rumor about second president John Adams was being whispered all around the country. According to the story, Adams had sent Charles C. Pinckney, one of his top generals, to England to bring back four young women as mistresses, two for the president and two for the general. When asked about the rumor, the president could have flatly denied it or expressed outrage at the mere mention of it. Instead, he replied:

I do declare, if this be true,
General Pinckney has kept them all for himself,
and cheated me out of my two.

Throughout history, politicians have been the object of vicious rumors and unflattering stories, invented by opponents and spread in hushed tones. When considering how best to respond, the most successful politicians have discovered that wit and humor may be the most effective method of stopping the rumors in their tracks.

A wonderful example occurred during John F. Kennedy's 1960 run for the presidency, when his campaign began to be dogged by rumors that his wealthy father was planning to use the family fortune to "buy the election." As the rumor began to develop traction, it threatened to distract Kennedy and take his campaign off message. Speaking at the annual Gridiron dinner in Washington, DC, the handsome young candidate seized the initiative by announcing that he had just received a telegram from his father. The fictional telegram, which effectively ended the rumors, read:

> JACK, DON'T BUY A SINGLE VOTE MORE THAN NECESSARY.
> I'LL BE DAMNED IF I'M GOING TO PAY FOR A LANDSLIDE.

During Ronald Reagan's reelection campaign in 1984, the seventy-three-year-old president was the oldest sitting chief executive in U.S. history. As his first term was drawing to a close, rumors circulated about his tendency to doze off in cabinet meetings and critics began to accuse him of "government by anecdote." In opinion polls, many Americans—especially the "Reagan Democrats" who had supported him in the last election—began to question his capacity to endure the demands of a second term. In his first debate with Democratic challenger Walter Mondale, Reagan put in a lackluster appearance and seemed in danger of letting the election slip away. In the second debate, held in Kansas City on October 21, 1984, the age issue was on everybody's mind. Early in the debate, *Baltimore Sun* reporter Henry Trewhitt surfaced the issue:

> *Mr. President, I want to raise an issue that I think has been lurking out there for two or three weeks, and cast it specifically in national security terms. You already are the oldest president in history, and some of your staff say you were tired after your most recent encounter with Mr. Mondale. I recall that President Kennedy had to go for days on end with very little sleep during the Cuban missile crisis. Is there any doubt in your mind that you would be able to function in such circumstances?*

The president had been prepared for the moment, replying:

> Not at all, Mr. Trewhitt, and I want you to know that
> I will not make age an issue of this campaign.
> I am not going to exploit for political purposes
> my opponent's youth and inexperience.

The remark drew a hearty laugh from the audience and even an admiring nod from the challenger (Mondale later admitted that it might have been the turning point of the campaign). Reagan's perfectly executed reply, just like the Kennedy telegram a few decades earlier, was a perfect example of a truism in politics—humor is often the best way to defuse an issue or disarm an opponent. Thirty years later, Reagan's words are remembered as the best sound bite of the 1984 campaign and one of the most effective replies in political history.

While many examples of political repartee are humorous, some are deadly serious. The best example in recent history occurred in the 1988 debate between Lloyd Bentsen, the Democratic VP candidate, and his Republican opponent, Dan Quayle. During the campaign, the maturity and intelligence of Quayle, a forty-one-year-old senator from Indiana, had come into question. In the debate, the moderator asked the handsome young senator what he would do if he were called upon to succeed to the presidency. Quayle was well prepared, and he tried to lay the matter to rest by saying, "I have as much experience in the Congress as Jack Kennedy did when he sought the presidency." Bentsen broke in with one of the most devastating political replies of all time:

> **Senator, I served with Jack Kennedy.**
> **I knew Jack Kennedy.**
> **Jack Kennedy was a friend of mine.**
> **Senator, you're no Jack Kennedy.**

The ability to forge quick and clever replies also has been extremely useful in dealing with another feature of the political process: hecklers. Politicians who allow themselves to be rattled by hecklers instantly lose credibility, giving voters the impression that they might wither under pressure if elected to office. By contrast, those who are able to exhibit grace—or better, wit—under pressure have almost always earned the admiration and the favor of the electorate.

Al Smith served four terms as governor of New York State before becoming the first Roman Catholic to run for the presidency (he was defeated in the 1928 election by Republican Herbert Hoover). Known as the Happy Warrior, Smith was a colorful campaigner and a charismatic speaker. One day, though, he uncharacteristically hesitated in the middle of a speech, apparently rattled by the remarks of a heckler. As Smith paused, the heckler poured it on, saying, "Go ahead, Al, don't let me bother you. Tell 'em all you know. It won't take long." Smith regained his composure and won back the crowd when he replied:

> **If I tell 'em all we both know,**
> **it won't take me any longer.**

For several decades in the middle of the twentieth century, Adlai Stevenson was one of the most eloquent voices in American political life. Twice the Democratic Party's unsuccessful candidate for president, he was named U.S. ambassador to the United Nations during the Kennedy administration. In Dallas in 1963 for a United Nations Day speech, Stevenson was interrupted again and again by a heckler who challenged the ambassador to state his beliefs. Stevenson ignored the first few interruptions, but got an admiring round of applause when he finally put down his speech, looked in the direction of the heckler, and said:

> **I believe in the forgiveness of sin**
> **and the redemption of ignorance.**

Sometimes politicians give good repartee, and sometimes they get it. In the middle of a campaign speech in the early 1900s, Theodore Roosevelt was interrupted by a heckler who kept saying, "I'm a Democrat!" Roosevelt departed from his prepared remarks, inquiring, "May I ask the gentleman why he's a Democrat?" The man answered, "My grandfather was a Democrat, my father was a Democrat, and I'm a Democrat." "My friend"—Roosevelt pressed forward confidently—"suppose your grandfather had been a jackass and your father was a jackass, what would you be then?" To the delight of fellow Democrats in the audience, the man shot back:

A Republican!

Politics has always been a rough-and-tumble affair, with lots of mudslinging, rumor mongering, and backstabbing. But amidst all the tangling and turmoil, there have also been many bright and light moments, when wit and charm and eloquence have won the day. We'll celebrate those moments in the remainder of this chapter on *political repartee*.

★ ★ ★ ★ ★ ★ ★ ★ ★ ★

In the first half of the twentieth century, Latin America experienced great political turmoil and many banana republics went to great lengths to stifle revolutionary activity. While all of this was going on, diplomatic relations with other countries went on as usual. At a reception in Washington, DC, a Latin American diplomat said, "Our most popular sport is bullfighting." A DC society matron, who overheard the comment, broke in to observe disdainfully, "I've always thought that was revolting." The diplomat cleverly replied:

No, that's our second most popular pastime.

★ ★ ★ ★ ★ ★ ★ ★ ★ ★

As World War II came to an end, Clement Attlee replaced Winston Churchill as prime minister of England, serving in that role until 1951. In his early years, Attlee was a member of the Fabian Society and, as prime minister, presided over the establishment of a welfare state in Great Britain. During the war, Attlee supported Churchill and served in a number of posts in his cabinet. The liberal Attlee often disagreed with the conservative Churchill, however, and he sometimes bridled at Churchill's imperious ways. At one cabinet meeting, Attlee attempted to raise a matter for discussion, but Churchill squelched him by saying that the topic had been decided in a previous meeting. Attlee, who'd grown tired of Churchill's long-winded orations, remarked:

A monologue is not a decision.

★ ★ ★ ★ ★ ★ ★ ★ ★ ★

From 1966 to 1999, William F. Buckley Jr. interviewed politicians of every stripe on *Firing Line*. A brilliant man with a piercing wit, Buckley often sought out liberal guests to serve as a foil for his conservative views. The economist John Kenneth Galbraith appeared on the show many times, but declined a request one day by saying to Buckley, "I'm sorry, but that week I'll be teaching at the University of Moscow." Buckley took full advantage of the opening, saying to his liberal colleague:

Oh, what do you have left to teach them?

★ ★ ★ ★ ★ ★ ★ ★ ★ ★

In 1965, William F. Buckley Jr. ran for mayor of New York City on the ticket of the newly formed Conservative Party. While nobody gave him much of a chance to win, his candidacy brought panache and humor to the campaign. During a televised debate, Buckley was asked by the moderator if he would like to use his sixty-second rebuttal period to reply to his opponents. Buckley declined, and got a huge laugh when he replied:

I am satisfied to sit back in silence and contemplate my own former eloquence.

Later in the campaign, a reporter asked Buckley, "What's the first thing you will do if you are elected mayor?" The next day, every paper in the city headlined his reply:

Demand a recount.

★ ★ ★ ★ ★ ★ ★ ★ ★ ★

In May 2004, First Lady Laura Bush appeared on *The Tonight Show with Jay Leno*. Leno was up to his usual tricks, kidding around with Mrs. Bush and trying to get a glimpse into the private side of a very public person. At one point, he said, "Now, you were in Las Vegas last night, I imagine partying until dawn? Did you gamble at all while you were there? Did you pull a slot machine? Did you go to a Chippendales show?" The audience laughed at the teasing nature of Leno's questions, but they howled when the First Lady looked Leno squarely in the eye and deadpanned:

Jay, what happens in Vegas stays in Vegas.

It was a fabulous extemporaneous moment, and Leno was visibly impressed, saying, "Wow, that's the last answer I expected to hear." Leno continued to press the First Lady for private tidbits, asking, "When was the last time you and your husband had a disagreement on an issue?" Once again, Mrs. Bush got a big laugh when she replied, "Jay, what happens in the White House stays in the White House."

★ ★ ★ ★ ★ ★ ★ ★ ★ ★

Hattie Caraway of Arkansas, the first woman elected to the U.S. Senate, never made a single Senate speech while serving in that body from 1931 to 1944 (Winston Churchill called her the Sitting Hen). Commenting on her undistinguished Senate career, one observer described her as "the quiet grandmother who won nothing, lost nothing, and did nothing." When she was once asked why she never made a speech on the floor of the Senate, her reply made people wish she had said more during her political career:

I haven't the heart to take a minute from the men. The poor dears love it so.

☆ ☆ ☆ ☆ ☆ ☆ ☆ ☆ ☆ ☆ ☆

In 1995, several years after stepping down as secretary of defense in the first Bush administration, Dick Cheney became CEO of Halliburton, a huge Texas-based construction company. During his tenure, the company's performance skyrocketed, and there were many reports of "sweetheart" deals made with old friends back in Washington. When Cheney was picked as the VP candidate by George W. Bush in 1999, he unloaded his Halliburton stock, reaping a profit of more than $5 million. As the campaign got under way, Democratic strategists believed they could use this information to their advantage. They were also confident that their VP candidate, the squeaky-clean Joe Lieberman, was the perfect man to make the case that Cheney was just another multimillionaire Republican who had manipulated the system to his advantage. At the vice presidential debate in 1999, Lieberman tried to make a point about the healthy Clinton economy and Cheney's newfound wealth when he said, "I'm pleased to see, Dick, from the newspapers that you're better off now than you were eight years ago." Cheney's response may not have been completely accurate, but it was the perfect rejoinder:

> **And I can tell you, Joe, that the government
> had absolutely nothing to do with it!**

Realizing his first punch had not landed, Lieberman saw in Cheney's answer another opportunity to score a point. This time, he said, "I can see my wife, and I think she's saying, 'I think he should go out into the private sector.'" Once again, Cheney rose to the occasion, providing the cleverest reply of the 1999 campaign:

> **Well, I'm going to try to help you do that, Joe!**

☆ ☆ ☆ ☆ ☆ ☆ ☆ ☆ ☆ ☆ ☆

In 1904, twenty-nine-year-old Winston Churchill made two important decisions. He left the Conservative Party to join the ranks of the liberals and he grew a mustache in an attempt to look older and more distinguished. One day, a female constituent ran into Churchill on a London street and said with disdain, "Mr. Churchill, I approve of neither your politics nor your mustache." The master of repartee replied:

**Do not worry, Madam,
you are unlikely to come in contact with either.**

★ ★ ★ ★ ★ ★ ★ ★ ★ ★ ★

A frequent visitor to Washington, DC, before and during World War II, Winston Churchill always lodged at the White House Executive Mansion during his stays. At the end of 1941, during a critical three-week stay following the attack on Pearl Harbor, Churchill sent a telegram to Clement Atlee, saying:

**WE LIVE HERE AS A BIG FAMILY IN THE GREATEST INTIMACY
AND INFORMALITY. AND I HAVE FORMED THE VERY HIGHEST REGARD
AND ADMIRATION FOR THE PRESIDENT.**

During his stays, Churchill would often work very late into the night—frequently with a drink in hand—well after everyone else had gone to bed. The next day, he would sleep late, often not arising until almost noon. One day, Franklin D. Roosevelt went to Churchill's chambers in the middle of the day, expecting to find the prime minister at work. Churchill, however, had only recently awakened and was just stepping out of the bathtub when he found himself standing stark naked in the presence of a startled American president. In this undignified situation, Churchill managed to maintain his aplomb, saying:

**The prime minister of England has nothing to hide
from the president of the United States.**

★ ★ ★ ★ ★ ★ ★ ★ ★ ★ ★

After the United States formally declared war on Japan and Germany in 1941, the English people breathed a collective sigh of relief. The Battle of Britain had taken a huge toll, and the entire country felt enormous gratitude toward America in general and to President Roosevelt in particular. Churchill, who also had great fondness for the American president, spent years pleading for his support. He also believed that, were it not for Pearl Harbor, the Americans might have continued to stay out of the fight. One day during the war, Churchill was talking with the aging Edward Marsh, his former private secretary and now a distinguished man of letters. Marsh was effusive in his praise for FDR, saying, "I'm in favor of kissing him on both cheeks." Churchill, who thought Marsh was carrying things a little too far, replied:

Yes, but not on all four.

★ ★ ★ ★ ★ ★ ★ ★ ★ ★

While serving in Congress in the early years of the nineteenth century, Daniel Webster of Massachusetts and Henry Clay of Kentucky developed a friendly rivalry. One day, as they were sitting in front of the National Hotel in Washington, a man driving a pack of mules passed by. Webster, the quintessential Yankee, saw an opportunity to take a jab at his Southern colleague. "Clay, there goes a number of your Kentucky constituents." Clay slowly examined the scene before him and calmly replied:

Yes, they must be going up to Massachusetts to teach school.

★ ★ ★ ★ ★ ★ ★ ★ ★ ★

One day in Congress, Alexander Smyth, one of Henry Clay's political adversaries, was in the middle of a long and rambling political harangue when he turned to Clay and charged, "You, sir, speak for the present generation; but I speak for posterity." Clay slowly rose from his seat, looked squarely at Smyth, and countered:

Yes, and you, sir, seem resolved to speak until the arrival of your audience.

★ ★ ★ ★ ★ ★ ★ ★ ★ ★ ★

Early in the 1992 presidential campaign, the seven Democratic presidential candidates were referred to by Republicans as the Seven Dwarfs. One of the candidates was Arkansas governor Bill Clinton, a former Rhodes scholar and a bright new star in the Democratic Party. At a campaign stop one day, Clinton was introduced as the most intelligent of the presidential candidates. A master at self-deprecation, Clinton wowed the crowd when he observed with a smile:

Isn't that like calling Moe the most intelligent of the Three Stooges?

★ ★ ★ ★ ★ ★ ★ ★ ★ ★ ★

Just after the 1992 Republican National Convention, Vice President Dan Quayle revealed plans to be "a pit bull" in the upcoming campaign. When presidential candidate Bill Clinton was asked for his reaction to the announcement, he replied:

That's got every fire hydrant in America worried.

★ ★ ★ ★ ★ ★ ★ ★ ★ ★ ★

Shortly after George H. W. Bush was elected the forty-first U.S. president, former Texas governor John B. Connally was asked what he thought about President Bush's claim that he was a Texan. Instead of commenting on Bush's Connecticut background, preppie roots, and Ivy League education, Connally simply observed:

All hat and no cattle.

★ ★ ★ ★ ★ ★ ★ ★ ★ ★ ★

During his thirty-plus years in Congress, Everett Dirksen of Illinois established a reputation as a conservative Republican, but not an ideologue (he was instrumental in breaking a filibuster that threatened passage of the Civil Rights Act of 1964). His rich orotund voice and florid oratorical skills became a kind of trademark, and even earned him the nickname The Wizard of Ooze. He also had a marvelous sense of humor. While debating a bill one day, an opposing senator interrupted with an objection. Dirksen brought smiles to colleagues on both sides of the aisle when he quickly responded:

Sir, you are interrupting the man I most like to hear.

★ ★ ★ ★ ★ ★ ★ ★ ★ ★

During the nineteenth century, the political and personality clashes between William Gladstone and Benjamin Disraeli dominated English politics, and it was widely believed that the two men loathed one another. In a famous story, Disraeli was once asked to describe the difference between a misfortune and a calamity. Seizing the opportunity to take a potshot at his adversary, he replied:

Well, if Gladstone fell into the Thames,
that would be a misfortune;
and if anybody pulled him out,
that, I suppose, would be a calamity.

★ ★ ★ ★ ★ ★ ★ ★ ★ ★

One day, Benjamin Disraeli and some colleagues were discussing John Bright, a liberal member of the House of Commons who was at the time also serving in Prime Minister William Gladstone's cabinet. Disraeli disparaged Bright in some rather harsh terms, which provoked a reaction from one of the other men. "I wouldn't be so hard on Bright," he advised. "After all, he is a self-made man." Disraeli replied:

I know he is, and he adores his maker.

✶ ✶ ✶ ✶ ✶ ✶ ✶ ✶ ✶ ✶

In the summer of 1988, competing for the Republican presidential nomination, Bob Dole was asked by a reporter what he thought about the vice presidency. Dodging the thrust of the question, he replied, "It's inside work with no heavy lifting." Later that summer, after losing the race for the nomination to George H. W. Bush, Dole was asked by a reporter how he was handling the defeat. Taking refuge in humor, he said:

Contrary to reports that I took the loss badly, I slept like a baby—every two hours I woke up and cried.

✶ ✶ ✶ ✶ ✶ ✶ ✶ ✶ ✶ ✶

In the 1960s, after working fourteen years as an editor at *Vogue* magazine, the fifty-something Millicent Fenwick became involved in politics via the civil rights movement. Blessed with exceptional intelligence, striking good looks, and a keen wit, she rose rapidly in the ranks of the Republican Party. Elected to Congress in 1974 at age sixty-four, she became a media darling. During her four congressional terms she emerged as one of the most colorful politicians in American history (many believe she was the model for the character of Lacey Davenport in Garry Trudeau's *Doonesbury* series). Fenwick once attended a hearing in which a conservative male congressman attacked some proposed equal rights legislation that Fenwick supported. During his polemic, the sexist senator tried to bolster his case by saying, "I've always thought of women as kissable, cuddly, and smelling good." The irrepressible congresswoman quickly responded:

That's what I've always thought about men, and I hope for your sake that you haven't been disappointed as many times as I've been.

★ ★ ★ ★ ★ ★ ★ ★ ★ ★

In 1972, Jesse Helms became the first Republican senator in North Carolina history. Known for his staunch conservative views, he soon became a lightning rod for liberals in the same way that Ted Kennedy did for conservatives. In 2002, after thirty years in the Senate, Helms announced that he would not seek reelection, citing health reasons. Soon after the announcement, he had heart-valve surgery. As he was recovering, Helms was asked by a reporter about the challenges he was facing. In good humor, he replied:

**It's no piece of cake, but it sure beats
listening to Ted Kennedy on the Senate floor.**

Kennedy took the shot in good humor, sending Helms a note saying, "I would be happy to send you tapes of my recent Senate speeches if that will help you to a speedy recovery!"

★ ★ ★ ★ ★ ★ ★ ★ ★ ★

In October 1929, nine months into the first year of Herbert Hoover's presidency, the stock market collapsed and the nation was thrown into the Great Depression. Hoover was no believer in government activism, but he did try several measures to stimulate economic recovery, all without success. One day, he was complaining to former president Calvin Coolidge about the failure of his initiatives. Coolidge tried to console the president, saying, "You can't expect to see calves running in the field the day after you put the bull to the cows." Hoover, though deeply discouraged, said with a wry smile:

No, but I would at least expect to see some contented cows.

✴ ✴ ✴ ✴ ✴ ✴ ✴ ✴ ✴ ✴ ✴

In his early press conferences as the new U.S. president, John F. Kennedy often read prepared answers from index cards. This was a somewhat stilted departure from the press conferences he held as a senator, which were far more informal and freewheeling. One day, a reporter asked him why he had decided to read prepared answers at press conferences. The new president punningly replied:

Because I am not a textual deviant.

✴ ✴ ✴ ✴ ✴ ✴ ✴ ✴ ✴ ✴ ✴

During World War II, Lieutenant (j.g.) John F. Kennedy was the skipper of the torpedo boat PT-109 in the South Pacific. In August 1943, his boat was rammed by a Japanese destroyer, killing two U.S. sailors and throwing the remaining crew into the dangerous waters, which had been set aflame by burning gasoline. Lieutenant Kennedy placed the life strap of one injured crewman between his teeth and swam for four hours, finally arriving safely on a small island in the South Seas. For his valor, Kennedy was awarded a Purple Heart and the Navy/Marine Corps Medal. His exploits were chronicled in a best-selling book *(PT-109)*, later made into a movie starring Cliff Robertson. During the presidential campaign in 1960, much was made of Kennedy's war record. At one campaign stop, a little boy asked, "How did you become a war hero?" JFK's self-deprecating answer, eagerly recorded by the press, charmed the entire country:

It was involuntary. They sank my boat.

✴ ✴ ✴ ✴ ✴ ✴ ✴ ✴ ✴ ✴ ✴

The only Welshman ever to serve as prime minister of England, David Lloyd George headed up a coalition government at the end of World War I. Called the Welsh Wizard, he was rarely at a loss for words. Once, however, he came close.

Beginning a speech at a campaign stop, he said, "I am here . . ." and then paused for a moment, suggesting that he had forgotten the name of the city in which he was appearing. One more time, he said, "I am here . . ." and paused again. As the audience fidgeted, a heckler from the audience hollered out, "So am I." The crowd laughed heartily, and the prime minister was in danger of losing his audience. But he quickly won them back when he looked at the man and said:

**Yes, but there is a difference.
I am *all* here.**

✴ ✴ ✴ ✴ ✴ ✴ ✴ ✴ ✴ ✴

After John Kerry wrapped up the Democratic Party's nomination for president in the early months of 2004, rumors surfaced that he might stun the political world by selecting Arizona's Republican senator John McCain as his running mate. For many observers, it seemed like a political Dream Team. Kerry and McCain were close personal friends and both were decorated Vietnam War veterans. And even though they belonged to different political parties, their political beliefs were reasonably compatible. While McCain pooh-poohed the idea from the beginning, the rumors persisted. Appearing on Conan O'Brien's late-night television show in the summer of 2004, McCain was once more asked the question, "Do you want to become the vice president?" He delighted the audience with his answer:

**I spent several years in a North Vietnamese POW camp,
kept in the dark, fed with scraps.
Do you think I want to do that all over again?**

✴ ✴ ✴ ✴ ✴ ✴ ✴ ✴ ✴ ✴

While serving as prime minister of Australia from 1949 to 1966, Robert Gordon Menzies presided over a country experiencing rapid economic growth and increased prominence on the world stage. His Liberal Party was often at odds with the socialist leanings of Australia's powerful Labor Party, and Menzies was a frequent target of protesters. During a speech one day, he was interrupted by a heckler who shouted, "I wouldn't vote for you if you were the Archangel Gabriel!" The prime minister gave it right back:

If I were the Archangel Gabriel, madam, you would scarcely be in my constituency.

* * * * * * * * * * *

While serving as press secretary to Lyndon B. Johnson in 1965, Bill Moyers—also an ordained Baptist minister—was asked to say grace at a White House dinner. As he said the grace, Moyers spoke in a soft and reverent voice. LBJ struggled to hear the words, but was seated too far away to make them out. Finally, he bellowed, "Speak up, Bill! Speak up!" Moyers slowly looked up and softly reminded LBJ:

I wasn't addressing you, Mr. President.

* * * * * * * * * * *

After a tough Republican loss in the New York State elections in 1862, Abraham Lincoln was asked how he felt. His reply, quoted in *Leslie's Illustrated Weekly* on November 22, 1862, has been recalled by many other defeated candidates ever since. He remarked:

Somewhat like the boy in Kentucky who stubbed his toe while running to see his sweetheart. The boy said he was too big to cry, and far too badly hurt to laugh.

* * * * * * * * * * *

Abraham Lincoln had many misgivings when he appointed General Joseph Hooker as commander of the Army of the Potomac in the middle of the Civil

War, and he soon regretted his decision. Not only did Hooker lose some pivotal battles, he carried himself in a manner that Lincoln found offensive. One day, Hooker sent a dispatch to Lincoln reporting on the progress his army was making against Confederate troops. In the report, he identified his location as "headquarters in the saddle." Reading the report, Lincoln sighed at Hooker's transparent attempt to look good and observed to an aide:

The trouble with Hooker is that he's got his headquarters where his hindquarters ought to be.

★ ★ ★ ★ ★ ★ ★ ★ ★ ★ ★

On September 29, 1960, British prime minister Harold Macmillan addressed the United Nations General Assembly. In the middle of his remarks, Soviet premier Nikita Khrushchev removed a shoe and began pounding on the table—a traditional Russian way of expressing displeasure with a speaker. The Soviet premier had done this even more famously on an American trip a year earlier, when he uttered his famous "We will bury you!" line. This time, the Soviet leader's actions startled the assembly and threatened to take the spotlight off the speaker. But the unflappable Macmillan rose to the occasion, calmly looking over at an interpreter and requesting:

Could I have that translated, please?

★ ★ ★ ★ ★ ★ ★ ★ ★ ★ ★

In 1981, as he was recuperating in his hospital bed after the unsuccessful assassination attempt, President Ronald Reagan was reassured by an aide that the government was functioning normally. Reagan, who had been in incredible spirits during the entire ordeal, cleverly displayed his conservative view of government when he quipped:

What makes you think I'd be happy about that?

* * * * * * * * * *

After attending Baylor University on a debating scholarship, Ann Richards worked as a teacher before entering politics, serving as a county commissioner and then as state treasurer before becoming governor of Texas in 1991. She stepped grandly on to the national stage with her rousing address at the 1988 Democratic National Convention (the speech in which she said, "Poor George, he can't help it. He was born with a silver foot in his mouth"). Throughout her career, she could always be counted on for a candid observation or colorful quip. While serving as state treasurer, there was a big brouhaha about the presence of a Christmas crèche in the Texas Capitol Building. When it was decided the religious display was to be removed, a journalist asked Richards how she felt about the decision. In her clever reply, she deftly avoided the controversy, but ensured that her words would appear on every single newscast later that evening:

> **I hate to see them take that crèche out of the Capitol.**
> **It could be the only chance we'll ever have**
> **to get three wise men in that building.**

* * * * * * * * * *

In 1952 and 1956, Adlai Stevenson was the Democratic Party's candidate for president, both times defeated soundly by the Republican Party's Dwight D. Eisenhower, a war hero and man with a "common" touch. Stevenson's obvious intelligence and thoughtful manner gave him a special appeal to intellectuals and academics, but he came across as cerebral to the average person (he was the first politician to be pejoratively described by the epithet *egghead*). At a stop during the 1952 campaign, a supporter cried out, "You have the support of all thinking Americans!" Stevenson, who ranks as one of the wittiest of all American politicians, quipped:

> **Madam, that is not enough.**
> **I'm going to need a majority.**

★ ★ ★ ★ ★ ★ ★ ★ ★ ★ ★

Even though he had a reputation for being cold and somewhat aloof, George Washington could be quite amiable with people who knew him well, especially his comrades in arms. While serving as commander of the Continental Army, Washington and a group of officers were enjoying an after-dinner drink and warming themselves at the hearth of an inn. As the fire crackled behind him, Washington began to move away from the heat. As he did, one of his officers commented in jest, "Doesn't it behoove a great general to be able to stand fire?" Washington charmingly replied:

> **Yes, but it doesn't look good
> for a general to receive it from behind.**

★ ★ ★ ★ ★ ★ ★ ★ ★ ★ ★

Before becoming the twenty-eighth president of the United States, Woodrow Wilson was the president of Princeton University and the governor of New Jersey. While serving as governor in 1911, aides informed him of the death of John Kean, the state's U.S. senator, and a member of the Republican Party. As Wilson began the search for a replacement—from his own Democratic Party, of course—he took a phone call from a high-ranking member of the New Jersey Republican Party. When the man said, "Governor, I would like to take the senator's place," Wilson replied:

> **Well, you may quote me as saying
> that's perfectly agreeable to me
> if it's agreeable to the undertaker.**

written repartee

While most comebacks and retorts are delivered orally, written replies also occupy a special place in the history of repartee. Unlike oral comebacks, which are usually delivered immediately, examples of *written repartee* are not created under duress or the pressure of time. And while they lack the immediacy of wit under pressure, they still impress.

A legendary example involves two familiar names, George Bernard Shaw and Winston Churchill. Shaw, best remembered today as a great playwright, was almost as well known in his time for his political beliefs (an avowed socialist, he was a founding member of the Fabian Society). In the early years of the twentieth century, Shaw was no fan of Churchill, at the time a rising star in England's Conservative Party. Shortly before the opening of his 1913 play *Pygmalion,* Shaw sent Churchill a telegram that read:

> RESERVING TWO TICKETS FOR YOU FOR MY PREMIERE.
> COME AND BRING A FRIEND—IF YOU HAVE ONE.

Churchill quickly responded with a telegram of his own to Shaw:

> IMPOSSIBLE TO BE PRESENT FOR FIRST PERFORMANCE.
> WILL ATTEND THE SECOND—IF THERE IS ONE.

Another classic reply appears in a handwritten note from one of history's most admired figures. While Mark Twain was visiting England in the late 1890s, rumors were rampant throughout America that the great writer had fallen on hard times and was dangerously ill. In 1897, the editor of the *New York Journal* sent two separate cables to the paper's London correspondent:

IF MARK TWAIN DYING IN POVERTY IN LONDON SEND 500 WORDS.
IF MARK TWAIN HAS DIED IN POVERTY SEND 1000 WORDS.

The journalist went to Twain's lodgings and found him in excellent health and in good spirits. When he showed the telegrams to Twain, the two men had a good laugh. Twain then drafted a handwritten note and asked the correspondent to pass it on to the editor of the paper back in New York. The note read: "James Ross Clemens, a cousin of mine, was seriously ill two or three weeks ago in London but is well now. The report of my illness grew out of his illness." Twain's note then ended with the now-famous words:

The report of my death was an exaggeration.

A few months later, the *New York Journal* published an article under the headline "Mark Twain Amused" and formally printed these words for the first time. As often happens, the story was embellished as time passed. In one version, Twain was said to have read his own obituary in the paper. This is false. In another version, Twain was said to have cabled his reply to the paper. This is also false. And, finally, many versions have erroneously reported that Twain said, "The reports of my death are *greatly* exaggerated."

As it turns out, Twain himself is responsible for some of these errors. In 1906, nearly a decade after the event in question, the sixty-nine-year-old Twain was formally chronicling the event for his autobiography. In his recollection, which we now know to be faulty, he didn't even mention the handwritten note, but he wrote of telling the journalist, "Say the report is an exaggeration." A few months later, revising his own draft, he inserted the word *greatly*. He even recalled, falsely, that this response was cabled to New

York. When Twain's nearly decade-old recollection appeared in print, it was the version people chose to remember, even though it was not true.

Some of the best examples of written repartee aren't replies in the strict sense of the word, but responses to situations or important life events. After Mary Sherwood, wife of playwright Robert E. Sherwood, gave birth to her first child, she received a warm and witty telegram from family friend Dorothy Parker:

> CONGRATULATIONS MARY,
> WE ALL KNEW YOU HAD IT IN YOU.

When Groucho Marx celebrated his seventy-first birthday in 1961, he received letters and telegrams from friends and fans all around the world. Few, however, could hold a candle to the cable he received from good friend Irving Berlin:

> THE WORLD WOULD NOT BE IN SUCH A SNARL
> HAD MARX BEEN GROUCHO INSTEAD OF KARL.

And, finally, when the American writer John O'Hara learned in October of 1962 that his good friend John Steinbeck had been awarded the Nobel Prize in literature, he immediately sent him a telegram that said:

> CONGRATULATIONS. I CAN THINK OF ONLY
> ONE OTHER AUTHOR I'D RATHER SEE GET IT.

Witty written replies have also shown up in an area most people would not describe as particularly amusing: accounts payable. One of the first employees of the newly formed General Electric Company in 1893, Charles Steinmetz was responsible for many of the technical advances that made wide-scale electrification of America possible. After his retirement from GE, Steinmetz was called back to do some emergency troubleshooting. A complex system of machinery was malfunctioning and could not be repaired by the current staff of engineers. When Steinmetz showed up, he slowly walked around the equipment, performed several simple tests here and there, and then used a piece of chalk to mark an "X" on a side panel. Sure enough, when GE engineers disassembled that portion of the equipment, they found the problem and repaired it. When the company received Steinmetz's statement a few weeks later, corporate bean counters blanched at what they considered an exorbitant fee: $10,000. They asked Steinmetz to send them an itemized bill. A few days later, the revised statement arrived:

Making chalk mark:	$ 1.00
Knowing where to place it	9,999.00
TOTAL	$10,000.00

Examples of *written repartee* have appeared in letters and telegrams, on walls and billboards, and even in response to items in questionnaires and on application forms. More examples follow in the remainder of the chapter.

★ ★ ★ ★ ★ ★ ★ ★ ★ ★

During America's bicentennial celebration in 1976, the Procrastinators Club of America sent a letter of complaint to the Whitechapel Bell Foundry in London, the firm that had forged the original Liberty Bell in 1752. In their good-natured complaint, the club inquired about a warranty and requested a replacement for the most famous cracked bell in history. It was a clever publicity ploy, garnering the club much press and serving as a perfect example of the group's motto, "Don't do today what you can put off till tomorrow." What club leaders didn't expect, however, was the clever reply from executives at the four-hundred-year-old company. Proving the firm was every bit as good at customer service as the Procrastinators Club was at putting things off, they replied:

We would be happy to provide a replacement bell.
Kindly return the damaged bell to us in its original packaging.

∗ ∗ ∗ ∗ ∗ ∗ ∗ ∗ ∗ ∗ ∗

In the early days of telegraph history, it was decided that ambiguity would be reduced if the end of a sentence was indicated by keying "stop" instead of "period." Many years later, that decision inspired a witty young man to send an unambiguous telegram to his newlywed buddy:

> **CONGRATS ON YOUR WEDDING STOP**
> **VERY HAPPY FOR YOU AND BRIDE STOP**
> **HAPPY HONEYMOON DON'T STOP.**

∗ ∗ ∗ ∗ ∗ ∗ ∗ ∗ ∗ ∗ ∗

A message board in front of a church prominently displayed the words "If tired of sin, come in." Underneath, an anonymous sinner appended the rejoinder:

> **If not, call 555-4321.**

∗ ∗ ∗ ∗ ∗ ∗ ∗ ∗ ∗ ∗ ∗

The Forbes Book of Great Business Letters, a collection of some of the most fascinating correspondence in history, also describes one of the most questionable pay-raise requests of all time. The executive editor at Monocle Periodicals in New York City sent his publisher a telegram that read:

> **MUST HAVE RAISE OR COUNT ME OUT.**

The publisher apparently didn't think the editor was worth it, sending a reply telegram that read:

> **ONE, TWO, THREE, FOUR, FIVE, SIX, SEVEN, EIGHT, NINE, TEN.**

★ ★ ★ ★ ★ ★ ★ ★ ★ ★ ★

Among his many other talents, George Bernard Shaw also enjoyed a reputation as a master coffee brewer. One day he received a letter from an English clergyman who requested his coffee recipe. The letter looked legitimate, but Shaw suspected it might be a ruse. He sent the clergyman his recipe with an accompanying note: "I hope this is an honest request and not a surreptitious mode of securing my autograph." A few weeks later, Shaw received a return letter from the clergyman. Opening the envelope, he immediately noticed a snippet of paper containing his signature, obviously cut with a scissors from his original letter. The parson's handwritten note said:

Please accept my thanks for the recipe.
I wrote in good faith, so allow me to return
what is obviously to you infinitely prized,
but which is of no value to me, your autograph.

★ ★ ★ ★ ★ ★ ★ ★ ★ ★ ★

Today, the word *news* is treated as a singular word (as in "The news is good"), but this was not always the case. In the nineteenth century, when the word was beginning to come into vogue, it was commonly considered a plural word (Queen Victoria once wrote, "The news from Austria are very sad"). The pioneering American publisher Horace Greeley was a firm believer that it should be considered a plural word and would always correct his staff when they—in his view—mistakenly said, "Is there any news?" He once cabled a reporter:

ARE THERE ANY NEWS?

The reporter found a way of sticking it to his stickler boss, cabling back:

NOT A NEW.

★ ★ ★ ★ ★ ★ ★ ★ ★ ★ ★

A penurious foreign editor of a major American newspaper once sent a telegram to a free-spending overseas reporter: SENT $400. PLEASE ACCOUNT. Several days later the anonymous reporter's reply came back:

RECEIVED $400. SPENT $400. REGARDS.

★ ★ ★ ★ ★ ★ ★ ★ ★ ★ ★

During a South American tour of the play *La Tosca* in 1905, the internationally acclaimed Sarah Bernhardt injured her leg while jumping off the parapet in the final scene. The injury was never properly treated and, when gangrene set in ten years later, the leg had to be amputated. Within months, the indomitable actress was bolstering the spirits of French soldiers at the front lines, carried about by aides on a transportable litter. News of the actress's great courage only enhanced her reputation and she soon began getting telegrams from around the world, some quite bizarre. The manager of the Pan-American Exposition in San Francisco sent a cable in which he offered $100,000 for permission to display her leg. The great actress might have been offended by such a macabre request, but she saw it as an opportunity to respond with a most clever reply:

WHICH LEG?

★ ★ ★ ★ ★ ★ ★ ★ ★ ★ ★

After a so-so career as a player and manager, Branch Rickey became one of the greatest executives in baseball history. As general manager (GM) of the St. Louis Cardinals in the 1920s and '30s, he invented the "farm system" for developing players. In 1945, as GM of the Brooklyn Dodgers, he broke the game's color barrier by signing Jackie Robinson. While GM for the Dodgers, he sent a telegram to Bobby Bragan, manager of the Dodgers' farm team in Fort Worth, Texas. The telegram read:

> DO YOU NEED A SHORTSTOP OR IS PRESENT INFIELD OKAY?

Bragan wired back:

> YES.

Annoyed at this nonanswer, Rickey fired back a telegram:

> YES WHAT?

Intimidated by Rickey's telegram, the shaky Bragan cabled back:

> YES SIR!

★ ★ ★ ★ ★ ★ ★ ★ ★ ★

After the birth of his first son, the film producer Irving Thalberg received a telegram from his good friend Eddie Cantor. In his congratulatory message, Cantor found a way of relating the modern practice of film editing to the ancient ritual of circumcision:

> CONGRATULATIONS ON YOUR LATEST PRODUCTION.
> AM SURE IT WILL LOOK BETTER AFTER IT'S BEEN CUT.

★ ★ ★ ★ ★ ★ ★ ★ ★ ★

In the early 1920s, well before she became a well-known novelist, playwright, and radio and television personality, Ilka Chase married the actor Louis Calhern. In the fashion of the time, Chase ordered stationery with "Mrs. Louis Calhern" inscribed at the top. As with so many show business nuptials, the marriage was very short-lived, and Chase was unable to use the stationery. Within a few months, Chase's ex-husband decided to try his luck again, and married the actress Julia Hoyt. Chase, known for her offbeat sense of humor, wrapped up the stationery and sent it to Hoyt. Cleverly suggesting that Hoyt's marriage to Calhern might be as brief as her own was, she wrote:

Dear Julia, I hope these reach you in time.

★ ★ ★ ★ ★ ★ ★ ★ ★ ★ ★

Winston Churchill may have been the most prolific writer among all of history's world leaders. His first book was published when he was twenty-seven and he continued churning them out until well into his eighties. Like many powerful personalities, he resisted the editing efforts of his publishers. During the final editing of a manuscript, a punctilious editor aroused Churchill's ire by rather clumsily rewording a sentence so that it would not end in a preposition. According to the *Oxford Companion to the English Language,* Churchill scrawled a note to the editor in the margin of the manuscript:

This is the sort of bloody nonsense up with which I will not put.

★ ★ ★ ★ ★ ★ ★ ★ ★ ★ ★

After his presidency, Calvin Coolidge decided to hang up his political spurs and see what politics looked like from the other side of the fence. Completing the application for membership in the Washington Press Club, he came to the "Occupation" category and wrote "Retired." In the next section, marked "Comments," he wrote:

And glad of it.

★ ★ ★ ★ ★ ★ ★ ★ ★ ★ ★

The author of the classic "Wynken, Blynken, and Nod,"Eugene Field became known as the Child's Poet for his lighthearted and engaging verse. Also a respected journalist and columnist for the *Chicago Daily News*, Fields was occasionally asked to provide feedback on the literary creations of aspiring writers. In the early 1890s, a poet sent Field a poem titled "Why Do I Live?" and asked for his opinion. The poem was long and tedious, but Field read it through to the very end. Reflecting on his painful reading experience—and keeping the title of the poem in mind—Field sent the poet a note saying:

Because you send your poem by mail.

✻ ✻ ✻ ✻ ✻ ✻ ✻ ✻ ✻ ✻

During one of his stints in Hollywood, the actor John Gielgud was invited by friend Carol Channing to an event at which she was scheduled to present some awards. Unable to attend because of a viral infection, Gielgud penned a note to Channing:

Sorry, love, cannot attend.
Gielgud doesn't fielgud.

✻ ✻ ✻ ✻ ✻ ✻ ✻ ✻ ✻ ✻

After Cary Grant's film debut in 1932, he went on to become one of the most debonair actors of all time, starring in some of Hollywood's most popular films with some of the most glamorous leading ladies. As Grant aged, he continued to be paired with beautiful young actresses, leading many people to wonder how old he actually was. One day, a magazine editor sent Grant's agent a telegram:

HOW OLD CARY GRANT?

Grant intercepted the note and, demonstrating wit to match his charm, cabled back:

OLD CARY GRANT FINE. HOW YOU?

✶ ✶ ✶ ✶ ✶ ✶ ✶ ✶ ✶ ✶

When Graham Greene turned sixty in 1964, he had achieved about as much success as a writer could hope for. Best-selling novels like *The Third Man*, *Our Man in Havana*, and *The Quiet American* had been made into films, and he felt he was at the top of his game. In 1968, he sent a completed manuscript of his latest book, *Travels with My Aunt*, to his publisher in New York. A few weeks later, he received a cable saying:

> **TERRIFIC BOOK, BUT WE'LL NEED TO CHANGE TITLE.**

Greene cabled back:

> **NO NEED TO CHANGE TITLE.**
> **EASIER TO CHANGE PUBLISHERS.**

✶ ✶ ✶ ✶ ✶ ✶ ✶ ✶ ✶ ✶

Alec Guinness starred in some of Hollywood's most famous films, including *The Bridge on the River Kwai* (winning him the 1958 Oscar for Best Actor), *Lawrence of Arabia*, and the *Star Wars* movies, in which he played Ben Obi-Wan Kenobi (he hated those *Star Wars* roles, once describing the entire series as "frightful rubbish"). After returning a script earlier in his career, he received a handwritten note from a disappointed studio head, saying: "We tailored it just for you." Guinness sent back a note saying:

> **But no one came to take my measurements.**

✶ ✶ ✶ ✶ ✶ ✶ ✶ ✶ ✶ ✶

When he died at his Cannes home in 1972, British oil tycoon Nubar Gulbenkian was one of the world's wealthiest men. He inherited a fortune from his multi-millionaire father and, as director of the Iraq Petroleum Company, continued to have the Midas touch the rest of his life. A man who appreciated the finer things in life, Gulbenkian was once completing a market research form when he came to the section: "Position in life." He answered:

Enviable.

✶ ✶ ✶ ✶ ✶ ✶ ✶ ✶ ✶ ✶ ✶

Before becoming a novelist, Ernest Hemingway was a journalist. Between the two World Wars, he spent many years in Paris, serving as European correspondent for the *Toronto Star* and later for William Randolph Hearst's International News Service. While writing for the Hearst syndicate, he occasionally bridled at some of the company's efforts to rein him in. In 1928, while on assignment in Constantinople, he got a cable from Frank Mason, chief of the Paris bureau. The company was trying to balance the books, wrote Mason, and needed a complete accounting of Hemingway's expenses, including his original receipts. The free-spirited journalist was able to tell his boss where to go while also cleverly sidestepping the telegraph company's prohibition against profanity:

SUGGEST YOU UPSTICK BOOKS ASSWARDS.

✶ ✶ ✶ ✶ ✶ ✶ ✶ ✶ ✶ ✶ ✶

George S. Kaufman, the playwright and Algonquin Round Table wit, received the first of his two Pulitzer Prizes for the 1931 musical comedy *Of Thee I Sing* (written with Morrie Ryskind; music and lyrics by George and Ira Gershwin). Kaufman attended a performance one afternoon and was dismayed to see actor William Gaxton murdering some of the play's best lines. He rushed out of the theater to send Gaxton a telegram, which he had delivered to the actor's dressing room during the intermission. It read:

AM SITTING IN THE LAST ROW.
WISH YOU WERE HERE.

⋆ ⋆ ⋆ ⋆ ⋆ ⋆ ⋆ ⋆ ⋆ ⋆ ⋆

The country's most glamorous couple in the early 1960s, John and Jackie Kennedy were often hounded by reporters. While Jack used the press to his advantage, Jackie tangled with them constantly (she once had Secret Service agents confiscate film from a journalist who took pictures of her children without permission). After acquiring a new German shepherd puppy, Jackie was on a flight back to Washington after a brief stay at the Kennedy compound in Hyannisport. A journalist in the back of the plane sent her a note asking what she intended to feed the new puppy. She sent back a note that said:

Reporters.

⋆ ⋆ ⋆ ⋆ ⋆ ⋆ ⋆ ⋆ ⋆ ⋆ ⋆

Barry Goldwater, the Republican senator from Arizona, was an amateur photographer and, by all accounts, was quite talented. In the early 1960s, he snapped a photograph of President John F. Kennedy and sent it to the White House with a note asking for a presidential inscription. A few days later, the White House sent the photograph back to Goldwater, with a handwritten inscription from JFK:

For Barry Goldwater,
Whom I urge to follow the career for which
he has shown so much talent—photography.
From his friend, John Kennedy.

⋆ ⋆ ⋆ ⋆ ⋆ ⋆ ⋆ ⋆ ⋆ ⋆ ⋆

Rudyard Kipling was one of the most respected and successful writers in history. One piece of verse alone—his 1910 poem "If"—was translated into twenty-seven languages. In 1992, the *Guinness Book of World Records* called it the "most successful poem" in history. After Kipling was awarded the Nobel Prize in literature in 1907, a journalist reported that he was earning about a dollar a word, a huge amount at the time. Shortly after the article appeared, Kipling received a letter from a man who, for years, had been bugging him for an autograph. It read: "I see you get a dollar a word for your writing. I enclose a check for one dollar. Please send me a sample." Kipling happily complied. He sent the autograph-seeker a postcard that said:

Thanks.

★ ★ ★ ★ ★ ★ ★ ★ ★ ★

After receiving the Nobel Prize in literature in 1930—the first American writer so honored—Sinclair Lewis became an object of great interest, some of it quite fascinating. One day, a letter arrived at his home, written by a young woman who said she would like to serve as his secretary. In the letter, she said she would do anything for him, adding for emphasis, "And when I say anything, I mean anything." The letter was intercepted by Lewis's second wife, Dorothy, a well-regarded journalist. Mrs. Lewis took it on her own to respond to the young woman, writing in her letter that Lewis already had a secretary. She wrote that he also had a wife who did everything else for him, adding:

And when I say everything, I mean everything.

★ ★ ★ ★ ★ ★ ★ ★ ★ ★

During the Civil War, Abraham Lincoln received a letter from a woman asking for "a sentiment" from the president, along with his signature. Annoyed at the presumption of her request—especially during such a critical time for the nation—he wrote back:

**Dear Madam: When you ask from a stranger
that which is of interest only to yourself, always enclose a stamp.
There's your sentiment, and here's my autograph. A. Lincoln.**

✳ ✳ ✳ ✳ ✳ ✳ ✳ ✳ ✳ ✳ ✳

Harry Cohn, who ran Columbia Pictures from 1924 until his death in 1957, was well deserving of the nickname given to him by Ben Hecht: "White Fang." He spied on employees with a hidden microphone system, pressured employees to rat on one another, and sacked employees at will. Like all control freaks, though, he couldn't control everything. During the filming of the 1934 film *The Captain Hates the Sea,* Cohn and film director Lewis Milestone did everything they could to limit the alcohol of the hard-drinking lead actor, John Gilbert. As it turns out, the other cast members were also heavy drinkers, and they kept the star (and themselves) well lubricated. As production delays mounted, Cohn got more and more upset. Finally, he fired off a telegram to Milestone:

HURRY UP! THE COST IS STAGGERING.

Milestone cabled back to Cohn:

SO IS THE CAST.

✳ ✳ ✳ ✳ ✳ ✳ ✳ ✳ ✳ ✳ ✳

During his forty-year writing career, Ogden Nash became one of America's most popular writers, producing dozens of volumes of light, whimsical, and wickedly charming verse (like "Candy/Is dandy/But liquor/Is quicker"). One day, Nash opened his mail to find a copy of one of his books along with a note from his friend Tom Carlson. The dog, Carlson explained, had chewed up his original copy of the book, which had been autographed by the author. "Would you please sign this copy?" asked Carlson. Nash returned the book with the inscription:

**To Tom Carlson or his dog,
depending on whose taste it best suits.**

★ ★ ★ ★ ★ ★ ★ ★ ★ ★

In the 1930s, many famous writers were lured to Hollywood by movie moguls eager to improve the quality of their screenplays and their guest lists. One hotly pursued writer was Eugene O'Neill, who had earned three Pulitzer Prizes in the 1920s (he would later earn a fourth for *Long Day's Journey into Night* in 1957, and the biggest of them all, the Nobel, in 1936). Unlike many of his colleagues, O'Neill wanted nothing to do with Hollywood. One day he received a cable from a major studio executive asking him to write a screenplay for a planned Jean Harlow film. The cable asked him to reply in a collect telegram of no more than twenty words. O'Neill responded:

**NO NO NO NO NO NO NO
NO NO NO NO NO NO NO
NO NO NO NO NO O'NEILL**

★ ★ ★ ★ ★ ★ ★ ★ ★ ★

In the early 1900s, Max Reger was a prominent German composer, pianist, and organist. When he wasn't teaching composition at the Munich Academy of Music and Leipzig University, he was an active performer in venues throughout Europe and Russia. After a 1906 performance, he received a scathing review from one of the noted music critics of the day, Rudolph Louis. The next day, Louis received a handwritten note from Reger. The note, which has become the stuff of legend in musical history, read:

**I am sitting in the smallest room in my house.
I have your review before me.
In a moment it will be behind me.**

★ ★ ★ ★ ★ ★ ★ ★ ★ ★

William Randolph Hearst is known as America's first newspaper magnate (at one point owning twenty-eight major newspapers around the country), but he was in reality the head of a vast communications empire that also included radio stations, film companies, and a major international news service. In the 1890s, he became interested in acquiring a number of East Coast newspapers, including the *New York Tribune*, owned by Whitelaw Reid. Not noted for his softness or sensitivity, Hearst sent Reid a telegram that bluntly asked:

HOW MUCH WILL YOU TAKE FOR THE TRIBUNE?

Reid, who had no interest in selling his paper to Hearst or anyone else, sent a return cable saying:

THREE CENTS ON WEEKDAYS.
FIVE CENTS ON SUNDAYS.

✶ ✶ ✶ ✶ ✶ ✶ ✶ ✶ ✶ ✶ ✶

William Howard Taft holds the distinction of being, at 350 pounds, the fattest of all U.S. presidents. In 1900, nine years before he became the twenty-seventh U.S. president, Taft was appointed chief administrator for the Philippines by Theodore Roosevelt. One day, he received a telegram from his friend Elihu Root, who was serving as secretary of war at the time. It read simply:

HEARD YOU WERE SICK.

Taft immediately replied that he had been sick, but was feeling much better after a recent trip to the mountains. In fact, he reported, he was feeling invigorated after a twenty-five-mile horseback ride at an elevation of 5,000 feet. The next day, Taft got a second telegram from Root. This one inquired:

HOW IS THE HORSE?

* * * * * * * * * *

While browsing one day in a used bookstore in London, George Bernard Shaw happened upon one of his old books. Opening the book, he was surprised to discover it was one he had previously given—and personally inscribed—to a friend: "To So-and-So, With esteem, George Bernard Shaw." Instantly sensing a rare opportunity, Shaw snapped up the book, had it gift wrapped, and arranged for it to be delivered to his friend. Before doing so, however, he added a few words after the original inscription:

**With renewed esteem,
George Bernard Shaw.**

* * * * * * * * * *

A close friend of T. S. Eliot and Ezra Pound, English writer Osbert Sitwell was also a member of one of England's most prominent literary families. Even though a person of aristocratic birth, he occasionally liked to tweak the pretensions of the members of his social class. In his 1929 *Who's Who* application, Sitwell poked a little fun at the selection committee by answering the "Education" question this way:

During the holidays from Eton.

* * * * * * * * * *

Miami reporter Milt Sosin was an eyewitness to modern history, interviewing a young Fidel Castro before the Cuban Revolution, witnessing the Jack Ruby slaying of Lee Harvey Oswald, and, at age eighty, scooping every other reporter in the nation by breaking the news that Manuel Noriega was about to be indicted on drug charges by the U.S. government. The crusty and cantankerous Sosin was openly disdainful of editors and top executives at the *Miami News*, often referring to them as "amateurs." At a staff meeting one day, an editor who had been critical of the writing style of the beat reporters demanded, "I want you to start writing short and punchy paragraphs." Disgusted, Sosin stormed out of the meeting, headed straight for his typewriter, and banged out a note that he posted on the paper's bulletin board:

Quit. That's what reporter Milt Sosin did today.

★ ★ ★ ★ ★ ★ ★ ★ ★ ★ ★

Igor Stravinsky wrote the music for the ballet portion of Billy Rose's *Seven Lively Arts,* an ambitious undertaking that included ballet, opera, vaudeville, jazz, Broadway, concert music, and modern painting. After the Philadelphia opening, Rose felt the Stravinsky portion could be improved if Robert Russell Bennett, the famous orchestrator, would take a look at it and make a few modifications. Since he didn't want to insult the great Stravinsky, he delicately composed a telegram that said:

> YOUR MUSIC GREAT SUCCESS. COULD BE SENSATIONAL
> SUCCESS IF YOU WOULD AUTHORIZE
> ROBERT RUSSELL BENNETT TO RETOUCH ORCHESTRATIONS.
> BENNETT ORCHESTRATES EVEN THE WORK OF COLE PORTER.

A few days later, Rose received a cable from Stravinsky that read:

> SATISFIED WITH GREAT SUCCESS.

★ ★ ★ ★ ★ ★ ★ ★ ★ ★ ★

The philosopher George Santayana once observed, "To knock a thing down, especially if it is cocked at an arrogant angle, is a deep delight of the blood." Nobody subscribed to this sentiment more than Mark Twain, who was always eager to annoy the arrogant and puncture the pompous. One day, while checking into a luxurious Canadian hotel, Twain noticed that the gentleman who had registered just before him had written, "Mr. So-and-So and valet." Twain wrote on the hotel register:

Mark Twain and valise.

★ ★ ★ ★ ★ ★ ★ ★ ★ ★ ★

Mark Twain traveled all over the globe in search of adventure and material for his writing. Some friends, knowing that Twain was traveling abroad, but not sure exactly where, sent him a birthday card addressed simply: "Mark Twain, God knows where." A month later, they received a letter, unsigned, from Italy that said only:

He did.

★ ★ ★ ★ ★ ★ ★ ★ ★ ★ ★

In the seventeenth century, the French philosopher Blaise Pascal wrote, "I have made this letter longer than usual because I lack the time to make it shorter." Ever since, countless writers have echoed the notion that it takes a long time to produce a short piece. One such writer was Mark Twain, who once received a telegram from a magazine editor that read:

NEED TWO-PAGE SHORT STORY IN TWO DAYS.

Twain immediately cabled back:

NO CAN DO TWO PAGES TWO DAYS.
CAN DO THIRTY PAGES IN TWO DAYS.
NEED THIRTY DAYS TO DO TWO PAGES.

★ ★ ★ ★ ★ ★ ★ ★ ★ ★ ★ ★

Like many famous novelists, English writer Evelyn Waugh began his career as a journalist. During World War II, he served as a war correspondent in Ethiopia. One day, his editor sent him a cable asking him to substantiate a rumor that an American nurse had been blown up in an Italian air raid. The telegram to Waugh was written in classic cable-ese:

REQUIRE EARLIEST NAME LIFE STORY PHOTOGRAPH AMERICAN NURSE UPBLOWN.

Discovering the rumor to be false, Waugh cabled back:

NURSE UNUPBLOWN.

★ ★ ★ ★ ★ ★ ★ ★ ★ ★ ★ ★

In 1883, *Punch* magazine reported that Oscar Wilde and the artist James McNeill Whistler recently had been seen discussing the relative merits of two prominent female actresses. Wilde and Whistler—two of the greatest wits of their era—enjoyed an early friendship but began to feud as the years passed. Wilde found the *Punch* article amusing and cabled Whistler:

PUNCH TOO RIDICULOUS. WHEN YOU AND I ARE TOGETHER WE NEVER TALK ABOUT ANYTHING EXCEPT OURSELVES.

It was a perfect opportunity for Whistler to engage in a bit of one-upmanship with one of history's great egotists. He immediately cabled back:

NO, NO, OSCAR, YOU FORGET. WHEN YOU AND I ARE TOGETHER, WE NEVER TALK ABOUT ANYTHING EXCEPT ME.

★ ★ ★ ★ ★ ★ ★ ★ ★ ★

In Paris for the shooting of the 1957 film *Love in the Afternoon,* director Billy Wilder was asked by his wife, Audrey, to find her a bidet, a bathroom convenience not widely available in America at the time. Wilder checked all around town, but couldn't find a firm that would export one. Finally, he cabled her:

IMPOSSIBLE TO OBTAIN BIDET.
SUGGEST HANDSTAND IN SHOWER.

★ ★ ★ ★ ★ ★ ★ ★ ★ ★

At the end of the nineteenth century, the English writer Israel Zangwill was chronicling Jewish life for his own people and helping Gentile readers learn more about Jewish life and culture. The author of the expression "the Melting Pot," which he used to describe America, Zangwill was fond of engaging in wordplay with his literary friends. One day, Andrew Lang, the Scottish poet and writer, sent a note to Zangwill asking him if he was planning to attend an upcoming social event. Zangwill replied:

If you, Lang, will,
I, Zangwill.

round table repartee

As World War I was drawing to a close, three staff writers at *Vanity Fair* magazine—Dorothy Parker, Robert Benchley, and Robert E. Sherwood—were regular luncheon customers at the fashionable Algonquin Hotel in Midtown Manhattan. One day in 1919, they decided to hold a "welcome home" reception for their friend and colleague, Alexander Woollcott, who had just arrived back in New York after a stint as a war correspondent for *Stars and Stripes*, the U.S. Army's newspaper for American soldiers.

As the *Vanity Fair* trio and their literary friends gathered around a large round table in the Rose Room of the hotel, they "welcomed" Woollcott in a manner that might almost be described as a "roast." The room was filled with banners welcoming him home, but every banner contained a deliberate misspelling of his name. As the evening progressed, the assembled wits playfully ridiculed Woollcott's many affectations, like his penchant for beginning war dispatches with such florid prose as "From my seat in the theater of war. . . ." The barbs and zingers were all delivered in good humor, of course, and the entire experience was so enjoyable that, at the end of the festivities, one member of the group suggested the idea of meeting daily.

Over the next decade, the small cadre of friends began to meet almost every day for lunch at the hotel. They were regularly joined by another half-dozen people, mainly writers and show business personalities, and occasionally by another dozen or so people. Within a short period, the group became the talk of the town, as reports of their bon mots were reported in New York City's daily newspapers (many in columns written by the participants themselves). While the members of the group referred to themselves as the Vicious Circle, the press dubbed them the Algonquin Round Table, which is how this fascinating collection of wits is now known to history.

Here and there in previous chapters, I've already presented replies from these wits and wordsmiths. In this chapter, we'll focus on the most prominent members of the group and feature more great examples of *Round Table repartee*.

★ ★ ★ ★ ★ ★ ★ ★ ★ ★

Franklin Pierce Adams moved from Chicago to New York City in 1904 at age twenty-two. After a few years as a beat reporter, he began writing "The Conning Tower," a column that was so popular that he became one of the few writers in history—another being George Bernard Shaw (GBS)—to be well known only by his initials: FPA. Often called the father of the syndicated newspaper column, Adams helped establish the popularity of the Algonquin Round Table by featuring their witticisms so frequently in his column. In 1938, he became a panelist on the enormously popular radio show *Information Please,* where his wit and erudition could be appreciated by an audience in the millions.

★ ★ ★ ★ ★ ★ ★ ★ ★ ★

Adams was once asked by fellow Round Table member George S. Kaufman to escort Kaufman's wife, Beatrice, to a party. Shortly after their arrival, Mrs. Kaufman was sitting on a cane chair when the seat gave way. In that instant, as Beatrice's bottom went through the seat of the chair and her rear end was inches from the floor, her legs flew upward in the most awkward way. As she struggled to free herself from this embarrassing position, the rest of the partygoers were momentarily frozen in a stunned silence. Adopting a tone of mock sternness, FPA broke the tension when he said:

I've told you a hundred times, Beatrice, that's not funny!

☆ ☆ ☆ ☆ ☆ ☆ ☆ ☆ ☆ ☆ ☆

Shortly after fellow Round Table member Alexander Woollcott came out with his book *Shouts and Murmurs*, Adams bought a copy and asked the author for a personal inscription. As Woollcott was writing in the book, he mused in good humor, "Ah, what is so rare as a Woollcott first edition?" Adams teasingly replied:

A Woollcott second edition.

☆ ☆ ☆ ☆ ☆ ☆ ☆ ☆ ☆ ☆ ☆

Adams and his friend Herbert Bayard Swope were discussing literature with visitors from Europe when somebody mentioned the contribution of the German poet and playwright Heinrich Wilhelm von Kleist. Swope was reasonably well read, but was completely unfamiliar with the name. "Who's Kleist?" he asked. Before any of the guests could answer, FPA piped in with his own guess:

The Chinese Messiah?

☆ ☆ ☆ ☆ ☆ ☆ ☆ ☆ ☆ ☆ ☆

By 1921, the occasional pickup poker games of the early Round Table group were formalized into regular Saturday night affairs. Held in a suite at the hotel that was provided free of charge by the marketing-savvy manager, Frank Case, the players dubbed themselves "The Thanatopsis Literary and Inside Straight Club." For almost a decade, the games were a fertile ground for clever quips and snappy replies, many of which ended up in newspaper columns the following Monday morning. The actor Herbert Ransom, a regular at many of the games, was the butt of many jokes because he was unable to maintain a "poker face" when holding a good hand. One night, his facial expressions were so transparent that FPA announced to the rest of the players:

Anyone who looks at Ransom's face is cheating.

★ ★ ★ ★ ★ ★ ★ ★ ★ ★ ★

While attending Harvard University, Massachusetts native Robert Bench-ley honed his satirical skills as two-time editor of the *Harvard Lampoon*. After graduation, he moved to New York City, where he was, by his own admission, such a terrible newspaper reporter that he decided to try his luck at book reviews and dramatic criticism. In 1919, he was hired by *Vanity Fair,* where he met Dorothy Parker and Robert E. Sherwood. In 1920, he became a theater critic for *Life* magazine, where he worked until he joined the staff of *The New Yorker,* where he worked until 1940. One of America's greatest humorists, he wrote fifteen volumes of humorous sketches and essays, many best-sellers. Benchley had aspirations of becoming a serious writer, and never fully appreciated his success. (Sadly, there is some truth in his famous observation: "It took me fifteen years to discover that I had no talent for writing, but I couldn't give it up because by that time I was too famous."). He eventually moved to Hollywood, where he became a national celebrity for producing and starring in scores of short subject films (he won an Oscar for his 1935 film *How to Sleep*).

★ ★ ★ ★ ★ ★ ★ ★ ★ ★ ★

After lunching at the Algonquin Hotel one day, Benchley and his companions walked through the lobby and out the front door. Still engaged in conversation with his friends, Benchley offhandedly said to the uniformed man standing by the front door, "My good man, would you please get me a taxi?" The man immediately took offense and replied indignantly, "I'm not a doorman. I happen to be a rear admiral in the United States Navy." Benchley instantly quipped:

All right then, get me a battleship.

✶ ✶ ✶ ✶ ✶ ✶ ✶ ✶ ✶ ✶ ✶

During their years at *The New Yorker*, Benchley and Dorothy Parker loved to tease the magazine's founder, Harold Ross. Arriving in Venice during his first-ever European vacation, Benchley was inspired by the site. He immediately sent a telegram to Ross:

> **STREETS FULL OF WATER.**
> **PLEASE ADVISE.**

✶ ✶ ✶ ✶ ✶ ✶ ✶ ✶ ✶ ✶ ✶

At six-feet-seven, playwright Robert E. Sherwood was the tallest member of the Round Table. One day, a stranger to the group asked Benchley if he knew Sherwood. Benchley hopped on the seat of a nearby chair, raised his hand above his head, and replied:

> **Do I know him?**
> **Why I've known Bob Sherwood**
> **since he was *this* high.**

✶ ✶ ✶ ✶ ✶ ✶ ✶ ✶ ✶ ✶ ✶

During their late-night parties, the members of the Round Table played many inventive word and language games, including one where they composed their own humorous epitaphs. One night, Benchley attended a Hollywood party in which the hostess invited the guests to play the same game. When his turn came around, Benchley was ready with his own creation: "This is all above me." An actress seated next to Benchley, a woman famous for her many marriages and affairs, struggled to come up with something for herself. Finally, she confessed, "I simply can't think of anything." Benchley was quick to offer his suggestion:

> **At last she sleeps alone.**

★ ★ ★ ★ ★ ★ ★ ★ ★ ★

In 1926, while serving as a drama critic for *The New Yorker*, Benchley attended the premiere of a play titled *The Squall*, which featured the frequent use of "pidgin" English on the part of the actors. Growing increasingly annoyed, Benchley whispered to his companion that he had heard just about enough. At that moment, a young female performer fell to her knees at the feet of the male lead character and said, "Me Nubi. Nubi good girl. Me stay." Benchley bolted out of his seat and, heading for the aisle, said to his companion:

Me Bobby. Bobby bad boy. Me go!

★ ★ ★ ★ ★ ★ ★ ★ ★ ★

Checking out of a hotel one day, Benchley searched out all the hotel staff who had made his visit enjoyable and expressed his appreciation with generous tips. As Benchley was making his final exit, he was approached by a doorman who had scarcely even seen Benchley during his stay. Having heard about the generous tips the famous guest had given the rest of the staff, the doorman extended his hand and said, "Aren't you going to remember me, Mr. Benchley?" As Benchley walked away, he smiled and said cheerfully:

**Why, of course.
I'll write you every day.**

★ ★ ★ ★ ★ ★ ★ ★ ★ ★

Benchley didn't drink at all in college, and in his midtwenties was even known to lecture his hard-drinking friends on the evils of alcohol. But, like millions of Americans during Prohibition, he became a heavy drinker as the decade wore on. At one point, he was admonished by recently sober friend F. Scott Fitzgerald, who said with concern, "Don't you know that alcohol is slow poison?" Benchley cavalierly replied:

So who's in a hurry?

✳ ✳ ✳ ✳ ✳ ✳ ✳ ✳ ✳ ✳ ✳

The only native New Yorker to become a regular Round Table member, the Brooklyn-born Heywood Broun went to college at Harvard, but fell short of graduation by only a few credits (most say he spent too many days at the ballpark cheering on Tris Speaker and the Boston Red Sox). Moving back to New York City, he began his career as a sportswriter, a line of work he dabbled in his entire career. He became best known, however, as a fiery journalist, an outspoken political commentator, and an influential drama critic. Noted for espousing progressive causes—like supporting the defendants in the Sacco-Vanzetti case—he ran unsuccessfully for Congress on the Socialist ticket in 1930. A "union man," he helped establish the American Newspaper Guild, serving for a time as its president. In 1935, he began writing a regular column for *The New Republic,* which he did until his death at age fifty-one in 1939.

✳ ✳ ✳ ✳ ✳ ✳ ✳ ✳ ✳ ✳ ✳

A man of strongly held opinions, Broun rarely held back in expressing them. In 1917, he was sued by actor Geoffrey Steyne after writing that his recent stage performance was the "worst to be seen in the contemporary theater." The case was eventually dismissed, but while the suit was pending, the paper's lawyers cautioned Broun to choose his words a bit more carefully in the future. Broun complied, but in his own way. Before the suit was settled, Broun had a chance to see Steyne in another play. This time he wrote in his review:

Mr. Steyne's performance was not up to its usual standard.

✳ ✳ ✳ ✳ ✳ ✳ ✳ ✳ ✳ ✳ ✳

Early in his career, Broun was assigned to interview Reed Smoot of Utah, the first Mormon elected to the U.S. Senate. A conservative Republican, Smoot was one of the "irreconcilables," a group of senators and congressmen steadfastly opposed to the U.S. joining the League of Nations. When the liberal Broun asked the conservative senator for an interview, Smoot replied, "I'm sorry, I have nothing to say." Broun replied:

I know. Now can we get down to the interview?

★ ★ ★ ★ ★ ★ ★ ★ ★ ★ ★

During a surprise thunderstorm, Broun and a colleague were forced to take shelter in a Manhattan dive that was not up to their usual standard. When the wine came, it was also not of the highest quality, provoking Broun to sigh:

Oh well, any port in a storm.

★ ★ ★ ★ ★ ★ ★ ★ ★ ★ ★

On June 14, 1934, Broun was covering the fight when twenty-five-year-old Max Baer, the American challenger, defeated Italy's Primo Carnera, the reigning heavyweight champ. At six feet, six inches tall and weighing over 260 pounds, Carnera was an imposing figure (and the biggest champ in boxing history). Baer shocked the sporting world when he pummeled the heavily favored Carnera, dropping him to the canvas twelve separate times before knocking him out in the eleventh round. During the devastating tenth round, Baer overwhelmed Carnera, knocking him down again and again. Each time Carnera went down, however, he staggered back to his feet. A sportswriter sitting next to Broun (some say it was Grantland Rice), leaned over and said: "The big fella certainly can take it." Broun replied:

Yes, but he doesn't seem to know what to do with it.

★ ★ ★ ★ ★ ★ ★ ★ ★ ★ ★

George S. Kaufman became interested in the theater in his early teens, writing his first play at age fourteen. At nineteen, he followed his family from

Pittsburgh to Paterson, New Jersey, where he began writing humorous sketches for local papers (even though he had no formal middle name, he initialed his pieces *GSK*, emulating his hero, Franklin Pierce Adams). With Adams's help, he landed his first column in 1912 and by 1917 was a columnist and drama critic for the *New York Times*. He achieved great success as a playwright, with many of his plays becoming Broadway hits (two won Pulitzer Prizes). He also wrote screenplays for many Hollywood films, including a number of Marx Brothers classics. A regular panelist on the radio show *Information Please*, he was also a fixture on the television quiz show *This Is Show Business*. A stroke in 1950 left him almost blind and partially paralyzed, but he remained active until the late 1950s. When he died of a stroke in 1961, at age seventy-one, many recalled the epitaph he had created for himself forty years earlier: "Over my dead body."

∗ ∗ ∗ ∗ ∗ ∗ ∗ . ∗ ∗ ∗ ∗

As a child, Kaufman was informed that a particularly unpleasant aunt was coming to visit. When he expressed his displeasure, his parents gave him the standard parental lecture, ending with the predictable admonition, "It wouldn't hurt to be nice, would it?" The precocious boy was said to have replied:

That depends on your threshold of pain.

∗ ∗ ∗ ∗ ∗ ∗ ∗ ∗ ∗ ∗ ∗

After settling into his apartment in New York City, the Pennsylvania-raised Kaufman was surprised to find so many of his city friends dining late in the evening, hours after he had eaten. One night around 8:30 P.M., he got a telephone call from his friend, the journalist Herbert Bayard Swope. When Swope asked, "What are you doing for dinner tonight?" Kaufman answered:

Digesting it.

∗ ∗ ∗ ∗ ∗ ∗ ∗ ∗ ∗ ∗ ∗

The producer of such classic Broadway plays as *The Front Page* and *Our Town*, Jed Harris was a colorful character who loved to shock people by doing unexpected or even outrageous things. When Kaufman showed up for a meeting at Harris's office one day, he was momentarily startled to see a totally nude Harris sitting at his desk. The average person might have been nonplussed, but Kaufman kept his composure, calmly saying:

Jed, I believe your fly is open.

* * * * * * * * * * *

One day, a speculator tried to convince Kaufman and some other Round Table members to buy shares in a gold mine somewhere out West. Trying a little too hard to impress the potential investors, he said, "The mine is so rich, you can actually pick up chunks of gold from off the ground." Adopting an air of incredulity, Kaufman said with a straight face:

You mean, I'd have to *bend over?*

* * * * * * * * * * *

A regular at the Thanatopsis poker games, Kaufman was also an avid bridge player. Known to occasionally take the game too seriously, one night he berated his partner for poor play. The castigated partner didn't take the abuse lying down, challenging Kaufman, "All right, George, how would you have played the hand?" Kaufman's answer brought guffaws from the other players:

Under an assumed name.

Another night, after a series of losses at the bridge table, Kaufman's partner excused himself to go to the bathroom. As the poor-playing partner headed for the men's room, the frustrated Kaufman yelled after him:

**For the first time tonight,
I'll know what you have in your hand.**

✳ ✳ ✳ ✳ ✳ ✳ ✳ ✳ ✳ ✳ ✳

New Jersey native Dorothy Parker never got the Ivy League education of many of her Round Table colleagues (she attended the Blessed Sacrament Convent School in Manhattan), but she was every bit an intellectual equal. In 1916, at age twenty-two, she was hired as a caption writer at *Vogue* magazine (it was here she wrote her immortal caption for an underwear spread, "Brevity is the soul of lingerie"). In 1917, she wangled a job as drama critic at *Vanity Fair*. Fired three years later for a caustic review, she began writing freelance short stories and light verse. She produced a number of best-sellers, beginning with the book of poetry *Enough Rope* in 1926. In 1927, she began writing for *The New Yorker*, an association she would maintain throughout her professional life. In 1933, she and husband Alan Campbell moved to Hollywood, where they wrote many screenplays, including *A Star Is Born*. A petite woman with a demure appearance, she had a rapier wit that could be devastating (Alexander Woollcott once described her as "a combination of Little Nell and Lady Macbeth"). In the 1920s and '30s, she became something of a cultural icon, the prototype of the modern, liberated woman.

✳ ✳ ✳ ✳ ✳ ✳ ✳ ✳ ✳ ✳

The luncheon meetings of the Round Table frequently extended into the late afternoon, when the group would often adjourn to the home of one of the members. At these evening affairs, Parker excelled at the group's parlor games (she composed two epitaphs for herself: "Excuse my dust" and "This one's on me"). In another favorite game called "I Can Give You a Sentence," someone would toss out an unusual word and challenge the others to use it in a sentence. The best efforts usually involved creative puns. One night, someone suggested the word "horticulture." After a moment's silence, Parker hollered out, "I've got one!" Her creation that night won the plaudits of the group and went on to become one of her most celebrated quotes:

**You may lead a whore to culture,
but you can't make her think.**

★ ★ ★ ★ ★ ★ ★ ★ ★ ★ ★

At a Manhattan party one night, Parker noticed a young man who didn't appear to be enjoying himself. Striking up a conversation with him, she discovered he was a poor little rich kid who was bored to be at a party attended by people so far below him on the social ladder. At one point, he looked around the room and said contemptuously, "I simply cannot bear fools." In her acidly sweet tone, Parker replied:

How odd, your mother could.

★ ★ ★ ★ ★ ★ ★ ★ ★ ★ ★

During the early years of *The New Yorker* magazine, editor Harold Ross was so frugal that even the simplest office supplies were sometimes hard to come by. One day, Ross was upset that Parker had not come to the office to work on an article that was overdue. When he asked her if she had an excuse, she deadpanned:

Someone else was using the pencil.

★ ★ ★ ★ ★ ★ ★ ★ ★ ★ ★

Working as a screenwriter during her Hollywood days, Parker would often be invited on movie sets to offer advice to cast and crew. One day a director whispered to Parker, "Don't you think our leading lady should wear a brassiere in this scene?" She advised:

God, no! You've got to have something in this show that moves.

✷ ✷ ✷ ✷ ✷ ✷ ✷ ✷ ✷ ✷

During her stay in Hollywood, Dorothy Parker became annoyed when the English actor Herbert Marshall made repeated references to his busy schedule, pronouncing the word "SHED-yuhl," in the British fashion. Finally, she blurted out:

I think you're full of skit!

✷ ✷ ✷ ✷ ✷ ✷ ✷ ✷ ✷ ✷

One day, Alexander Woollcott was agonizing over what to do with his old and ailing cat. Realizing he had to put the animal down, he sought Parker's advice on how to proceed, saying, "I don't have the faintest idea how to go about it." Great wits sometimes have to choose between sensitivity and cleverness. Parker, never one to score high on the empathy scale, advised:

Try curiosity.

✷ ✷ ✷ ✷ ✷ ✷ ✷ ✷ ✷ ✷

At a party celebrating the ninety-second birthday of W. E. B. DuBois, the prominent African-American intellectual, Parker was seated next to the distinguished guest. During the entertainment portion of the evening, an African ceremonial dance featured spears that were being thrust about wildly, some coming uncomfortably close to DuBois. After one too many close calls, Parker leaned over and whispered into the ear of the honored guest:

Watch out, mate, or you'll never see ninety-three.

✷ ✷ ✷ ✷ ✷ ✷ ✷ ✷ ✷ ✷

Alexander Woollcott grew up in New Jersey, where he was unmercifully teased for his endomorphic body and thick spectacles. At Hamilton College, he adopted an Oscar Wilde–like persona (he often played female roles in school plays, describing himself as "half God, half woman"). After graduating in 1909, he became a *New York Times* reporter, and five years later the paper's drama critic. A big man with a disheveled appearance and a tendency to dress oddly, he shocked his friends when in 1917 he volunteered to serve in the Great War. Not fit for any kind of military service (one officer called him "the pregnant mermaid"), he was soon transferred to the U.S. Army newspaper *Stars and Stripes*, where he served out the war as a correspondent. His many antics—which included the hanging of a cast-iron frying pan across his chest for protection—made him something of a living legend. Returning home after the war, he became the most influential drama critic of his time. With his caustic wit, he could sink a Broadway production (friend Marc Connelly once said that "Rancor was Woollcott's only form of exercise"). In 1929, he began hosting his own radio show, *The Town Crier*, where his talent as a raconteur combined with his resonant voice to make him a household name during the 1930s.

★ ★ ★ ★ ★ ★ ★ ★ ★ ★ ★

The author of countless wisecracks and witty sayings (like "All the things I really like to do are either illegal, immoral, or fattening"), Woollcott's best remarks appeared with regularity in New York City newspaper columns. Many of the lines attributed to him were actually written by a New York comedy writer named Irving Mansfield, hired by Woollcott to produce material for him. As sometimes happens with writers, Mansfield went through a dry spell, resulting in a sudden decline in the number of times Woollcott's name was being mentioned in local papers. Concerned about the development, Woollcott sent a note to Mansfield, saying:

Whatever happened to my sense of humor?

★ ★ ★ ★ ★ ★ ★ ★ ★ ★ ★

A bachelor his entire life, Woollcott had numerous married friends who embraced him as a member of their own families. Never married or a parent himself, he served as a godfather to the children of his friends nineteen separate times. After the baptism of the daughter of actress Helen Hayes and her husband, Charles MacArthur, Woollcott was heard to mutter:

Always a godfather, never a god.

★ ★ ★ ★ ★ ★ ★ ★ ★ ★

Noted for his brutal honesty as a critic, Woollcott could be extremely charming in his dealings with people outside the theater. After delivering a lecture one evening, he was approached by an elderly woman who told him how much she had enjoyed his talk. As Woollcott graciously shook the lady's hand, she continued, "I was encouraged to speak to you because you said you loved old ladies." Woollcott smoothly replied:

Yes, I do, but I also like them your age.

★ ★ ★ ★ ★ ★ ★ ★ ★ ★

In 1924, Woollcott bought a little island in Lake Bomoseen in the mountains of Vermont. It soon became "the" summer place to go for numerous New York celebrities, who willingly paid Woollcott a thousand-dollar initiation fee and a one-hundred-dollar annual fee for a bucolic retreat that included nude swimming, cribbage, witty word games, and croquet (Woollcott's most strenuous form of exercise). One day, Harpo Marx decided to spend a weekend at Woollcott's cottage. When Marx arrived in a rickety Model T Ford, Woollcott exclaimed, "What in the hell are you driving?" Marx answered, "This is my town car." Woollcott replied:

What was the town? Pompeii?

9

relationship repartee

While discussing the topic of male-female relationships at one of my leadership seminars a few years ago, I remarked that many husbands think their wives talk too much. I even quoted a former client who had said, "With my wife, no detail is too small." As people chuckled at the line, a woman near the back of the room raised her hand, eager to speak. "My husband and I are about to celebrate our fortieth wedding anniversary," she said. "But when we were first married, he used to drive me crazy. Often, when I was in the middle of saying something, he would interrupt and say, 'Honey, does this story have a point?'" Several months into the marriage, the woman went on to say, she came up with a riposte that was so impressive, the couple still chuckle about it four decades later. When her husband, one last time, asked his offensive question, she simply replied:

> **Yes it does, dear,**
> **and if you bend over,**
> **I'm gonna give it to you right now.**

The line got a big laugh, especially from the women in the audience, and it got me thinking about the comebacks, rejoinders, and other fascinating replies that emerge as men and women attempt to overcome the differences between the two sexes and establish an intimate relationship.

A spectacular example happened to economist and presidential adviser

John Kenneth Galbraith when he was a teenager living on the family farm in rural Ontario. One summer day, he and the attractive daughter of a neighboring farmer were deep in conversation while sitting on the top rail of a fence overlooking a herd of cattle. Just as the conversation was starting to move in an intimate direction, a bull entered the corral and began servicing one of the cows. Young Galbraith figured it was the perfect time to make his move. While observing the mating behavior of the animals, he leaned closer to the object of his affection and said in a slightly suggestive tone, "That looks like it would be fun." The young woman hesitated for a moment, and then completely deflated the young suitor with one simple comment:

Well . . . it's your cow.

A story told by Nunnally Johnson further illustrates the point. The screenwriter for such classic films as *The Grapes of Wrath*, *The Desert Fox*, *The Three Faces of Eve*, and *The Dirty Dozen*, Johnson was lunching one day at a restaurant with his girlfriend. Just after he ordered the house specialty, a combination seafood platter, she uttered the dreaded words, "We have to talk." Ten minutes later, as the food arrived, she was in the middle of a litany of complaints about Johnson: his selfishness, insensitivity, failure to prioritize the relationship, tendency to take her for granted, and so forth. As she was talking, Johnson listened without comment or defensiveness. But not wanting his food to get cold, he began digging into the culinary delicacy before him. This was not exactly the time for multitasking, however, and the girlfriend exploded. "Just look at you!" she exclaimed. "Our very lives are at a crossroad, and there you sit, smacking your lips like a pig." It was a scene right out of a movie. And so was Johnson's reply:

I'm sorry. If I would've known it was going to be like this, I would've ordered something I didn't like.

When couples finally tie the knot and embark on the adventure of marriage, many of the pretenses of the courtship ritual are dropped, and some of the annoying tendencies that have always existed—but never fully manifested—begin to emerge. Somewhere in the middle of Walter Matthau's forty-year marriage to his wife, Carol, the couple went to a party where he became fascinated by an actress with unusually thick legs. She was also a woman of indeterminate age, and Walter was having a devil of a time gauging how old she was. He went on about her legs and her age so many times that Carol accused him of being fixated on the subject. Near the end of the evening, he mentioned it one more time and the exasperated Carol blurted out:

For God's sake, Walter,
why don't you just chop off her legs and read the rings?

Marital banter has always been fascinating, but when husbands and wives become parents and a couple is transformed into a family, the clever lines that have emerged rival the snappiest dialogue of the best stage plays and sitcoms.

One evening in the 1930s, Joseph Kennedy gathered together his wife, Rose, and the rest of the Kennedy children to discuss the family's financial situation. It was a typical family meeting, with the father lecturing and the children squirming uncomfortably in their seats. The entire country was going through hard times, the elder Kennedy said, and he was concerned that the children were taking the family's good fortune for granted and spending his hard-earned money too freely. He even tried to induce a little guilt by saying, "No one appears to have the slightest concern for how much they spend. I just don't know what's going to happen after I'm gone." He then singled out one of the Kennedy girls and reprimanded her for her lavish spending habits. The severity of his words stung rather deeply, and soon sent her running from the room in tears. When she returned a few moments later, the teenage John Kennedy got up from his seat, put a consoling arm around his sister's shoulder, and said:

Now, now, there's nothing to worry about.
While you were gone, we came to the conclusion
that the only solution is to have Dad work harder.

The tension in the room was immediately broken and howls of laughter erupted from the entire clan (including, it is said, from a relieved father, Joe). It was an early example of the famous Kennedy wit, which an entire nation would greatly admire a few decades later.

While the most celebrated examples of relationship repartee have come from celebrities, many remarkable replies have been authored by little-known people in the seclusion of their homes. This past year, I got a note from Ken Logsdon, a subscriber to *Dr. Mardy's Quotes of the Week*, a weekly e-newsletter I send out every Sunday morning to people all around the world. When he found out I was working on this book, he wrote to tell me how much he admired a clever comeback he'd just heard from his wife, Lynnette. The Logsdons have an art collection they dearly love, but which is not esteemed as highly by their teenage daughters. When the family was gathered in the living room one day, sixteen-year-old Emily was seen examining the paintings. Finally, she looked over at her mother and asked, "When you die, can we sell all these?" Stunned by the bluntness of the question, Ken's mouth dropped open and he was stumped for words. But not Lynnette. She nonchalantly replied:

If they belong to you.

It was the perfect rejoinder, and one especially appreciated by eighteen-year-old Katy Logsdon, who'd been observing the conversation. She honored her mother's comeback with the ultimate teenage compliment, simply saying, "Ouch!"

The relationships between men and women, husbands and wives, and parents and children have long been a rich source of material for people interested in repartee, as you will continue to see in the remainder of this chapter.

⋆ ⋆ ⋆ ⋆ ⋆ ⋆ ⋆ ⋆ ⋆ ⋆

While serving as secretary of state in the early 1950s, Dean Acheson had many opportunities to display his diplomatic skills, some quite unexpected. While he was walking through a Washington hotel lobby one day, a well-dressed, gray-haired woman approached him and whispered in a flustered manner: "I'm sorry to bother you, but I'm due at a meeting in a few minutes and the zipper on my dress appears to be stuck. I wonder if you could help me out." Acheson graciously complied with the woman's request and, like a true gentleman, made sure he averted his eyes as he did so. The grateful woman thanked Acheson for his help and added with pride, "By the way, I think you should know that I am a vice president of the Daughters of the American Revolution." With diplomatic flair, Acheson replied:

> **My dear lady, what a moment ago was a rare privilege**
> **now appears to have been a really great honor.**

★ ★ ★ ★ ★ ★ ★ ★ ★ ★ ★

As the twentieth century began, the German pianist and composer Eugène d'Albert was well known throughout Europe. He was also beginning to establish another reputation as a serial husband (he was married six times). At a reception just after his fifth marriage, he introduced his new bride to an old friend. When attending the weddings of oft-divorced and much-married people, guests are often at a loss for words, but not this witty gentleman. Shaking the groom's hand, he said:

> **Congratulations, Eugène,**
> **you have rarely introduced me**
> **to so charming a wife.**

★ ★ ★ ★ ★ ★ ★ ★ ★ ★ ★

One of history's most famous theatrical families, the Barrymore acting legacy started in 1875, when English actor Maurice Barrymore arrived in New York and became a hit on the Broadway stage. Maurice and wife, Georgiana Drew, also an actress, produced three children—Ethel, John, and Lionel—who would become such acclaimed theatrical stars they were dubbed the Royal Family of Broadway.

When Maurice died in 1905, the three siblings—all in their twenties—gathered at the funeral. As the casket was being lowered into the grave, a problem occurred with the lowering mechanism and the casket had to be brought up again before it could be lowered properly. Just before it began its second descent, Lionel whispered to brother John:

How like father—a curtain call.

    ★ ★ ★ ★ ★ ★ ★ ★ ★ ★ ★

In the early decades of the twentieth century, English writer and caricaturist Max Beerbohm was celebrated as one of London's great wits, right up there with Shaw, Wilde, and Whistler. One day, as Beerbohm and a friend were discussing a mutual acquaintance whom Max hadn't seen in years, the friend casually mentioned that she was exactly the same and, in fact, hadn't changed a bit. Beerbohm wryly observed:

I'm sorry to hear that.

    ★ ★ ★ ★ ★ ★ ★ ★ ★ ★ ★

Mrs. Patrick Campbell was a great presence on the English stage in the late nineteenth and early twentieth centuries. After playing the role of Eliza in Shaw's 1914 play, *Pygmalion*, she formed a deep and long friendship with the author, carried out mainly via wonderfully interesting letters they wrote to one another. Mrs. Campbell was a temperamental actress, which made her the terror of many directors and fellow actors, but she could also be witty and charming and downright irresistible. One day a reporter asked her the loaded question, "Why is it that women have no sense of humor?" She thought about the question for a moment and replied:

God did it on purpose
so we may love you men
instead of laughing at you.

⭑ ⭑ ⭑ ⭑ ⭑ ⭑ ⭑ ⭑ ⭑ ⭑

After serving as secretary of the treasury in Abraham Lincoln's wartime cabinet, Salmon P. Chase was elevated to the Supreme Court in 1864, where he served as the sixth chief justice of the United States until his death in 1873. Shortly after the Civil War, Chase, a fervent abolitionist, was introduced to a beautiful Southern belle at a Washington dinner party. In a pronounced Southern drawl, the young beauty said provocatively, "I must warn you, Mr. Chief Justice, that I'm an unreconstructed rebel." Chase may have been approaching sixty, but he proved he could still be quite the charmer, replying:

> **In your case, madam,
> reconstruction—even in the slightest—
> would be nothing short of sacrilege.**

⭑ ⭑ ⭑ ⭑ ⭑ ⭑ ⭑ ⭑ ⭑ ⭑

While serving as ambassador to England in the early 1900s, Joseph Choate and his wife attended a London party in which the hostess suggested a game in which people were asked to name the person they would most like to be if they were not themselves. When it came time for Choate to reply, he glanced over at his wife as he was standing up, and provided an answer truly fitting a great diplomat:

> **If I could not be myself,
> I would like to be—
> Mrs. Choate's second husband.**

⭑ ⭑ ⭑ ⭑ ⭑ ⭑ ⭑ ⭑ ⭑ ⭑

The fifty-six-year marriage of Winston and Clementine Churchill was successful in large part because of Clementine's wifely devotion and her ability to accept some of his challenging personal traits: occasional tantrums, extremely exacting standards, and notorious tardiness. When once asked about her husband's tardiness, she replied:

Winston's a sporting man;
he always gives the train a chance to get away.

★ ★ ★ ★ ★ ★ ★ ★ ★ ★

After leading his beleaguered nation through the darkest days of World War II, Winston Churchill was voted out of office in the elections of 1945. It was a shock to the world, and it stunned the Grand Old Man of English politics, who had underestimated the appeal of the Labor Party's program of economic and social reform. As a dejected Churchill was trying to absorb the meaning of the defeat, his wife, Clementine, tried to console him by saying, "Perhaps it's a blessing in disguise." Able to retain his sense of humor during this depressing moment, Churchill replied:

Perhaps, but at the moment,
it seems quite effectively disguised.

★ ★ ★ ★ ★ ★ ★ ★ ★ ★

During his many decades in Congress, Henry Clay of Kentucky was unusually adept at thinking on his feet, a trait that served him as well in his personal affairs as it did in his political life. At a Washington social gathering in the early 1800s, he ran into a beautiful lady he had met some months earlier. As they began conversing, Clay confessed that he had forgotten her name. Adopting a tone of mock offense, the woman said, "You mean you don't remember my name, Mr. Clay?" Ever the politician, he smoothly replied:

No, for when we last met,
I was sure your beauty and accomplishments
would very soon compel you to change it.

✶ ✶ ✶ ✶ ✶ ✶ ✶ ✶ ✶ ✶ ✶

Many wives complain that their husbands don't talk enough, and few wives had greater justification than Grace Coolidge, wife of the thirtieth U.S. president. Coolidge was extremely taciturn, well deserving his "Silent Cal" nickname. Returning from church one Sunday morning, Coolidge was asked by the First Lady, "What did the preacher speak about today? "Sin," replied the laconic president. Frustrated with the lack of detail, Mrs. Coolidge persisted, "Well, what did he say about it?" The president, apparently enjoying the moment, said simply:

He was against it.

✶ ✶ ✶ ✶ ✶ ✶ ✶ ✶ ✶ ✶ ✶

A vaudeville comedienne, Ina Claire became a big star in both the *Ziegfeld Follies* and *The Gold Diggers*. While she also did a few silent films—and "talkies" a few years later—she focused her career on the Broadway stage. In 1929, she married matinee idol John Gilbert, one of the biggest film stars of the silent era. Just after the wedding, a reporter asked Claire, "How does it feel to be married to a celebrity?" The stage star coyly replied:

I don't know.
Why don't you ask my husband?

✶ ✶ ✶ ✶ ✶ ✶ ✶ ✶ ✶ ✶ ✶

The nineteenth-century French writer Alfred de Musset was almost as well known for his romantic relationship with the famous female writer George Sand as he was for his literary endeavors. When Sand dumped him for another man, he became so furious he wrote a pornographic novel featuring a thinly veiled version of her. His relationship with Sand helped establish his reputation as a great lover, making him attractive to other French women. One day, a vain and self-absorbed actress approached him and said seductively, "People tell me that you boast of having slept with me." The poet offered a memorable rebuff:

Pardon me, but I have always boasted of the exact opposite.

★ ★ ★ ★ ★ ★ ★ ★ ★ ★ ★

After glasnost and perestroika opened up the former Soviet Union to the freewheeling journalistic practices of the West, Mikhail Gorbachev was asked by a reporter, "What effect on history do you think it would have made if, in 1963, President Khrushchev had been assassinated instead of President Kennedy?" This was not a question for which Gorbachev could have been prepared, but he proved as adept as any witty Western politician when he answered with a straight face:

**I don't think Mr. Onassis
would have married Mrs. Khrushchev.**

★ ★ ★ ★ ★ ★ ★ ★ ★ ★ ★

Born in 1898 to one of New York City's wealthiest families, Peggy Guggenheim inherited a fortune at age twenty-one, which she used to become one of the most influential art patrons of the twentieth century. While living in Paris and London in the 1920s and '30s, she associated with avant-garde writers and artists, acquiring a massive modern art collection (one biographer estimated that she spent around $350,000 for a collection that was valued at more than $350 million when she died in 1979). Guggenheim led a Bohemian lifestyle that resulted in a number of marriages and the taking of numerous lovers. When an interviewer once asked, "How many husbands have you had?" she answered:

Do you mean my own or other people's?

Some time later, the much-married actress Zsa Zsa Gabor was asked the same question, and she replied: "You mean apart from my own?" It is not known if Gabor was familiar with Guggenheim's earlier reply.

★ ★ ★ ★ ★ ★ ★ ★ ★ ★

In 1902, Alma Schindler, a beautiful and free-spirited Viennese pianist, married composer Gustav Mahler, a man twenty years her senior (he called her "my wild creature"). After Mahler's death a decade later, Schindler embarked on a lifetime of romantic and erotic adventures with some of the era's most famous men, including architect Walter Gropius, singer Enrico Caruso, writer Franz Werfel, and numerous other writers, painters, and composers (she once said, "Nothing is better than sperm from a genius"). While she was married to Mahler, the couple went to a party that was also attended by the German playwright Gerhart Hauptmann and his wife. At one point, thinking he was out of earshot of his wife, Hauptmann whispered to the irresistible beauty, "Alma, in another life, we two must be lovers. May I make a reservation now?" Unfortunately for Hauptmann, his wife overheard the conversation and immediately took charge of the situation. As she grabbed her husband's arm to lead him away, she said:

Come, darling, I'm sure Alma will be booked up there, too.

★ ★ ★ ★ ★ ★ ★ ★ ★ ★

After emigrating from Russia to the United States in 1906, the impresario Sol Hurok introduced millions of Americans to the Bolshoi Ballet and such classical stars as Artur Rubinstein, Isaac Stern, Maria Callas, and Andrés Segovia. In 1953, the sixty-five-year-old Hurok attended a screening of *Tonight We Sing*, a film based on his 1946 autobiography by the same title. The film revealed an interesting fact about Hurok's life—because of the enormous amount of time required to tend to the needs of his famous clients, he and his new wife were never able to take a honeymoon. As the film ended, Hurok was clearly moved. He leaned over and tenderly whispered to his wife, "Emma, we have to go on that honeymoon." Emma gently reminded her husband:

Sol, that movie was about your first wife.

✳ ✳ ✳ ✳ ✳ ✳ ✳ ✳ ✳ ✳ ✳

The Pittsburgh-born George S. Kaufman and his wife, Beatrice, who grew up in Rochester, New York, were walking down Fifth Avenue one day when they kept running into old friends and acquaintances from her hometown. Finally, Mrs. Kaufman exclaimed, "All of Rochester seems to be in New York this week." Kaufman, always looking for an opportunity to exercise his wit, mused:

Hmmm, what an excellent time to visit Rochester.

✳ ✳ ✳ ✳ ✳ ✳ ✳ ✳ ✳ ✳ ✳

In the early 1960s, President Kennedy and wife, Jackie, flew to Cape Cod for a weekend of relaxation. One afternoon at the Hyannisport Golf Course, JFK grew frustrated as he watched his wife struggling to get her ball out of a sand trap. Every time she took a swing, the ball moved several feet up the side of the trap and then trickled back down to its original position. "Open the club face!" he instructed brusquely. "Follow through!" After observing a few more unsuccessful swings, the impatient JFK jumped from the cart, snatched the club from his wife, and said, "Let me show you how to do it!" After a mighty swing and a huge explosion of sand, the ball advanced a few feet and then trickled back into the trap. It was an embarrassing moment for the president, who could hear muffled snickers from nearby Secret Service agents. The snickers turned to guffaws, however, when JFK handed the club back to the First Lady and said:

There, that's how you do it.

✳ ✳ ✳ ✳ ✳ ✳ ✳ ✳ ✳ ✳ ✳

President John F. Kennedy and his father, Joseph, were once proudly watching JFK's daughter, Caroline, at play. As they sat side by side on comfortable lawn chairs, no words passed between the two men for quite some time. Finally, the elder Kennedy said, "Caroline's very bright, Jack." Then, after a pause, he added, "Smarter than you were at that age." The president adopted a similar thoughtful demeanor and, without looking over at his dad, said, "Yes, she is." Then, after a pause of his own, he added:

But look who *she* has for a father.

✴ ✴ ✴ ✴ ✴ ✴ ✴ ✴ ✴ ✴

In 1960, after the noted intellectuals Arthur Schlesinger Jr. and John Kenneth Galbraith announced that they were joining the presidential campaign of John F. Kennedy, a *Boston Globe* reporter called Schlesinger's wife and asked her if she was also supporting Kennedy. No, she reported, she was backing Adlai Stevenson. The newspaper published this interesting tidbit the very next day. Several days later, Schlesinger received a letter from Robert F. Kennedy, JFK's campaign manager, in which he described several campaign-related matters. In a handwritten postscript at the bottom of the letter, RFK demonstrated the well-known Kennedy wit when he wrote:

Can't you control your wife?
Or are you like me?

✴ ✴ ✴ ✴ ✴ ✴ ✴ ✴ ✴ ✴

Shortly before World War II, the pianist and wit Oscar Levant ran into friend Moss Hart at a New York party. Even though Hart was only in his midthirties, he was already being hailed as one of America's great playwrights, and there is no doubt that he was enjoying his celebrity status. Until he married Kitty Carlisle in 1946, he was routinely described as one of America's "most eligible bachelors" and generally seen with a beautiful young woman on his arm—almost always a different young woman. That evening, Hart was accompanied by the beautiful actress Edith Atwater. When Levant spotted the handsome young couple, he walked up and said:

**Ah, here comes Moss Hart
and the future . . . Miss Atwater.**

✳ ✳ ✳ ✳ ✳ ✳ ✳ ✳ ✳ ✳

Chico (correctly pronounced "CHICK-oh") Marx, the oldest of the brothers, got his nickname from his penchant for chasing young women (i.e., chicks) early in his life. Although the Marx Brothers made millions over the years, Chico was often in financial straits because of a lifelong gambling problem (his wife, Betty, insisted that they rent rather than own a home for fear of Chico's losing their house in a card game). Over the years, his interest in the ladies also created a few marital problems. At a club one night, Betty angrily accused Chico of kissing another woman on the dance floor. His defense may not have convinced his wife, but it has pleased fans of repartee ever since:

**I wasn't kissing her,
I was whispering in her mouth.**

✳ ✳ ✳ ✳ ✳ ✳ ✳ ✳ ✳ ✳

One of Hungary's most popular and prolific writers, Ferenc Molnár set a goal early in his career of producing one play and one novel every year (one of his works was adapted by Rodgers and Hammerstein as the musical *Carousel* and another was adapted by Tom Stoppard as *Rough Crossing)*. During one of his three marriages, Molnár and his wife got into a huge argument in front of an old friend. Astonished at the vituperative quality of the fight, the friend broke in and asked, "Is this the way you two always argue?" The couple immediately ceased hostilities and a calm filled the air. Molnár then explained:

**Of course. It saves time.
Now that we've both unburdened ourselves
we can enjoy some delicious silence.**

✶ ✶ ✶ ✶ ✶ ✶ ✶ ✶ ✶ ✶

Paul Newman and Joanne Woodward were married in 1958, a year after they met on the set of *The Long Hot Summer*. One of America's most famous couples, in a few years they may celebrate a Hollywood rarity—a golden wedding anniversary. He once said of her, "Joanne is one of the last of the great broads." And she said, "Being married to Paul is being married to a most considerate, romantic man." When an interviewer once asked Newman why, given the numerous temptations, he never strayed, his answer drew "aaahs"of appreciation from married women all around the world:

Why fool around with hamburger when you have steak at home?

✶ ✶ ✶ ✶ ✶ ✶ ✶ ✶ ✶ ✶

Algonquin Round Table wit Dorothy Parker married second husband Alan Campbell in 1933. The couple lived and worked together until 1947, when they divorced. Three years later, they remarried. At the second wedding reception, a family friend gushed about how wonderful the day was: "People who haven't spoken to one another in years are talking to one another today," she said. Parker immediately added:

Including the bride and groom.

✶ ✶ ✶ ✶ ✶ ✶ ✶ ✶ ✶ ✶

U.S. presidents and other heads of state have long struggled with the behavior of their children, but none more famously than Theodore Roosevelt. Alice Roosevelt was seventeen when her father was inaugurated in 1901 and she soon became a media darling. She was dubbed Princess Alice by the press, and newspapers all over America chronicled her many antics, which included going on unchaperoned dates (shocking at the time), smoking on the White House roof, and once jumping into a swimming pool fully clothed. She retained her unconventional ways into adulthood and was known in her later years as "Washington's other monument." During her father's first term, Alice frequently barged into meetings the president was having with staff and visiting dignitaries. When the writer Owen Wister—an old friend from Roosevelt's Harvard days—complained about it one day when he was visiting, the exasperated president replied:

> **I can be president of the United States
> or I can control Alice.
> But I cannot do both.**

★ ★ ★ ★ ★ ★ ★ ★ ★ ★

In the latter half of the nineteenth century, Charles Russell was an Irish lawyer and politician who was so well regarded by Queen Victoria that she appointed him Queen's Counsel. In 1884 he became lord chief justice of England, the first Catholic in that position since the Reformation. While solemn on the bench, he was good-humored and witty in person. A woman once asked him, "What is the maximum punishment for bigamy?" Well before jokes about the subject became popular, Lord Russell answered without hesitation:

> **Two mothers-in-law.**

★ ★ ★ ★ ★ ★ ★ ★ ★ ★

In 1898, while recuperating from an illness, George Bernard Shaw married Charlotte Payne-Townshend, an Irish heiress who had been nursing him back to health. It was a marriage of convenience (once described as a "celibate marriage") but not an unhappy one. They remained together until she died in 1943. Shaw was one of the wittiest men of all time, but he was once outperformed in the confines of his own home. As the couple enjoyed their afternoon tea one day, Shaw said to his wife, "Isn't it true, my dear, that male judgment is superior to female judgment?" Mrs. Shaw sweetly replied:

**Of course, dear.
After all, you married me, and I you.**

★ ★ ★ ★ ★ ★ ★ ★ ★ ★

Richard Brinsley Sheridan may have been one of the best-known playwrights of his time, but he was notoriously bad at managing his money and continually in debt. While he didn't appear to mind the indebtedness all that much, his wife and family were often embarrassed by creditors knocking at the door. One day, in the middle of a fierce and bitter argument with his son Tom, Sheridan said, "I'll cut you off without a shilling!" Tom immediately struck back:

But, Father, where will you borrow the shilling?

A few years later, Tom Sheridan told his father that he was going to follow in his dad's footsteps and run for Parliament. Unlike the elder Sheridan, who was a staunch Liberal, Tom said he planned to proclaim his independence of party. He even suggested that his vote might be for sale to the highest bidder by saying, "If I were in Parliament, I would write on my forehead, 'To Let.' " Not impressed, the witty father replied:

And under that, add *Unfurnished*.

★ ★ ★ ★ ★ ★ ★ ★ ★ ★

The legendary literary couple Thomas and Jane Carlyle had one of history's most famous "difficult" marriages. He was emotionally distant, completely absorbed in his work, in the grip of what today is called an obsessive-compulsive disorder, and was infatuated with a woman other than his wife. She had married a man she admitted she didn't love, had her own emotional connections with men other than her husband, was a notorious busybody, and got so overinvolved with household help that she went through thirty servants in thirty years. Their troubled relationship was so apparent to friends and colleagues that many wondered why they stayed together. One day, as Alfred, Lord Tennyson and some friends were discussing the Carlyles' situation, a member of the group stated that the marriage was a big mistake and suggested that if each of them had married someone else, they might have achieved happiness. Tennyson immediately jumped in with his contrary opinion:

> **I totally disagree with you.**
> **By any other arrangement,**
> **four people would have been unhappy instead of two.**

★ ★ ★ ★ ★ ★ ★ ★ ★ ★

When Margaret Thatcher became the first female prime minister of England in 1979, much of the press focused on her marriage to English businessman Denis Thatcher. Many wondered what it must be like to be the husband of such a powerful and no-nonsense leader, nicknamed the Iron Lady. Shortly after the couple moved into their residence at 10 Downing Street, a reporter asked Mr. Thatcher, "Who wears the pants in your house?" He replied instantly, "I do." And then he added with a smile:

> **I also wash and iron them.**

★ ★ ★ ★ ★ ★ ★ ★ ★ ★

After U.S. president Harry Truman referred to a Republican politician's speech as "a bunch of horse manure," an aide suggested to First Lady Bess Truman that she might want to tell her husband to "tone down" his language. She replied, "You don't know how many years it's taken me to get him to say 'horse manure'!" Another wife who struggled with her husband's salty language was Olivia Clemens, wife of Mark Twain. After years of unsuccessful nagging, she decided one day to try a different tack. Having heard Twain cuss a blue streak after he cut himself while shaving, Mrs. Clemens spent the rest of the day repeating those very same profanities, hoping the endless repetition would get her husband to see what he sounded like and, hopefully, motivate him to clean up his act. Twain patiently let her have her fun throughout the day, but when she did it once again before bedtime, he calmly observed:

**You have heard the words, my dear,
but you will never master the tune.**

senior citizen repartee

On his seventy-fifth birthday on November 30, 1950, Winston Churchill was in great spirits and in rare form. When members of the press arrived, they swarmed around the honored guest, peppering him with questions. When one reporter shouted out, "Do you have any fear of death?" the avuncular Churchill got a hearty laugh when he replied:

> **I am ready to meet my Maker.**
> **Whether my Maker is prepared for the ordeal of meeting me**
> **is another matter.**

In the middle of the festivities, an awestruck photographer gingerly approached the old man and said with the greatest respect, "I hope, sir, that I will shoot your picture on your hundredth birthday." Churchill stepped back, looked the young man over carefully, and replied in distinctive Churchillian fashion:

> **I don't see why not, young man.**
> **You look reasonably fit and healthy.**

If mental quickness deteriorates with age, you'd never know it from the spectacular replies that elders have authored over the years. In 1883, Eubie

Blake was born to former slaves in Baltimore, Maryland. Showing an early talent for the keyboard, the teenage Blake began playing in local cafes and brothels. One of the first African American performers to appear on the professional stage without minstrel makeup, his "Charleston Rag" helped establish ragtime as a unique American art form. Although he smoked since childhood and—strangely—refused to drink water, he lived to be 100 years old. While celebrating his birthday, a reporter asked, "How do you feel, Mr. Blake?" The great showman replied:

> **If I'd known I was going to live this long,
> I'd have taken better care of myself!**

The irrepressible Blake often entertained interviewers and fans with clever quips and provocative observations. On the occasion of his ninety-seventh birthday, an interviewer asked him, "At what age does the sex drive go?" He answered:

> **You'll have to ask somebody older than me.**

There's no reason to believe Blake knew about it, but a similar version of this great reply had been offered more than a century earlier by the eighty-year-old Countess of Essex and recorded for posterity by Jane Carlyle, wife of the English man of letters Thomas Carlyle. In a letter to a friend, Mrs. Carlyle admired the cleverness of the Countess's reply when she was asked by a young man, "When does a woman have done with love?" She replied, "Ask someone older than me."

Art Linkletter was fond of saying that the two best interview subjects were children under ten and people over seventy. Both, he said, say exactly what's on their minds—children because they don't know any better and seniors because they've stopped censoring their true thoughts for fear of what people might think. In one of Linkletter's favorite stories, an elderly widow was approached by the funeral director just prior to the services for her recently deceased husband. Gently taking the widow's hand in his, he unctuously asked,

"How old was your husband, dear?" "Ninety-eight" she replied. "Two years older than me." "So, you're ninety-six?" the undertaker commented, almost as if he were talking to a child. The woman replied sweetly:

Yes, hardly worth going home, is it?

In 1999, the eighty-seven-year-old Linkletter described a priceless senior reply, all the more special because it was not meant to be funny. While speaking to a Pittsburgh group about the importance of keeping a sense of humor despite the tragedies and problems that life brings, he recalled visiting a nursing home as part of his campaign to help fight Alzheimer's disease. Approaching an elderly female resident, Linkletter asked, "Do you know who I am?" Mistaking the celebrity for one of the home's residents, she replied:

**No, but if you go to the front desk,
they'll be sure to tell you.**

Some of history's best replies have occurred during the last days of life, many on deathbeds. As he lay dying at age eighty-four, Voltaire was visited by a pious clergyman who exhorted him to repudiate the devil. Not about to make a deathbed conversion, the witty freethinker replied with a question of his own:

Is this a time to be making enemies?

A similar exchange was recorded at the deathbed of Henry David Thoreau, a deeply spiritual person who read the Bible and sacred writings of other religious traditions, but rejected organized religion. As he lay dying of tuberculosis, friends and family gathered around him. When Thoreau's aunt, a strict Calvinist, asked, "Henry, have you made your peace with God?" he replied:

I was not aware we had ever quarreled.

Shocked by her nephew's impious answer, the devout aunt pressed the matter further, inquiring, "But aren't you concerned about the next world?" Thoreau was ready for this question as well, replying with a soft tone of resignation:

One world at a time.

Great elder replies have spanned the gamut of topics: politics, sex, relationships, stereotypes, the joys of aging, and occasionally the aging of joys. Let's examine more *senior citizen repartee* in the remainder of the chapter.

★ ★ ★ ★ ★ ★ ★ ★ ★ ★ ★

Roy Acuff became a regular performer at the *Grand Ole Opry* starting in 1938. Along with his Smoky Mountain Boys, he set the tone for country-and-western music until the 1950s. After he stopped performing, he was active in the music business—and Tennessee politics—until he died at age eighty-nine. When he turned eighty-three, Acuff was asked, "How's your health?" He replied:

My health is good;
it's my age that's bad.

★ ★ ★ ★ ★ ★ ★ ★ ★ ★ ★

John Quincy Adams was the first son of a president to also be elected to the nation's highest office, becoming the sixth U.S. president in 1825. After his defeat in the 1828 presidential election, he took some time off before returning to political life as a Massachusetts congressman from 1831 until his death in 1848. Two years before his death, a serious stroke limited him enormously, but he continued to serve in Congress. Shortly before his death, Adams was visited by a friend who asked him how he was doing. The declining Adams offered a memorable metaphorical reply:

I inhabit a weak, frail, decayed tenement;
battered by the winds and broken in upon by the storms,
and from all I can learn,
the landlord does not intend to repair.

★ ★ ★ ★ ★ ★ ★ ★ ★ ★ ★

When reporters interview people who've turned 100, they often get stale answers or hackneyed clichés. But not always. A few years ago, a reporter interviewed a woman on her birthday. When asked, "What's the best thing about being 104?" she answered:

No peer pressure.

★ ★ ★ ★ ★ ★ ★ ★ ★ ★ ★

At the Boston Marathon a few years ago, a reporter discovered that a man who had just crossed the finish line was seventy-five years old. Marveling over the accomplishment of a man of that age running twenty-six miles, he asked, "Do you think running will add years to your life?" The aging athlete replied:

I don't know, but it's certainly added life to my years.

★ ★ ★ ★ ★ ★ ★ ★ ★ ★ ★

On his seventy-fifth birthday, a well-known actor was interviewed by a journalist (most versions of the story cite John Barrymore as the actor, but he died at age sixty, making him an unlikely candidate). The actor was still appearing regularly on stage and in films, leading the reporter to ask, "Is acting as much fun as it used to be?" The actor replied:

Young man, I am seventy-five.
Nothing is as much fun as it used to be.

★ ★ ★ ★ ★ ★ ★ ★ ★ ★

The French opera composer Daniel Auber was active until his 1871 death in Paris at age eighty-eight. Late in his life, he began to sense his mortality. Attending the funeral of an old friend, he remarked:

I believe this is the last time I'll take part as an amateur.

One day, an old friend ran into Auber at the Paris Opéra and said, "My friend, we're all getting older, aren't we?" Auber nodded his head in agreement, adding:

Well, there's no helping it.
Aging seems to be the only available way to live a long time.

★ ★ ★ ★ ★ ★ ★ ★ ★ ★

Milton Berle broke into show business at age five in the 1914 silent film classic, *The Perils of Pauline*. After years on the vaudeville circuit and a few decades as a radio and screen talent, he began his towering television career in 1948. By 1951, he was considered so valuable that NBC signed him to a thirty-year contract, paying him an annual salary of $100,000, whether he appeared or not. Berle performed for more than eight decades, his comedic skills showing no diminishment with age. In his ninetieth year in 1998, he was interviewed by Larry King, who said, "You don't look ninety." When Berle replied, "I don't feel it," King asked, "How old do you feel?" Berle wisecracked:

I feel like a twenty-year-old—
but there's never one around.

★ ★ ★ ★ ★ ★ ★ ★ ★ ★

The greatest actress of her era, the "Divine Sarah" Bernhardt was famous not only in her native France, but throughout the world. She had many lovers during her lifetime, including Victor Hugo and the Prince of Wales (before he became Edward VII). Shortly before her death at age seventy-nine in 1923, she lived on the upper floor of a Paris apartment building. She was visited one day by a male admirer, who arrived at her door out of breath from climbing the stairs. "Why do you live so high up?" he inquired. No longer the great beauty with irresistible sensual appeal, she replied coyly:

It's the only way I can still make the hearts of men beat faster.

★ ★ ★ ★ ★ ★ ★ ★ ★ ★ ★

After his American film debut in 1929, French actor Maurice Chevalier began a three-decade association with Hollywood that would see him appear in such classic films as *Gigi*, *Can-Can*, and *Fanny*. His reputation took a dive during World War II as he continued to perform in German-occupied France, but his career rebounded after the war. Famous for his suave and debonair manner (and ever-present straw hat and cane), he received a special Academy Award in 1958. On his seventy-second birthday in 1960, an interviewer asked him, "How do you feel about getting older?" He answered:

**Considering the alternative,
it's not too bad at all.**

★ ★ ★ ★ ★ ★ ★ ★ ★ ★ ★

Winston Churchill always had an eye for the ladies, a trait that did not change as he grew older. During a particularly severe English winter in the 1950s, the aging Churchill was informed by an aide of a story that had London buzzing—a London man in his late seventies had been arrested in Hyde Park for making improper advances toward a young woman. When the news was brought to him, Churchill queried the aide, "Over seventy-five, you say?" "Yes sir," said the aide.

"And below zero?" "Yes sir," the aide confirmed. Churchill reflected for a moment and observed:

> ## Over seventy-five and below zero!
> ## Makes you *proud* to be an Englishman!

★ ★ ★ ★ ★ ★ ★ ★ ★ ★

After having been out of office for five years, the seventy-six-year-old Winston Churchill led the Conservative Party back to power in 1951. He served as prime minister until 1955, when failing health forced his resignation. Many of the newer—and much younger—members of Parliament began to ungenerously refer to Churchill as the "Old Man." One day, Churchill overheard a new M.P. whisper to another, "They say the old man's getting a bit past it." He quickly chimed in:

> ## They say the old man's getting deaf as well.

As he got older, Churchill retained his sense of humor, despite many of the predictable problems associated with aging. When told by a friend that his fly was open, he suggested it was no big deal, saying with resigned acceptance:

> ## A dead bird does not leave its nest.

★ ★ ★ ★ ★ ★ ★ ★ ★ ★

In 1989, several months before he turned sixty, the balding Sean Connery was named the Sexiest Man Alive by *People* magazine. He accepted the honor with good humor, saying, "For the first time, I'm speechless," and suggesting that Russian president Mikhail Gorbachev would have been his choice. Shortly after receiving the award, Connery was asked by a reporter how it felt to be the sexiest man alive. He replied, "Well, there are very few sexy ones that are dead." During the next year, the award came up in virtually every interview the actor did. In one interview, a female reporter said, "I have been told that after the age of sixty, balding men are very sexual and sensuous. Do you believe that?" Connery answered with a sly smile:

**I wouldn't know.
It's been years since I've been in bed
with anybody over sixty who's balding.**

✳ ✳ ✳ ✳ ✳ ✳ ✳ ✳ ✳ ✳ ✳

One of the most gifted orators of his time, the railroad-executive-turned-politician Chauncey Depew was asked to give after-dinner speeches until late in his life. One evening, the aging Depew was seated on a dais next to a beautiful young woman wearing a low-cut evening dress with delicate spaghetti straps. Even though more than a half-century older than his dinner companion, Depew could be quite charming, and the young woman was obviously enjoying the conversation. At one point, he leaned over and whispered flirtatiously in the young woman's ear, "My dear, what is keeping that dress on your body?" She gave Depew a look and whispered back:

**Only your age, Mr. Depew.
Only your age!**

✳ ✳ ✳ ✳ ✳ ✳ ✳ ✳ ✳ ✳ ✳

Chauncey Depew died in 1928, at age ninety-four. Active until well into his eighties, he was once asked by a reporter, "Do you engage in regular exercise?" In an answer that has been plagiarized by countless others ever since, he replied:

**I get my exercise by acting as a pallbearer
to my friends who exercise.**

✳ ✳ ✳ ✳ ✳ ✳ ✳ ✳ ✳ ✳ ✳

In 1979, two years before his death, the aging philosopher Will Durant met Norman Cousins, the former longtime editor of the *Saturday Review,* at a Dodgers baseball game in Los Angeles. Durant, the author of *The Story of Philosophy* and the monumental eleven-volume *Story of Civilization* was in his nineties, but still full of vitality. When old friend Cousins asked, "Are you ninety-four or ninety-five now?" Durant replied:

> **Ninety-four.**
> **You don't think I'd be doing anything as foolish as this**
> **if I were ninety-five, do you?**

★ ★ ★ ★ ★ ★ ★ ★ ★ ★

On January 20, 1961, eighty-six-year-old Robert Frost recited "The Gift Outright" at the inauguration of John F. Kennedy, becoming the first poet in history to receive such an invitation. It was a crisp, bright January morning, and the glare of the sun made it impossible for Frost to read the typed text. So he recited the poem from memory—an impressive feat for a man at any age—ending with a flourish by deliberately changing the final line in honor of the occasion. A few years earlier, Frost was on a train when a fellow passenger recognized him. "Congratulations on your longevity," the man cried out with a big smile. Frost shouted back:

> **To hell with my longevity. Read my books!**

★ ★ ★ ★ ★ ★ ★ ★ ★ ★

Actress Ruth Gordon will be remembered forever for two stellar performances— one as a fun-loving and freewheeling eighty-year-old in the 1972 film *Harold and Maude* and the other as a witch posing as a solicitous neighbor in the 1968 film *Rosemary's Baby* (for which she won the Oscar for Best Supporting Actress). When she stepped up to accept the Oscar, the seventy-something actress delighted the audience when she said:

> **I can't tell you how encouraging a thing like this is.**

✳ ✳ ✳ ✳ ✳ ✳ ✳ ✳ ✳ ✳ ✳

In 1935, at age sixty, English actor Edmund Gwenn moved to Hollywood, where he finished out a distinguished career (in 1947, he received an Oscar for his role as Kris Kringle in *Miracle on 34th Street*). Just before his death in 1959, the ailing Gwenn was visited by old friend George Seaton, who offered the comforting words, "It's tough, isn't it?" The eigthty-four-year-old Gwenn proved he still had some life left in him when he replied:

Yes it is, but it's not as tough as playing comedy.

✳ ✳ ✳ ✳ ✳ ✳ ✳ ✳ ✳ ✳ ✳

In 1931, on his ninetieth birthday, Supreme Court Justice Oliver Wendell Holmes, Jr., was asked by a journalist if he would reveal the secret of his success. Holmes answered: "Young man, the secret of my success is that at an early age I discovered I was not God." In a story that is also told of other lecherous old men, the ninety-year-old Holmes was once walking down the street with a colleague when a beautiful young woman strolled by. Holmes looked at the beauty, and then at his companion, and said with resignation:

, Oh, to be eighty again!

This line became part of popular culture when it showed up in *The Magnificent Yankee*, a 1950 film about Holmes. Playing the ninety-year-old Holmes, actor Louis Calhern says, "Do you know what I think when I see a pretty girl . . . ? Oh, to be eighty again!"

✳ ✳ ✳ ✳ ✳ ✳ ✳ ✳ ✳ ✳ ✳

In his midseventies, the writer and legendary Algonquin Round Table wit George S. Kaufman unexpectedly ran into an old friend he hadn't seen in many years.

Continuing to exhibit the mental quickness he had exhibited throughout his life, he exclaimed:

My God, Peggy, I thought we were both dead!

★ ★ ★ ★ ★ ★ ★ ★ ★ ★ ★

On his seventy-ninth birthday in 2003, the comedian Don Knotts was interviewed by CNN news anchor Kyra Phillips. When Phillips jestingly asked, "How is the love life?" Knotts said quizzically, "Huh?" Phillips persisted, repeating, "How is the love life?" There was no formal audience, but the stagehands and technicians broke out in hearty laughter when Knotts replied:

Hello? I'm seventy-nine!

★ ★ ★ ★ ★ ★ ★ ★ ★ ★ ★

On his seventy-fifth birthday Austrian-born concert violinist Fritz Kreisler was given a gala party in his adopted home of New York City. One friend, noticing that Kreisler's wife had avoided him the entire night, suspected the couple might be having a spat. Finally, she asked Mrs. Kreisler, "Why have you not sat by your husband tonight?" All long-married people will appreciate the warmhearted generosity of her delightful answer:

I want him to have a good time tonight, with other women fussing all over him. That's the best birthday gift I can give.

★ ★ ★ ★ ★ ★ ★ ★ ★ ★ ★

Maggie Kuhn, who founded the Gray Panthers in 1970 after being forced to retire at age sixty-five, continued to play a role in the organization until her death in 1990 at age eighty-nine. A tireless battler for the rights of the elderly, her work directly resulted in many significant victories, including nursing home reform, the end of forced retirement, and stiffer penalties for fraud against the elderly. A few years before her death, an interviewer asked her if she was enjoying life. She replied:

**I'm having a glorious old age.
One of my greatest delights is that
I have outlived most of my opposition!**

★ ★ ★ ★ ★ ★ ★ ★ ★ ★

During his presidency, James Madison always dressed in black and developed a reputation for being somewhat stiff and stodgy. In truth, he had a keen sense of humor and was fond of telling amusing—and often earthy—anecdotes. Shortly before his death in 1836 at age eighty-five, the ailing Madison was visited by an old friend, who found the former president confined to his bed in the family home. So weak he was hardly able to speak, Madison struggled to say a few words. The concerned visitor advised, "Please try not to talk while you're lying in bed." Madison was failing, but he found the strength to make a final playful pun:

I always talk most easily when I lie.

★ ★ ★ ★ ★ ★ ★ ★ ★ ★

Richard Monckton Milnes, also known as Lord Houghton, was a British politician and man of letters who greatly influenced the cultural climate of nineteenth-century England by helping popularize the works of Keats, Tennyson, Emerson, and other writers. He was also known as a discriminating diner. On his deathbed in 1885, the seventy-six-year-old gourmet was asked if he had anything he'd like to say. He brought a smile to those around him by replying:

My exit is the result of too many entrees.

✶ ✶ ✶ ✶ ✶ ✶ ✶ ✶ ✶ ✶ ✶

The subjects of the Stephen Sondheim-John Weidman musical *Bounce*, Wilson and Addison Mizner were two of America's most colorful characters in the 1920s. The brothers prospected for gold in Alaska, promoted—and rigged—prizefights, and perpetrated numerous confidence scams before Wilson turned to writing and Addison to architecture and real-estate development. In 1933, as Addison lay on his deathbed in Palm Beach, Florida, he received a spirit-lifting telegram from Wilson:

STOP DYING. AM TRYING TO WRITE A COMEDY.

A few months after Addison's death, Wilson's own health began to fail and he slipped into a coma. Just before he died in 1933, he awakened from the coma to discover a priest hovering over him. Not a religious man, Mizner was annoyed at the clergyman's presence. When the priest said, "Is there anything you'd like to say?" Mizner replied:

**Why should I talk to you?
I've just been talking to your boss.**

✶ ✶ ✶ ✶ ✶ ✶ ✶ ✶ ✶ ✶ ✶

The Paris-born Pierre Monteux served as conductor for major symphony orchestras all around the world, including Paris, London, Boston, New York, and San Francisco. Named permanent conductor of the London Symphony in 1960, he was interviewed on the BBC in 1964, shortly before his death at age eighty-nine. Acknowledging that music had been the passion of his life, the interviewer asked Monteux to describe his current passions. The aging but active conductor replied:

**I still have two abiding passions.
One is my model railway, the other, women.
But at the age of eighty-nine,
I find I am getting just a little too old—
for model railways.**

★ ★ ★ ★ ★ ★ ★ ★ ★ ★

In 1854, eighty-three-year-old poet James Montgomery died in his home on the outskirts of London. The Scottish-born Montgomery never became a major poet, but his verse was read with admiration by Lord Byron and other respected poets of the time. Just before his death, he was visited by a friend who asked, "How are you doing?" Montgomery, who never married but was still the object of interest on the part of many local ladies, retained his sense of humor up until the end, replying:

Hovering between wife and death.

★ ★ ★ ★ ★ ★ ★ ★ ★ ★

The Irish-born writer George Moore was at the center of the cultural life of London in the late 1800s, a friend to Yeats, Joyce, Shaw, Whistler, and Wilde. In his life and his works (notably *Confessions of a Young Man*), he cultivated the image of a promiscuous libertine, but many believed his tales of romantic intrigue were fabrications (one woman at the time wrote, "Some men kiss and do not tell . . . but George Moore told and did not kiss"). As he aged, he perpetuated the persona. On his eightieth birthday, a reporter asked, "How is it that you enjoy such excellent health in your eightieth year?" He answered:

**It's because I never smoked or drank or touched a girl—
until I was eleven years old.**

★ ★ ★ ★ ★ ★ ★ ★ ★ ★

A few years before his death, the versatile English actor Robert Morley was walking down a London street when he ran into an old friend, the actor Llewellyn Rees. It had been several years since the two men had seen one another, and Rees said, "It's nice meeting old friends. A lot of people think I'm dead." Proving that seniors can be as good at badinage as their younger associates, Morley examined Rees carefully and replied:

Not if they look closely.

* * * * * * * * * *

From 1973 to 2002, Georgia politician Tom Murphy served as speaker of the Georgia House of Representatives (the longest tenure of any speaker in U.S. history). In his twenty-seven-year career, Murphy had many memorable moments, but he is best remembered for a clever reply he made to Republican Congresswoman Anne Mueller in 1999. When Mueller rose to speak, she noticed that her microphone was turned off. "Mr. Speaker, will you please turn me on?" she requested. The august body roared with laughter when the aging but sprightly Murphy replied:

Thirty years ago, I would have tried.

* * * * * * * * * *

Born in one of the poorest sections of London, musical conductor Sir Malcolm Sargent showed early musical talent and rose to the top of England's musical scene. (He was knighted in 1947.) Late in his life, it was revealed that he fathered several illegitimate children and had numerous sexual partners, including some members of the Royal Family (one writer dubbed him the Maestro of Seduction). When he turned seventy in 1965, a reporter asked, "To what do you attribute your advanced age?" He wisecracked:

**Well, I suppose I must attribute it
to the fact that I have not died.**

* * * * * * * * * *

Frank Sinatra died in 1998 at age eighty-two. As it turns out, he was granted a birthday wish he had made a little over a year earlier. When asked on the eve of his eighty-first birthday what gift he would most like, he replied:

Another birthday.

⋆ ⋆ ⋆ ⋆ ⋆ ⋆ ⋆ ⋆ ⋆ ⋆ ⋆

One of the important early voices of the modern Libertarian movement, the Austrian economist Ludwig von Mises taught at New York University from 1945 to 1969 (when he retired at age eighty-seven he was the oldest active professor in America). A staunch believer in the power of free markets, he was one of the first people to predict the demise of the Communist system. He died in 1973 at age ninety-two. On his eighty-eighth birthday, when an interviewer asked him how he felt upon getting up in the morning, he said simply:

Amazed.

⋆ ⋆ ⋆ ⋆ ⋆ ⋆ ⋆ ⋆ ⋆ ⋆ ⋆

When she died in London in 1983 at age ninety, Dame Rebecca West was considered one of the major literary figures of the twentieth century. During a career that spanned more than seventy years she wrote such impressive prose that Shaw wrote "Rebecca can handle a pen as brilliantly as ever I could and much more savagely." Full of wit and energy her entire life, at age eighty-five she was browsing in a London shop when she selected a large green caftan off a clothing rack. When an unhelpful clerk standing nearby observed, "That's a maternity dress," West quipped:

One can always hope for miracles.

11

sports repartee

People who excel in the world of sports are generally far more gifted physically than they are verbally. Occasionally, however, sports figures have authored replies and rejoinders that are every bit as impressive as their athletic accomplishments. The best of these verbal gems have been passed along by admiring fans from generation to generation.

In 1923, British schoolmaster and mountaineer George Mallory went on a U.S. lecture tour to help raise funds for a third attempt on the previously unconquered north face of Mount Everest. During the tour, a reporter from the *New York Times* posed a question that was on the minds of many people: "Why do you want to climb Mount Everest?" Mallory answered:

Because it's there.

The following year, Mallory and climbing partner Andrew Irvine perished in their quest. Seventy-five years later, in 1999, their bodies were found, and it was not clear if they had scaled the mountain before they met their deaths.

Two years after Mallory's death, in 1926, Jack Dempsey lost the heavyweight boxing title to Gene Tunney. After the fight, Dempsey telephoned his wife from his dressing room. When she asked, "What happened?" he answered:

Honey, I just forgot to duck.

Even though dejected over the defeat, Dempsey was thinking at that moment about his wife's feelings and hoping his attempt at humor would lift her spirits. His words have been cited countless times over the years, but never more famously than when U.S. president Ronald Reagan reprised them in 1981. After the unsuccessful assassination attempt on his life, Reagan used Dempsey's line in an attempt to comfort wife Nancy when she arrived at the hospital.

Dempsey's remark to his wife and Mallory's answer to the question about climbing Mount Everest have become so much a part of our lives that they enjoy a kind of immortality. In the rest of this chapter, though, we'll focus more on clever lines than immortal ones. Most of the examples to follow are not well known beyond a small cadre of sports fanatics, even though they involve some of the most famous names in sports history.

In the 1920s, George Herman "Babe" Ruth was not only the greatest home run hitter the game had ever seen, he was also—by a large margin—the highest paid. In 1927, he made a staggering $70,000 (Yankees teammate Lou Gehrig made $8,000 that year). Ruth's highest annual salary was $80,000, which he made in 1930 and 1931, at a time when the country was slipping deeper and deeper into the Great Depression. Despite a monster year in 1931 (.373 batting average, 46 home runs, 163 runs batted in [RBIs]), team officials cited economic hard times when they asked Ruth to reduce his salary to $75,000 for the 1932 season. Ruth made headlines when he held out. At a press conference, a reporter pointed out that $80,000 was $5,000 more than President Hoover's salary. Ruth considered the question and said:

Maybe so, but I had a better year than he did.

In the 1930s, when the Dodgers were the toast of the town in Brooklyn, the team had a "Babe" of their own, a slugger by the name of Babe Herman. Far more proficient with his bat than his glove, Herman was viewed by many as a defensive liability (once, while trying to catch a fly ball, he missed it completely and the ball hit him squarely on the head). In 1931, the team decided to bolster its defensive capabilities by acquiring Fresco Thompson, a great glove man, but not exactly fearsome at the plate. When Thompson walked into the clubhouse, he discovered that he had been assigned the locker next to Herman's. As Thompson approached the locker, Herman said in a voice loud enough for the rest of his teammates to hear, "Damn, they're makin' me dress next to a .250 hitter!" All eyes were on Thompson to see whether he would crumble or rise to the occasion. Happily, someone was around to record his clever reply, which immediately won over Herman and the other members of his new team:

Damn, they're makin' *me* dress next to a .250 *fielder*!

Whether you're a sports fan or not, I think you'll enjoy the examples of *sports repartee* to be found below.

✴ ✴ ✴ ✴ ✴ ✴ ✴ ✴ ✴ ✴

In 1957, five years after the Boston Braves headed for greener pastures in Wisconsin, the Milwaukee Braves won their first World Series Championship, beating the New York Yankees in a tightly contested seven-game series. The team's success that summer was due in large part to twenty-three-year-old Henry Aaron, who led the league in home runs and RBIs, and was later named National League Most Valuable Player (MVP). During the series, Aaron strode up to the plate one day and assumed his normal batting stance. As he did, Yankees catcher Yogi Berra noticed that the bat's trademark was facing down, a highly unusual sight. Hoping to rattle the young ballplayer, Berra said, "Turn the bat around so you can see the trademark." Aaron replied calmly:

**I didn't come up here to read;
I came up here to hit.**

★ ★ ★ ★ ★ ★ ★ ★ ★ ★ ★

At a Manhattan party in the 1970s, heavyweight boxing champ Muhammad Ali was introduced to Isaac Stern, the internationally acclaimed violinist and, at the time, president of Carnegie Hall. In a warmhearted attempt to ingratiate himself with the boxer, Stern said, "You might say we're in the same business. We both earn a living with our hands." Ali looked Stern over and replied:

**You must be pretty good;
there isn't a mark on you.**

★ ★ ★ ★ ★ ★ ★ ★ ★ ★ ★

In the sport of boxing, one of the jobs of the corner man is to observe how boxers are performing and provide feedback on their performance. Sometimes, though, the corner man becomes more of a cheerleader than a coach, which is not necessarily what the fighter needs. In 1935, the former heavyweight champ Max Baer fought newcomer Joe Louis before a packed house in Yankee Stadium. Louis completely overpowered Baer, knocking him out in the fourth round. Writer Ernest Hemingway was in attendance and described the fight as the "most disgusting public spectacle outside of a public hanging" that he'd ever seen. At the end of the third round, one of Baer's corner men said, "Good goin', Max, he ain't laid a glove on ya!" Baer replied:

**Well then you'd better keep an eye on that referee,
'cause somebody out there is beatin' the hell out of me.**

★ ★ ★ ★ ★ ★ ★ ★ ★ ★ ★

One of the smallest goalies ever to play professional hockey, Don "Bobo" Beaupre enjoyed a seventeen-year career, twice named to the NHL All-Star Team. In 1980, he was the thirty-seventh overall pick in the draft, selected by the Minnesota North Stars. At five feet, eight inches tall and 149 pounds, the diminutive goalie's selection distressed local fans. At a press conference after he was signed, a reporter asked, "Do you think you're big enough to be a goalie in the NHL?" Beaupre was in his teens, but he had the composure of a veteran, replying:

**I just have to stop the puck,
not beat it to death.**

★ ★ ★ ★ ★ ★ ★ ★ ★ ★ ★

While playing for the Brooklyn Dodgers in 1936, Stanley George "Frenchy" Bordagaray showed up for spring training sporting a mustache, hoping to be the first player in more than twenty years with facial hair. Team officials ordered him to shave it off, and major league baseball would remain clean shaven until 1972, when Reggie Jackson successfully challenged the ban. Bordagaray had a fiery temperament and once flew into such a rage while arguing a call that he spit in the face of an umpire. The offense resulted in a $500 fine, considerable for the time. When a sportswriter asked Bordagaray what he thought about the size of the fine, he replied:

It was more than I expectorated.

★ ★ ★ ★ ★ ★ ★ ★ ★ ★ ★

In the 1950s, Southern California's exclusive Hillcrest Country Club attracted the biggest names in show business, including some of the greatest comedians of all time: the Marx Brothers, George Burns, Jack Benny, Danny Kaye, and George Jessel. One day, while Burns and Kaye were in the clubhouse getting ready to play, word came in that a member of the club had just dropped dead on the first tee. The attendant reported, "He just keeled over while taking some practice swings." Hearing the news, Burns looked over at Kaye and said:

See, I *told* you this was a tough course.

★ ★ ★ ★ ★ ★ ★ ★ ★ ★ ★

In 1954, a year before he was elected to the National Baseball Hall of Fame, New York Yankees legend Joe DiMaggio announced that he and sex symbol Marilyn Monroe were engaged to be married. The news rocked the sports world. Just before the marriage, former teammate Yogi Berra was asked if he thought the marriage would be good for baseball. Berra, who was just beginning to develop a reputation for his "Yogi-isms," proved he also had a great sense of humor, replying:

> **I don't know if it's good for baseball but**
> **it sure beats the hell out of roomin' with Phil Rizutto.**

* * * * * * * * * * *

Personal insults are part of every sport, including the civilized game of cricket. In a hotly contested match a few years ago, Ed Brandes, the heavyset tailender for the Zimbabwe team, was having his way with Glenn McGrath, the fast bowler for the Australians. Frustration finally boiled over for McGrath, who hollered out at Brandes, "Why are you so fat?" Brandes coolly replied:

> **Because every time I sleep with your wife,**
> **she gives me a biscuit.**

* * * * * * * * * * *

For seventy years, the cereal Wheaties has advertised itself as the Breakfast of Champions and featured prominent athletes on its boxes (Lou Gehrig was the first to appear in 1934). In the early years of the campaign, the presence of some fast-living and hard-drinking ballplayers raised a few eyebrows. Shortly after Jay Hanna "Dizzy" Dean appeared on the boxes in 1935, the dominating pitcher for the St. Louis Cardinals was asked by a sportswriter if he actually ate the cereal. He answered:

> **Sure I eat Wheaties for breakfast.**
> **A good bowl of Wheaties with bourbon can't be beat.**

★ ★ ★ ★ ★ ★ ★ ★ ★ ★

Today's most meagerly paid baseball players make staggering salaries compared to players from baseball's past. During Joe DiMaggio's star-studded career, he developed a reputation as a hard bargainer in contract negotiations, often driving his salary far beyond what the Yankees wanted to pay. When he signed with the Yankees in 1936, he turned down the club's paltry first offer and finally signed for $8,500, the most the team ever paid for a rookie. In his entire career, though, the Yankee Clipper's annual salary never went above $100,000. One day in the early 1990s, a reporter asked the aging DiMaggio, "How much do you think you'd be worth in today's market?" Not normally a boastful person, DiMaggio thought for a moment and said:

**I'd walk up to the team owner,
stick out my hand, and say, "Howdy, partner!"**

★ ★ ★ ★ ★ ★ ★ ★ ★ ★

No chief executive in American history did more to popularize the game of golf than Dwight D. Eisenhower. Elected in 1952 at age sixty-one, he served after two presidents—FDR and Truman—who were rarely seen engaged in recreational activities. Ike clearly loved the game and was often photographed on the links with celebrities and high-ranking government officials. After serving two terms as president, he retired from public life in 1961, allowing him to spend even more time at the game. Shortly after his retirement, a reporter asked him if his golf game had changed since he left the White House. The amiable ex-president replied:

Yes, a lot more people beat me now.

★ ★ ★ ★ ★ ★ ★ ★ ★ ★

In the tenth round of a heavyweight championship fight in 1994, challenger George Foreman delivered a crushing blow to the chin of the previously undefeated champ Michael Moorer, knocking him out. A few years earlier, Moorer had kayoed Evander Holyfield to become the first left-handed boxer to win the heavyweight title. Defending his title against Foreman, Moorer was ahead on the scorecards of all three judges going into the tenth round. When Foreman was declared the victor, chants of "Fix! Fix!" were heard from all around the arena. In a postgame interview, a reporter asked Foreman if the fight had been fixed. Holding up a clenched fist, the new champ said:

> **Sure the fight was fixed.**
> **I fixed it with a right hand.**

★ ★ ★ ★ ★ ★ ★ ★ ★ ★ ★

Before becoming a sportscaster, Joe Garagiola was a major league baseball player. Beginning with the St. Louis Cardinals in 1946, he ended his career in 1954 with the New York Giants and their colorful manager, Leo "The Lip" Durocher. Never a dominating hitter, Garagiola's final season was lackluster. During one particularly bad day, he struck out with the bases loaded. Later in the game, he had a chance to redeem himself as he once again came to the plate with the bases filled. This time, he hit into an inning-ending double play. On the bench, the manager was livid. As the dejected Garagiola arrived at the dugout, Durocher screamed:

> **C'mon, Garagiola, be a team player! Strike out!**

★ ★ ★ ★ ★ ★ ★ ★ ★ ★ ★

During his eighteen-year career with the New York Rangers, Rod Gilbert skated with a reckless abandon that endeared him to fans. With his movie star looks and charismatic personality, he was also a much-sought-after interview by sports reporters. One day, an interviewer asked him if hockey fights were the real thing

or just phony stunts. Gilbert said that hockey fights were indeed the real thing. He
then added:

**If they were fake,
you'd see me *in* more of them.**

★ ★ ★ ★ ★ ★ ★ ★ ★ ★

During the 1950s, Toots Shor's Manhattan restaurant was one of the most popular
eating spots on the planet, frequented by Joe DiMaggio and other Yankees
ballplayers, Frank Sinatra and members of his Rat Pack, and countless other stars
and celebrities. Shor may have been a great restaurateur, but he was a lousy
athlete. While golfing with his pal Jackie Gleason one day, he shot an abysmal
round of 211 on a par 72 course. As they were walking away from the final hole,
Shor asked his golfing partner, "What do you think I should give the caddy?"
Gleason instantly answered:

Your clubs.

★ ★ ★ ★ ★ ★ ★ ★ ★ ★

In his first year as football coach at Arkansas in 1977, Lou Holtz won Coach of the
Year honors as he took the Razorbacks to an 11–1 record and a victory over
Oklahoma in the Orange Bowl. As he was readying his team for the Orange Bowl
game, officials warned Holtz that he and his players might be bombarded by
orange-tossing fans as they came onto the field at the beginning of the game. Holtz
smiled and replied:

**It could be worse.
We could be going to the Gator Bowl.**

★ ★ ★ ★ ★ ★ ★ ★ ★ ★

Babe Ruth died at age fifty-three on August 16, 1948, two years after being diagnosed with throat cancer. The next two days, over 200,000 mourners paid their final respects as his body lay in state at Yankee Stadium. Ruth's funeral was held on August 19 at St. Patrick's Cathedral in Manhattan, with Cardinal Francis J. Spellman presiding. It was one of the hottest days of the summer. The pallbearers, all former Yankees teammates, included two famous drinking buddies, Joe Dugan and Waite Hoyt. Not accustomed to wearing a suit and tie, especially in such sweltering conditions, the perspiring Dugan leaned over in the middle of the service and whispered to Hoyt, "Christ, I'd give a hundred bucks for a cold beer." Hoyt, recalling the many nights of revelry the threesome had logged over the years, looked over at the coffin and then whispered back to Dugan:

So would the Babe.

★ ★ ★ ★ ★ ★ ★ ★ ★ ★ ★

After dwindling fan attendance forced the Milwaukee Braves to seek greener pastures in Atlanta in 1966, Milwaukee was left without a baseball club until 1970, when Bud Selig and a few partners brought major league baseball back to town. Like many expansion clubs, the new Milwaukee Brewers had few A-list players and they struggled mightily in the first few years. As the club began the 1972 season, a reporter asked general manager Frank Lane why he didn't make any trades during the off-season. The team was going through hard times, but Lane retained his sense of humor, answering:

We didn't want to weaken the rest of the league.

★ ★ ★ ★ ★ ★ ★ ★ ★ ★ ★

When he retired from playing to pursue a career as a television football analyst, Paul Maguire of the Buffalo Bills was the American Football League's all-time leader in number of punts and total yardage. Playing against the Houston Oilers at the Astrodome one Sunday afternoon, he punted the ball eleven times for an average of forty-five yards. After the game, a reporter asked Maguire what it was like to kick in football's first domed stadium. He replied:

> **I think both the placekicker and I got a little more distance**
> **in the second and fourth quarters**
> **when we had the air conditioning at our backs.**

⋆ ⋆ ⋆ ⋆ ⋆ ⋆ ⋆ ⋆ ⋆ ⋆ ⋆

In the 1960s, there was no more glamorous professional athlete than Joe Namath, the quarterback for the New York Jets. Known as Broadway Joe for his resplendent sartorial style and enjoyment of the night life, Namath's willingness to say whatever was on his mind made him a great interview in the minds of reporters. During Namath's career, an artificial grasslike ground covering known as Astroturf began to replace natural grass as the playing surface in a number of NFL stadiums. When asked by a reporter, "Do you prefer Astroturf or grass?" the freewheeling Namath wisecracked:

> **I don't know,**
> **I never smoked Astroturf.**

⋆ ⋆ ⋆ ⋆ ⋆ ⋆ ⋆ ⋆ ⋆ ⋆ ⋆

Before his NFL career, Joe Namath was an outstanding college quarterback for Coach Bear Bryant and the University of Alabama Crimson Tide. Bryant was a no-nonsense coach who generally showed little patience for the shenanigans of players. During a locker room meeting at the beginning of one football season, the coach gave his standard lecture: "This is a class operation. I want your shoes to be shined. I want you to have a tie on, get your hair cut, and keep a crease in your pants. I also want you to go to class. I don't want no dumbbells on this team. If there is a dumbbell in the room, I wish he would stand up now." After several moments, Namath slowly rose to his feet. When Bryant said, "Joe, how come you're standing up? You ain't dumb!" Namath replied:

Coach, I just hate like the devil
for you to be standing up there all by yourself!

✳ ✳ ✳ ✳ ✳ ✳ ✳ ✳ ✳ ✳ ✳

Born and raised in Czechoslovakia, Martina Navratilova defected to the United States at age nineteen to pursue personal freedom and a professional tennis career. From 1975 to 1994, she earned a reputation as one of the greatest tennis players of all time, and one of the game's fiercest competitors. While she often came across as serious and intense, she could also be delightfully witty. At the height of her career, the left-handed Navratilova was asked why she never insured her valuable left arm with Lloyds of London. She replied:

The answer is simple.
They wanted an arm and a leg.

✳ ✳ ✳ ✳ ✳ ✳ ✳ ✳ ✳ ✳ ✳

One of the NBA's most dominant players, Shaquille O'Neal has always suffered from one major weakness—his free-throw shooting ability. During his rookie season with the Orlando Magic, Shaq was struggling at the free-throw line in a game against the Los Angeles Lakers. Playing for the Lakers at the time was A. C. Greene, a cofounder of a group called Athletes for Abstinence. As Shaq was clanking a few free-throw shots off the rim, Greene tried to rattle him by saying, "You'll be all right as soon as you get some experience." Shaq retorted:

And you'll be okay as soon as you get some sex.

✳ ✳ ✳ ✳ ✳ ✳ ✳ ✳ ✳ ✳ ✳

In his twenty-two-year career, Hall of Fame pitcher Gaylord Perry won 314 games (he was the first pitcher to win the Cy Young Award in both leagues). While on the pitching staff of the San Diego Padres in 1978, Perry was joined by relief pitcher—

and future Hall of Famer—Rollie Fingers. One of the great "closers" in the game, Fingers saved 37 games in 1978, many for a grateful Perry. During a winning streak that summer, a reporter suggested to Perry that he was likely to win 300 games in his career and, with a little luck, might even be able to challenge Cy Young's all-time record of 511 victories. Perry reflected on the question before observing:

It'll never happen.
Rollie won't live that long.

★ ★ ★ ★ ★ ★ ★ ★ ★ ★

In 1956, Prince Rainier III of Monaco put his tiny principality (with a total area of less than three-fourths of a square mile) on the international map when he married the American actress Grace Kelly. The couple visited America many times during their marriage, often to great fanfare. On one trip through Texas, they were given a tour of Houston's Astrodome. Built in 1965, the Astrodome was the largest domed stadium ever built, occupying more than nine acres. During the tour, a guide asked his royal guest, "How would you like to have the Astrodome in Monaco?" The prince replied:

Marvelous. Then we could be the world's only indoor country.

★ ★ ★ ★ ★ ★ ★ ★ ★ ★

After hitting three consecutive home runs in the final game of the 1977 World Series, Reggie Jackson was dubbed Mr. October. A true money ballplayer, he was also one of baseball's great blowhards, famous for tooting his own horn and exaggerating his accomplishments. In the Yankees dugout one day, Jackson boasted to teammate Mickey Rivers, "My IQ is 160." Rivers, the team's leadoff hitter and centerfielder, was known as Mick the Quick for his base-stealing abilities. He demonstrated another kind of quickness when he shot back at Jackson:

Out of what, a thousand?

⋆ ⋆ ⋆ ⋆ ⋆ ⋆ ⋆ ⋆ ⋆ ⋆ ⋆

Baseball players are not noted for being great intellectuals, and it is undoubtedly true that many of them couldn't wait to get out of the classroom in order to pursue their true passion. Nobody captured this phenomenon better than Dan Quisenberry, the submarine-throwing relief pitcher who spent most of his career with the Kansas City Royals. When he was asked in a 1981 interview, "What do you like most about baseball?" he replied:

There is no homework.

In an interview a year earlier, Quisenberry was asked by a sportswriter what happened when his sinker ball was not working. The colorful ballplayer answered:

The batter still hits a grounder.
But in this case the first bounce is three hundred and sixty feet away.

⋆ ⋆ ⋆ ⋆ ⋆ ⋆ ⋆ ⋆ ⋆ ⋆ ⋆

Frustrated golfers with poor temper control have long treated their clubs with disrespect, throwing them into sand traps and water hazards, whacking them against the nearest tree or golf cart, and sometimes simply breaking them in two like a twig over their legs. One day, a sportswriter, noticing that PGA golfer Craig Stadler was using a new putter, asked him why he made the switch. Stadler, affectionately known as the Walrus for his oversized frame, answered with a smile:

Because the other one didn't float too well.

⋆ ⋆ ⋆ ⋆ ⋆ ⋆ ⋆ ⋆ ⋆ ⋆ ⋆

After a respectable fifteen-year baseball career, Casey Stengel spent the next twenty-four years coaching and managing a number of minor and major league clubs, never achieving much success. In 1949, he was named manager of the New York Yankees. Over the next twelve years, he led the team to ten American League titles and seven World Series championships. After a year of retirement, he managed the hapless New York Mets until his retirement in 1965. During his glory years with the Yankees, Stengel was asked the secret of his success as a manager. He replied:

**All you have to do is
keep the five players who hate your guts
away from the five who are undecided.**

★ ★ ★ ★ ★ ★ ★ ★ ★ ★

The worlds of sports and politics sometimes intersect in intriguing ways. In 1990, Germany beat England in a World Cup semifinal soccer game. The defeat upset the entire nation, including many in the intellectual and political worlds. After the defeat, Kenneth Clark, the noted English man of letters, attended a meeting at 10 Downing Street and said in passing to Margaret Thatcher, "Isn't it terrible about losing to the Germans at our national sport?" The prime minister put it all into perspective when she replied:

**I shouldn't worry too much;
we've beaten them twice this century at theirs.**

chiastic repartee

A towering figure in literary and cultural history, Dr. Samuel Johnson produced the *Dictionary of the English Language* in 1755, the most comprehensive dictionary published to date, and one that set the mold for all later dictionaries. While a voluminous writer himself, Johnson is known to the world primarily through the book of another man, Scottish writer James Boswell. In 1791, Boswell published *The Life of Samuel Johnson*, in which he detailed Johnson's verbal facility, trenchant wit, and storehouse of knowledge. The biography became so popular that Johnson's most frequently quoted words come from Boswell's biography and not from his own works. At one point, an aspiring—and apparently annoying—young writer pestered Johnson to read a first draft of his novel. Johnson finally relented, and then sent the man a note containing one of the most famous lines in literary history:

> **Your manuscript is both good and original;**
> **but the part that is good is not original,**
> **and the part that is original is not good.**

Johnson's clever reply is an example of *chiasmus* (pronounced ky-AZ-mus), a literary device in which the order of words is reversed in two parallel phrases. It shows up in some of history's most famous sayings:

It's not the men in my life,
it's the life in my men.

Mae West

One should eat to live,
not live to eat.

Cicero

When the going gets tough,
the tough get going.

Knute Rockne

Ask not what your country can do for you,
ask what you can do for your country.

John F. Kennedy

Examples of chiasmus have appeared in every aspect of life: religion, politics, literature, poetry, and sports. While the noun is *chiasmus*, the adjective is *chiastic* (ky-AZ-tick), and the adverb is *chiastically*.

Chiasmus derives from an ancient Greek word meaning "to mark with an *X*." If you lay out the two clauses of a chiastic saying parallel to one another and draw lines connecting the key words, the two lines intersect, making an *X*:

I introduced chiasmus to a popular audience in my 1999 book *Never Let a Fool Kiss You or a Kiss Fool You.* My goal in that book was to bring this fascinating literary device out of the closet of obscurity and into the world of popular usage. I'm making progress toward that goal. Since the book was published, three million individual visitors have logged on to my Web site: www.chiasmus.com.

Chiasmus shows up in some of the most impressive replies in human history. One of the first recorded examples goes back more than 2,500 years. In the fifth century B.C., Themistocles was one of the most powerful men in Athens. His daughter came to him one day distraught and desperately seeking his guidance. She had received two marriage proposals and was having great difficulty choosing between the two suitors. One young man, she said, was a person of impeccable character, but of limited means. The other was wealthy and of the same social class as her father, but of questionable character. "Whom should I choose, Father?" she pleaded. "Please tell me!" Themistocles wisely replied:

> **I would choose a man without money**
> **rather than money without a man.**

In many examples of chiastic repartee, one person reverses the words of another. In the fourth century B.C., the Greek philosopher Diogenes preached the virtues of the simple life. One of his contemporaries was the worldly philosopher Aristippus, a status-seeking sycophant who obtained a lofty position in the king's court by currying favor with the emperor. One day, as Diogenes was preparing his simple evening meal of lentils, the cocky Aristippus arrived on the scene and announced, "If you would only learn to flatter the king, you wouldn't have to live on lentils." Diogenes' reply belongs to the ages:

> **If you would only learn to live on lentils,**
> **you wouldn't have to flatter the king.**

Another example occurs in the 1970 book *The Crowning Privilege* by the English poet Robert Graves, where he writes, "I heard an answer today to the platitude: *there's no money in poetry*." The reply that Graves heard and admired was:

There's no poetry in money, either.

One of history's most famous chiastic replies was authored during the darkest days of the Civil War. As Abraham Lincoln met in the White House with a group of advisers, one man was heard to say, "God is on our side." Lincoln, who agonized over the carnage the war had brought to both sides, was exasperated by the comment, but he maintained his composure beautifully, replying:

We trust, sir, that God is on our side.
It is more important to know that we are on God's side.

A fascinating variation on the chiasmus theme occurs when the words of popular expressions are reversed, as in sayings like "A hangover is the wrath of grapes" or Kermit the Frog's motto "Time's fun when you're having flies." These are examples of *implied chiasmus*, because the original sayings that inspired them are not mentioned explicitly, but only implied.

One of my favorite examples of implied chiasmus is also one of the most celebrated replies in literary history. Early in his career, the then little-known George Bernard Shaw submitted a play to a well-known London producer, who flatly rejected it. A few years later, the producer sent a cable to Shaw, then a successful writer, saying:

WOULD LIKE TO PRODUCE PLAY AFTER ALL.

Shaw cabled his reply:

BETTER NEVER THAN LATE.

By reversing the words of the popular expression "Better late than never," Shaw found the perfect words to reject the ludicrous offer.

Shaw had the luxury of time to compose his reply, but many examples of implied chiasmus are created almost instantaneously. A famous example comes from the writer and critic George S. Kaufman. During one of his stints in Hollywood, he attended a farewell party for fellow playwright S. N. Behrman, who was scheduled to return to New York directly after the celebration. After the party, however, studio officials asked Behrman to stay on for an extra day or so to do some emergency rewriting. Not aware of the change in plans, Kaufman was startled to see Behrman at his desk the next morning. Kaufman may have been surprised, but he was not at a loss for words, instantly quipping:

Ah, forgotten but not gone.

Kaufman authored yet another inspired example of implied chiasmus when his daughter, a student at Vassar, told him that a friend of hers had eloped and was dropping out of school. After only a moment's reflection, he observed:

Ah, yes. A case of putting the heart before the course.

In both remarks, Kaufman brilliantly reversed the words of proverbial sayings. His second reply also reminds us that chiasmus is sometimes combined with other forms of wordplay, like punning. In such cases, it's not the words themselves that are reversed, but the *sounds* of words, as in the century-old toast, "Here's champagne to our real friends and real pain to our sham friends."

One of my all-time favorite chiastic replies was delivered more than fifty years ago in an episode of the popular radio comedy show *The Bickersons*. John Bickerson (played by actor Don Ameche) and his wife, Blanche (actress Frances Langford), became America's favorite feuding couple during radio's heyday. In one episode, the couple moved to a new apartment and were bickering—as usual—over whether or not John would carry Blanche across the threshold (a feat he had not performed in many years). Disappointed, Blanche said, "You're not as gallant as when you were a boy." John instantly replied:

You're not as buoyant as when you were a gal.

In some examples of chiasmus, the initial *letters* of words are reversed, as in the saying, "A magician pulls rabbits out of hats, a psychologist pulls habits out of rats." An impressive reply of this type has long been attributed to the acclaimed pianist and composer Ignacy Jan Paderewski (also, by the way, one of Poland's great statesmen). While on a London tour in the 1930s, Paderewski was introduced by a mutual friend to a famous English polo player. In making the introduction, the friend graciously said, "The two of you are both leaders in your respective spheres, even though the spheres are quite different." The great composer was said to have replied:

Perhaps not so different.
You are a dear soul who plays polo,
and I am a poor Pole who plays solo.

It's hard to imagine anybody spontaneously displaying such a feat of verbal virtuosity, but Paderewski's reply was first reported in the English press in 1936 and has been circulated by his fans and by language lovers ever since.

Other examples of *chiastic repartee* follow in the remainder of this chapter. In each and every case, you will notice some kind of reversal that qualifies the reply as an example of the literary device of chiasmus.

★ ★ ★ ★ ★ ★ ★ ★ ★ ★

As America moved into the twentieth century, George Ade became one of the era's most successful playwrights and humorists. His 1899 *Fables in Slang* became a best-seller and, in the next few decades, was followed by many sequels that summarized—and often satirized—the wisdom of the day. On a lecture tour in Indiana in the early 1900s, Ade checked into a hotel that was hosting a convention of clergymen. A companion, noticing the irony, asked the irreverent Ade how he felt being around so many members of the clergy. Cleverly reversing the words of the famous biblical story, Ade answered:

I feel like a lion in a den of Daniels.

★ ★ ★ ★ ★ ★ ★ ★ ★ ★ ★

After moving from Northern California to Alaska in the mid-1980s, a young woman had trouble meeting men. Drinking alone at a local nightspot one evening, she presented the problem to a female bartender, who happened to be a longtime resident of the state. "What are the chances of finding a good man around here?" the newcomer asked. The bartender looked around the room, which was filled with men, but as usual, men of questionable quality. Finally, she replied:

The odds are good,
but the goods are odd.

★ ★ ★ ★ ★ ★ ★ ★ ★ ★ ★

Jan Kiepura was a Polish singer who starred in a number of Broadway shows in the 1930s and '40s, including a successful run of *The Merry Widow*. After the opening performance, the excited but anxious Kiepura began to worry that his Polish accent might affect his chances of success in America. In his thick accent, he nervously asked his agent, "Do you tink I need to pow-lish up my Inglish?" The clever agent replied:

No, you need to English up your Polish.

★ ★ ★ ★ ★ ★ ★ ★ ★ ★ ★

Emmeline Pankhurst, the English suffragist, was fond of telling a story about an Englishwoman who had been jailed for her suffrage activities. In Pankhurst's own words: "Some of the guards—I think men who had never known what it was like to earn a living, who knew nothing of the difficulties of a man's life, let alone of the difficulties of a woman's life—came out, and they said: 'Why did you break our windows? We have done nothing.'" According to Pankhurst, the woman replied:

**It is because you have done nothing
I have broken your windows.**

✴ ✴ ✴ ✴ ✴ ✴ ✴ ✴ ✴ ✴

The character of Peter Pan first appeared in James M. Barrie's 1902 play *The Little White Bird* and then in the 1904 smash hit *Peter Pan*. The play was soon being performed in theaters all around the world, making the shy Barrie an international, although somewhat reluctant, celebrity. When the play premiered in New York in 1905, Barrie traveled to America, where he received numerous speaking invitations. After speaking at Smith College, a friend asked Barrie how it went. The diffident celebrity replied:

**To tell you the truth,
I'd much rather talk one thousand times to one girl
than talk one time to a thousand girls.**

✴ ✴ ✴ ✴ ✴ ✴ ✴ ✴ ✴ ✴

Henry Ward Beecher, brother of Harriet Beecher Stowe, was one of the best-known preachers of his time. A fervent abolitionist and an advocate of other controversial causes, he aroused the antipathy of many people in the years just before the Civil War. One Sunday morning, he found an envelope stuffed in the mailbox at his Plymouth church in Brooklyn. Inside the envelope, he found a letter containing a single word: "Fool!" During his sermon later that morning, Beecher related the incident to his congregation and offered one of the cleverest replies ever delivered from the pulpit:

**I have known many an instance of a man writing a letter
and forgetting to sign his name,
but this is the only instance I have ever known
of a man signing his name
and forgetting to write the letter!**

✶ ✶ ✶ ✶ ✶ ✶ ✶ ✶ ✶ ✶ ✶

While Dr. Samuel Johnson is remembered for being a great wit and wordsmith, he was also a big, physically awkward man who could be slovenly in appearance and uncouth in language. Revered by his biographer, James Boswell, Johnson was not so well regarded by Boswell's wife, Margaret. During Boswell and Johnson's famous 1773 tour of Scotland, the good doctor spent several days at the Boswell home in Edinburgh, actually displacing the couple from their own bed during his visit. While Mrs. Boswell treated the houseguest politely during his stay, she was put off by his ill manners and irritated by what she regarded as his unhealthy influence over her husband. In an argument after Johnson departed, Boswell tried to defend Johnson and the relationship the two men had formed. Margaret Boswell would have none of it, saying to her husband:

> **I have seen many a bear led by a man,**
> **but I have never before saw a man led by a bear.**

✶ ✶ ✶ ✶ ✶ ✶ ✶ ✶ ✶ ✶ ✶

In the 1920s, drama critic and Algonquin Round Table member Heywood Broun attended a play starring Tallulah Bankhead. Bankhead's stage performances could vary greatly in quality and, this particular evening, things were not going well. As the final curtain came down, Broun went backstage to meet with the actress. When she asked for his opinion about the play, he offered a famous example of implied chiasmus:

> **Don't look now, Tallulah, but your show is slipping.**

✶ ✶ ✶ ✶ ✶ ✶ ✶ ✶ ✶ ✶ ✶

One of history's greatest orators, Winston Churchill was often approached by aspiring politicians for advice on speechmaking. One day, a young M.P. cornered him and said, "Mr. Churchill, you heard my talk yesterday. Can you tell me how I could have put more fire into my speech?" Churchill had heard the man talk, as it turns out, and didn't think much of what he'd heard. He answered:

**What you should have done is
to have put your speech into the fire.**

⋆ ⋆ ⋆ ⋆ ⋆ ⋆ ⋆ ⋆ ⋆ ⋆ ⋆

Winston Churchill had a legendary fondness for a good cigar and a glass of brandy. And while there are many reports that he often didn't stop at one glass, there are few reports that it impaired his ability or affected his judgment. Still, some people were concerned about his alcohol intake. One day, after someone expressed such a concern, he replied:

**Always remember that
I have taken more out of alcohol
than alcohol has taken out of me.**

⋆ ⋆ ⋆ ⋆ ⋆ ⋆ ⋆ ⋆ ⋆ ⋆ ⋆

Having wrestled with his weight his entire life, Winston Churchill got progressively rounder and pudgier as he grew older. One day, he and his baby grandson were strolling down a London street when a friend came upon them and said, "Winston! How wonderfully your new grandson resembles you!" Churchill replied:

**All babies look like me.
But then, I look like all babies.**

⋆ ⋆ ⋆ ⋆ ⋆ ⋆ ⋆ ⋆ ⋆ ⋆ ⋆

A 1997 *New York Times* article on police stress quoted a city councilman as saying, "Too many cops wind up as ticking time bombs." Three days later, the paper published a letter to the editor from reader Stephen R. Conn, who questioned the councilman's logic and even suggested he had it backward. Conn said that a more accurate statement might be:

> ## Too many ticking time bombs wind up as cops.

* * * * * * * * * * *

A talented high school athlete, Kevin Costner originally dreamed of playing professional baseball, but became interested in acting while attending California State University at Fullerton. As his acting career progressed, his love of sports showed up in movies like *Bull Durham* and *Field of Dreams*. In the 1996 film *Tin Cup*, Costner played the role of a quirky golf pro named Roy McAvoy. An extremely talented golfer, McAvoy has an even bigger talent for making self-destructive decisions on the golf course. In one scene, when McAvoy's play is questioned by his good friend and caddy (played by Cheech Marin), he replies:

> ## When a defining moment comes along,
> ## you define the moment
> ## or the moment defines you.

* * * * * * * * * * *

The American sculptor Jo Davidson became one of the foremost portrait sculptors of his time, masterfully capturing in bronze such luminaries as Woodrow Wilson, FDR, Will Rogers, Albert Einstein, and Mohandas Gandhi. Before Gandhi consented to have his portrait done, he invited Davidson to his home for a visit. Davidson arrived with a portfolio, showing photographs of his best work. After examining the photographs, the Mahatma observed, "I see you make heroes out of mud." Davidson was well known for his ability to win the cooperation of even the most difficult subjects, and he won Gandhi over that very moment with his witty reply:

And sometimes vice versa.

★ ★ ★ ★ ★ ★ ★ ★ ★ ★ ★

In the late 1800s, Chauncey Depew was one of the stars of the Republican Party. A successful businessman, respected diplomat, and two-term U.S. senator, he was also a popular after-dinner speaker. One evening, he was introduced by a master of ceremonies who said, "Chauncey Depew can always produce a speech. All you have to do is give him his dinner and up comes his speech." Depew strolled up to the podium, thanked the emcee for his introduction, and delighted the audience when he said:

I only hope it isn't true
that if I give you my speech,
up will come your dinner.

★ ★ ★ ★ ★ ★ ★ ★ ★ ★ ★

Albert Einstein, a man with a common touch and an uncommon ability to express himself, was once asked by a reporter to explain the theory of relativity in layman's terms. Already a beloved figure, his answer was widely reported in the press, and only served to further endear him to an admiring world:

When a man sits with a pretty girl for an hour,
it seems like a minute.
But let him sit on a hot stove for a minute—
and it's longer than an hour.
That's relativity.

★ ★ ★ ★ ★ ★ ★ ★ ★ ★ ★

A genial man with a sharp mind, Charles W. Eliot was president of Harvard University for forty years. On the weekend of the annual Harvard–Yale football game in the late 1800s, Eliot and the distinguished Harvard alumnus Edward Everett Hale were walking through Harvard Yard on the way to the game. As a group of students passed by, one of them hollered out, "Where are you going, Dr. Eliot?" He answered:

To yell with Hale.

His reply went over the heads of most of the students in the group, but one perceptive undergraduate immediately recognized it as a brilliant phonetic reversal of "To hell with Yale." Eliot's words have since become a part of Harvard lore.

★　★　★　★　★　★　★　★　★　★

As he grew older, Jackie Gleason's gargantuan appetite and fondness for liquor resulted in serious weight gain. The extra weight didn't interfere with his acting ability, and may have helped him in some of his roles, notably as Minnesota Fats in the 1961 film *The Hustler* (for which he was nominated for an Oscar for Best Supporting Actor). As he packed on the pounds, though, the dramatic increase in his girth did affect another of his great passions: the game of golf. When once asked what his biggest golfing challenge was, he replied:

When I tee the ball where I can see it, I can't hit it.
And when I put it where I can hit it, I can't see it.

★　★　★　★　★　★　★　★　★　★

In the 1994 film *Robin Hood: Men in Tights,* Mel Brooks brilliantly spoofed Kevin Costner's 1991 film *Robin Hood: Prince of Thieves.* Both movies begin similarly, with Robin Hood imprisoned in a dark dungeon. In Brooks's version, Robin (played by Cary Elwes) is securely locked in chains alongside another prisoner (the musician Isaac Hayes, in a cameo role). Robin struggles in vain to free himself from the chains, finally concluding, "It's not going to be easy getting out of here. What we need is a great feat of strength." In a classic example of Mel Brooks dialogue, Robin's fellow prisoner says:

> **Feat of strength? *Au contraire.***
> **Now that you are here with me**
> **what we have is great strength of feet.**

Together, the two men press their feet against the iron bar, breaking free from the chains, allowing them to escape from their captors.

★ ★ ★ ★ ★ ★ ★ ★ ★ ★

The prime minister of Great Britain from 1970 to 1974, Edward Heath was replaced by Margaret Thatcher after he failed to lead the Conservative Party to victory in the 1974 elections. Early in his career, Heath was the subject of a highly derogatory editorial in a London newspaper owned by William Aitken, the Canadian-born English newspaper magnate better known as Lord Beaverbrook. When Heath ran into Beaverbrook several days later in the washroom of a private club in London, a contrite Beaverbrook extended his hand to Heath and said, "My dear chap, I've been thinking it over, and I was wrong in that editorial. Here and now, I wish to apologize." Heath replied:

> **Very well, but next time,**
> **I wish you'd insult me in the washroom**
> **and apologize in your newspaper.**

★ ★ ★ ★ ★ ★ ★ ★ ★ ★

In 1970, Dustin Hoffman starred in *Little Big Man*, a film based on Thomas Berger's 1964 novel about the Old West as seen through the eyes of 111-year-old Jack Crabbe, the only soldier to survive the Battle of the Little Big Horn. At one stage of his life, Crabbe is living the life of an Indian brave who, even though married to an Indian squaw, has allowed his wife's three unmarried sisters to share his tepee (it's quite a challenge for one man, but Crabbe proves equal to the task).

Shortly after adopting this unique living arrangement, Crabbe encounters an old rival from the tribe. Attempting to show his superiority over Crabbe, the rival describes how much he has acquired in his life, boasting, "I have a wife and four horses." Crabbe has the perfect rejoinder, however, and bests his rival by replying:

I have a horse and four wives.

★ ★ ★ ★ ★ ★ ★ ★ ★ ★ ★

At the 1976 Olympic games in Montreal, Bruce Jenner overwhelmed the decathlon field, winning the gold medal and setting a new world record. Soon after, he retired from sports competition to become a television commentator, advertising spokesperson, and motivational speaker. At the height of Jenner's popularity, another athlete getting a lot of attention was Joe Namath, the flamboyant quarterback of the New York Jets. One day, a sportswriter asked Jenner how he would compare his career with Namath's. He replied:

I spent twelve years training for a career
that was over in a week.
Joe spent one week training for a career
that lasted twelve years.

★ ★ ★ ★ ★ ★ ★ ★ ★ ★ ★

When Lyndon B. Johnson assumed the presidency after the death of John F. Kennedy, he inherited the controversial J. Edgar Hoover as director of the FBI. As a Washington veteran, LBJ knew that both of his predecessors, JFK and Eisenhower, wanted to fire Hoover, but decided against it for political reasons. After several months in office, it was clear that LBJ was also planning to retain Hoover. At a 1964 press conference, a reporter asked Johnson why he put up with the crotchety and difficult Hoover. LBJ replied in his typically coarse style:

Well, it's probably better to have him
inside the tent pissin' out
than outside pissin' in.

★ ★ ★ ★ ★ ★ ★ ★ ★ ★ ★

Shortly after he was appointed ambassador to Great Britain in 1938, Joseph P. Kennedy made headlines in London newspapers—and many American papers as well—when he hit a hole in one in his first golf game in England. The next day, he received a teasing telegram from sons Joe, Jr., and Jack, who were both at Harvard. The exact message of that first telegram remains a mystery, but based on the elder Kennedy's eventual reply, it's easy to imagine that it might have said something like this:

> **CONGRATS ON HOLE IN ONE.**
> **HOPE IT DOESN'T GO TO YOUR HEAD AND**
> **YOU FORGET ABOUT FAMILY BACK HOME.**

A day later, the Kennedy boys received a cable from their father. This one said:

> **I AM MUCH HAPPIER BEING THE FATHER OF NINE CHILDREN**
> **AND MAKING A HOLE IN ONE**
> **THAN I WOULD BE AS THE FATHER OF ONE CHILD**
> **AND MAKING A HOLE IN NINE.**

★ ★ ★ ★ ★ ★ ★ ★ ★ ★ ★

During his presidency, Abraham Lincoln was visited by Robert Dale Owen, a prominent spiritualist. A lengthy article on spiritualism was being much discussed at the time, and Owen asked the president for his opinion. Not favorably disposed to the topic, but not wanting to be rude, Lincoln was said to have replied:

> **Well, for those who like that sort of thing,**
> **I should think that is**
> **just about the sort of thing they would like.**

✶ ✶ ✶ ✶ ✶ ✶ ✶ ✶ ✶ ✶ ✶

During his long career in the movies, on television, and in his popular Las Vegas act, Dean Martin played the role of a lush so effectively that many people were convinced he was an alcoholic (the truth is, whenever he had had a drink in his hands on stage, it was usually filled with apple juice). In a famous routine, the comedian Marty Brill asked Martin why he drank so much. Martin answered, "I drink to forget." When Brill said, "That's sad," Martin added, "It could be a lot sadder." Taking the bait, Brill said, "What could be sadder than drinking to forget?" Martin quipped:

> **I could forget to drink.**

✶ ✶ ✶ ✶ ✶ ✶ ✶ ✶ ✶ ✶ ✶

One of the brightest lights of the Renaissance, Michelangelo was so acclaimed in his lifetime that he enjoyed something like a celebrity status (he was the first artist to have his biography published while he was still living, and there were actually two competing biographies of him). As a result of his fame, many stories were told about him. In one memorable anecdote, a wealthy patron commissioned Michelangelo to do a sculpture, and then complained that the sculptor was taking far too long to make only trifling changes in the piece. The artist gave a legendary reply:

> **Trifles make perfection,**
> **and perfection is no trifle.**

✶ ✶ ✶ ✶ ✶ ✶ ✶ ✶ ✶ ✶ ✶

In the early 1700s, Matthew Prior was a politician and diplomat who also achieved a certain distinction as a writer of light verse. In one of his compositions, he wrote that every poet is a fool. Alexander Pope, who was emerging as one of the leading poets of the time—and no fan of Prior's—retaliated with this clever chiastic verse:

> Sir, I admit your gen'ral rule
> That every poet is a fool;
> But you yourself may serve to show it,
> That every fool is not a poet.

✴ ✴ ✴ ✴ ✴ ✴ ✴ ✴ ✴ ✴

In the 1998 movie *The Horse Whisperer*, Kristin Scott Thomas plays the role of Annie MacLean, a sophisticated East Coast woman whose daughter has been traumatized (along with her horse) in a tragic accident. When the distraught mother hears about Tom Booker (played by Robert Redford), a Montana horse trainer with an almost mystical ability to communicate with horses, she tracks him down. In her first phone conversation with Booker, she says, "I hear you help people with horse problems." He replies:

> I don't help people with horse problems,
> I help horses with people problems.

✴ ✴ ✴ ✴ ✴ ✴ ✴ ✴ ✴ ✴

Even though he was not exactly a handsome man, George Bernard Shaw was something of a babe magnet to beautiful women all around the world. Among the great beauties with a major attraction to Shaw was the famed dancer Isadora Duncan. A big supporter of the eugenics movement, Duncan thought a child between her and Shaw would be quite a specimen. She once said to him, "Think of it! With my body and your brains, what a wonder it would be." Shaw cleverly reminded her:

> Yes, but what if it had your brains and my body?

★ ★ ★ ★ ★ ★ ★ ★ ★ ★ ★

Richard Brinsley Sheridan was one of eighteenth-century London's most sparkling figures—a respected politician, the author of such witty plays as *The School for Scandal* and *The Rivals*, and a captivating speaker. Despite his success, he was a horrible manager of his financial affairs and was constantly scrambling to pay off his debts. In one famous story, a tailor grew tired of asking Sheridan to pay off a long-overdue bill. Finally, he cornered the deadbeat celebrity and pleaded, "At least you could pay me the interest on the principal." Sheridan's reply has been celebrated for more than two centuries:

> **It is not my interest to pay the principal;**
> **nor is it my principle to pay the interest.**

★ ★ ★ ★ ★ ★ ★ ★ ★ ★ ★

In the 1933 film *I'm No Angel,* a middle-aged and slightly plump (but still saucy) Mae West plays opposite a young and handsome Cary Grant. She's a circus hootchie-kootchie dancer named Tira and he plays Jack Clayton, a millionaire businessman. The unlikely couple begin to get involved, but a misunderstanding breaks them up and she sues for breach of promise. In the final courtroom scene, Clayton contests the charges by bringing in a number of Tira's ex-lovers. When Clayton watches Tira demolish the witnesses in her hilarious cross-examinations, he is persuaded that she truly loves him and the case is dismissed. After the trial, a female reporter asks Tira, "Why did you admit knowing so many men in your life?" Ignoring the precise question, West delivers what was to become a signature line:

> **Well, it's not the men in your life that counts,**
> **it's the life in your men.**

★ ★ ★ ★ ★ ★ ★ ★ ★ ★ ★

In the 1938 film *Every Day's a Holiday*, Mae West plays the role of Peaches O'Day, an 1890s con artist woman who sells the Brooklyn Bridge and then flees New York City to avoid capture. She later returns to the city—disguised as Mademoiselle Fifi—and embarks on a campaign to expose a corrupt police chief and his crooked cops. In one scene, she is asked by actor Charles Winninger (playing a character named Van Reighle Van Pelter Van Doon), "Now tell me, Peaches, do you keep a diary?" In another classic reply, West answers:

> **I always say, keep a diary**
> **and someday it'll keep you.**

✳ ✳ ✳ ✳ ✳ ✳ ✳ ✳ ✳ ✳

Even though he was not temperamentally well suited to be an art teacher, James McNeill Whistler occasionally took in students to supplement his income. One day, an obstinate student challenged the advice of his teacher by insisting, "I paint what I see!" Whistler, also well known for his verbal artistry, quickly riposted:

Ah, yes! But the shock will come when you see what you paint.

oxymoronic repartee

In a 2004 book, I introduced the word *oxymoronica* to the reading public. By adding the suffix *-ica* (which shows up in words like *erotica* and *exotica*) to the word *oxymoron*, I was trying to coin a word to describe a collection of oxymoronic and paradoxical quotations.

When most people think of an oxymoron, they think of simple two-word constructions, like *jumbo shrimp, pretty ugly, old news,* or according to some, *military intelligence.* An oxymoron is formed when two words that don't normally go together are conjoined, creating a *compressed paradox.* A paradox is interesting because it is false and true at the same time. Paradoxical observations are often extraordinarily thought provoking, helping us see old realities in new ways. Somebody once said—quite wisely—that a paradox is a truth standing on its head to get our attention.

Some examples of oxymoronica contain a simple oxymoron, as in "Parting is such sweet sorrow." Before these words were written, the incongruent words *sweet* and *sorrow* had never been formally linked. But when the expression first showed up in Shakespeare's *Romeo and Juliet,* it became unforgettable. The words capture an eternal truth about the romantic experience—when young lovers leave one another's embrace, they experience a bittersweet emotion.

"Acting is happy agony," a famous observation from English actor Alec Guinness, is also a beautiful blending of two normally incompatible words.

Just like the Shakespeare line earlier, his words capture an essential paradoxical truth—appearing on stage can be, almost at the same time, absolutely terrifying and enormously satisfying.

The most impressive examples of oxymoronica don't contain a simple *contradiction in terms*; they contain what might be called a *contradiction in ideas*. Some of the most famous sayings in history are examples:

> **Less is more.**
>
> *Robert Browning*

> **The more things change, the more they remain the same.**
>
> *Alphonse Karr*

> **To lead the people, walk behind them.**
>
> *Lao-tzu*

If you examine these sayings, you will notice that each one is false at a literal level and true at a figurative one. They are perfect examples of oxymoronica (for more on the subject, go to www.oxymoronica.com).

Happily, oxymoronica also shows up in many extraordinary replies and remarks. In his 1995 book *Beckett's Dying Words*, the distinguished literary scholar Christopher Ricks wrote admiringly about the comment of a friend of his—a professor at a Canadian university—who was asked if there were any vacancies in the English department. The professor's reply was ingenious:

> **There are plenty of vacancies,**
> **but they're all filled.**

Vacant positions, of course, are empty, so the notion of an empty position being filled is oxymoronic. And for anyone familiar with employment practices in academia, where many tenured professors have gone to sleep on the job, the professor's reply speaks volumes about the caliber of the people who are currently occupying such positions.

Many oxymoronic replies are wonderfully witty. After receiving the Nobel Prize in 1922, the Danish physicist Niels Bohr invited friends and associates to a celebration party at his country cottage north of Copenhagen. The event was also well attended by members of the press. One reporter, noticing a horseshoe hanging on a wall, teasingly asked the famous physicist, "Can it be that you, of all people, believe a horseshoe will bring you good luck?" Bohr replied:

> **Of course not,
> but I understand it brings you luck
> whether you believe it or not.**

Other oxymoronic replies are not so much witty as they are profound, often capturing important human truths. A famous example was offered by the emperor Pyrrhus in 279 B.C. when he led a coalition of invading Greek forces against the Roman army. In one of the longest and most bitterly fought battles of the campaign, there were heavy losses on both sides. Finally, the battered Greek army defeated the Roman forces. In a celebration after the battle, Pyrrhus was congratulated on the victory. He reportedly said:

> **Another victory like this and we are ruined.**

These are among the most famous words ever uttered, cited countless times throughout history in the wake of extremely costly victories. The words of Pyrrhus live on in the eponymous expression *pyrrhic* (PEER-ick) *victory,* which refers to a win accompanied by such huge losses that it's difficult to truly consider it a triumph.

Another provocative oxymoronic reply occurred in 1815, shortly after Napoléon was deposed and the French monarchy was restored to power. One day, the new emperor Louis XVIII was discussing a draft budget with foreign minister Charles Maurice de Talleyrand. Examining the budget, Talleyrand was surprised to discover that it included no salaries for top deputies. He questioned the omission, but the king defended the idea, saying, "It is an honorary position. Deputies should perform their duties without payment." Talleyrand replied:

> ### Without any payment?
> ### Your Majesty, that would cost too much.

Talleyrand's response is part of a grand oxymoronic theme that might be called "Free things cost too much." The notion goes back centuries and shows up in many wonderful paradoxical observations, including a line from Shakespeare's *The Winter's Tale*: "You pay a great deal too dear for what's given freely."

Some of history's most famous oxymoronic replies have come from Samuel Goldwyn. The Polish-born Goldwyn emigrated to America as a teenager in the 1890s. With his brother-in-law, a vaudeville producer, Goldwyn joined forces with Cecil B. DeMille to produce the 1913 film *Squaw Man*, the first full-length feature film made in Hollywood. One of the industry's most successful film producers, Goldwyn constantly struggled with the intricacies of the English language. Whether he actually said most of the things attributed to him is highly doubtful, but there is no doubt that he had a tendency to mangle the language in ways that cracked people up. His reputation for what became known as "Goldwynisms" was spread by writers working in his studio, who invented colorful stories about his malapropisms and attributed them to him.

In one popular story, Goldwyn was in the middle of a tense and tough negotiation with some hard-nosed Hollywood investors. The meeting dragged on and on without resolution. Finally, when Goldwyn was pressured to make a decision, he relented, saying:

> ### I'll give you a definite maybe.

In another story, Goldwyn got into a heated argument with a corporate accountant who believed the studio was paying far too much for a particular actor (some say the actor was Cary Grant). Goldwyn ultimately conceded:

We're overpaying him, but he's worth it.

And in yet another Goldwyn story, the legendary producer got so upset at some policy decisions made at a 1933 meeting of the Motion Picture Producers and Distributors that he stormed out of the meeting saying:

Gentlemen, include me out.

Another figure noted for his misadventures with the English language was Yogi Berra, the Hall of Fame catcher for the New York Yankees. During his career, and up to the present day, Berra's colorful way of expressing himself, dubbed "Yogi-isms," delighted fellow players, writers, and fans.

One memorable Yogi-ism occurred in the mid-1950s, when major league baseball attendance declined and a number of clubs began to experiment with special promotions to get fans out to the park. One day, a number of players in the Yankees clubhouse were debating the effectiveness of such events. While some players voiced support for the idea, Berra wasn't so sure, commenting:

If the fans don't want to come to the ballpark, nobody's gonna stop 'em.

Another occurred in the 1961 World Series, when all the games were played in the afternoon. In one game, blinded by the late afternoon sun, Berra was charged with an error after he dropped a fly ball. When a reporter asked him after the game what had happened, he explained:

It gets late early out there.

In one more Berra story, during spring training in the late 1950s, a number of Yankees ballplayers were discussing where to eat in Fort Lauderdale. When one player highly recommended a particularly trendy restaurant, Berra observed:

Nobody goes there anymore. It's too crowded.

This remark, which ultimately became one of Berra's most popular quotes, was soon applied by Berra to Toots Shor's popular New York City restaurant, an eating spot frequented by Yankees ballplayers and other celebrities.

Many Berra and Goldwyn replies were not purposeful, so we'll examine more contributions from them in the upcoming chapter on "Inadvertent Repartee." In the rest of this chapter, we'll look at more examples of *oxymoronic repartee*.

★ ★ ★ ★ ★ ★ ★ ★ ★ ★

One of the most eminent scientists of his time, Louis Agassiz did as much as anyone to popularize the study of natural history. Born and educated in Europe, he visited America in 1846 and decided to stay. By 1848, he accepted a professorship at Harvard, where he taught for the next twenty-five years. In constant demand as a speaker, he rarely accepted such invitations, fearing they would detract from his scientific pursuits. Invited one day to speak to a group of scientists, he declined on the usual grounds. The gentleman making the invitation persisted, however, and assured the reluctant scientist that he would be generously remunerated. Agassiz declined again, this time explaining:

I cannot afford to waste my time making money.

★ ★ ★ ★ ★ ★ ★ ★ ★ ★

Bertrand Russell, the renowned British philosopher and freethinker, loved to tell a story that was told to him by a fellow philosopher, F. W. H. Myers, also a well-known atheist. At a dinner party, Myers asked a religious man sitting next to him what he thought was going to happen to him after he died. When the man said he really didn't want to talk about it, Myers pressed the issue. Finally, the man replied:

**Oh, I suppose I shall inherit eternal bliss,
but I wish you wouldn't talk about such unpleasant subjects.**

★ ★ ★ ★ ★ ★ ★ ★ ★ ★ ★

In 1929, Nancy Astor, an American-born socialite who had married into an English branch of the wealthy Astor family, won election to the House of Commons. The first woman in history to be seated in what had been an exclusive male preserve, Lady Astor quickly tried to establish her presence. She argued her positions with passion and often interrupted other speakers in the middle of their remarks. When she was called to task one day for interrupting a fellow M.P., she protested, "But I've been listening for hours." One member of the House was heard to reply:

Yes, we *heard* you listening!

★ ★ ★ ★ ★ ★ ★ ★ ★ ★ ★

Rock star David Bowie has been described as one of the great chameleons of pop music, famous for remaking his image to meet the tastes of the time. For many years, he was noted for his ambiguous sexuality and gender-bending stage personas. Often appearing on stage in some outrageous costume, an interviewer once asked him why he chose to wear a dress. He explained:

**You must understand that
this is not a woman's dress I'm wearing.
It's a man's dress.**

★ ★ ★ ★ ★ ★ ★ ★ ★ ★ ★

After graduating first in his class from the Harvard Law School in 1877, Louis Brandeis soon became known as the People's Attorney for representing individual citizens in suits against large corporate interests. A man of indefatigable energy, Brandeis was once criticized by a colleague for taking a vacation just before a big trial, a period when all the other attorneys in the case were working night and day. Brandeis explained his decision in a most interesting way:

**I require the rest.
I find that while I can do a year's work in eleven months,
I can't do it in twelve.**

✳ ✳ ✳ ✳ ✳ ✳ ✳ ✳ ✳ ✳ ✳

As a teenager in Spain during World War I, Luis Buñuel was heavily influenced by the works of Salvador Dalí and the ideas of Sigmund Freud as he shed his early Catholic upbringing and began to forge a career as a filmmaker. While living in Mexico late in his life, he was asked in an interview how he had been influenced by his early Jesuit training. He replied:

Thanks to God, I am still an atheist.

✳ ✳ ✳ ✳ ✳ ✳ ✳ ✳ ✳ ✳ ✳

Even though G. K. Chesterton and George Bernard Shaw were friends, they disagreed on religion, politics, and many other important topics. After Shaw published a particularly scathing attack on Chesterton's economic views, friends of Chesterton were disappointed at his failure to reply. When the writer Hilaire Belloc, a good friend, questioned the silence strategy, Chesterton demonstrated a deep understanding of his amiable adversary by saying:

**I have answered him.
To a man of Shaw's wit,
silence is the one unbearable repartee.**

✳ ✳ ✳ ✳ ✳ ✳ ✳ ✳ ✳ ✳ ✳

In early 1917, with World War I dragging on and things not going well for the French, President Raymond Poincaré asked the eminent and aging seventy-six-year-old Georges Clemenceau to form a new government. Since 1911, as a member of the Senate, Clemenceau had been critical of the way French military leaders had been dealing with the German threat. As resolute as Churchill would later prove to be during World War II, Clemenceau immediately took charge, naming himself minister of war as well as premier. In one of his early cabinet meetings, he outlined a program of action that surprised some of those sitting around the table. Finally, one brave minister questioned him, saying, "Sir, this is not in agreement with the thinking of the General Staff." A frustrated Clemenceau responded:

War is much too serious a thing to be left to the military.

★ ★ ★ ★ ★ ★ ★ ★ ★ ★

Born into a wealthy and cultivated French family, Jean Cocteau became one of France's most versatile talents, making his mark as a poet, novelist, playwright, actor, film director, and painter. He influenced, and was influenced by, some of the greatest artists of the twentieth century, including Picasso, Modigliani, and Stravinsky. In 1955, after he was initiated into the French Academy, he was asked why such an antiestablishment figure would accept membership in such an established institution. He said:

Since it's now fashionable to laugh at
the conservative French Academy,
I have remained a rebel by joining it.

★ ★ ★ ★ ★ ★ ★ ★ ★ ★

One of the most prominent artists of the twentieth century, Salvador Dalí was also one of the most flamboyant. A brilliant self-promoter, he was well aware of the power of a captivating quip. When he was once asked, "Is it hard to paint a picture?" he replied:

No, it is either easy or impossible.

✻ ✻ ✻ ✻ ✻ ✻ ✻ ✻ ✻ ✻

In the 1960s, French film director Jean-Luc Godard established himself as a leader of the New Wave of filmmaking. Films like *Jules and Jim* and *Breathless* broke new cinematic ground, but were often criticized for being inaccessible and difficult to follow. In 1981, *Time* magazine reported on a film symposium in which Godard and the French film director Georges Franju were panelists. During a discussion of film technique, Franju declared, "Movies should have a beginning, a middle, and an end." Godard quickly interjected:

Certainly. But not necessarily in that order.

✻ ✻ ✻ ✻ ✻ ✻ ✻ ✻ ✻ ✻

On August 12, 1994, major league baseball players went on strike, bringing baseball to a halt for the rest of the season. The strike, which lasted 235 days, ended in April of the next year when a federal judge issued an injunction against the owners. Just before the strike, baseball was enjoying one of the most exciting seasons in many years. The lowly Montreal Expos were leading their league by six games, Tony Gwynn was flirting with a .400 batting average, and a number of ballplayers were having banner years. Just before the walkout, Ken Griffey, Jr., was asked what he thought about the upcoming strike, especially since he and so many other ballplayers were doing so well. He replied:

**We picked a bad year
to have a good year.**

✻ ✻ ✻ ✻ ✻ ✻ ✻ ✻ ✻ ✻

With *Catch-22* and other novels, Joseph Heller became one of history's most successful writers. In a 1975 interview in *Playboy* magazine, interviewer Sam Merrill was surprised to discover that the wealthy writer was still teaching fiction—and even grading student papers—at the City College of New York. When Merrill asked, "Have you considered giving up teaching so you could spend more time on your writing?" Heller replied:

> ### If I gave up teaching,
> ### I would have no time at all for writing.

✶ ✶ ✶ ✶ ✶ ✶ ✶ ✶ ✶ ✶ ✶

During the 1930s, the playwright and wit George S. Kaufman and his wife, Beatrice, were invited to spend a Thanksgiving holiday weekend at the beautiful home of Averell Harriman, chairman of the board of the Union Pacific Railroad. The guest list that weekend was dazzling, and included Robert and Mary Sherwood, Heywood and Ruth Broun, Harold Ross, Peggy Pulitzer, Oscar Levant, and more. During the sumptuous Thanksgiving feast, one of the guests made the offhand comment, "What a play this gathering would make." While the rest of the guests were considering the intriguing possibility, Kaufman reflected:

> ### Ah, yes. I think I would title it *The Upper Depths.*

✶ ✶ ✶ ✶ ✶ ✶ ✶ ✶ ✶ ✶ ✶

The English economist John Maynard Keynes revolutionized the role that government played in economic affairs. A member of the Bloomsbury Group, he associated with many other English intellectuals and acquired some of their witty ways. One day, Lady Violet Bonham-Carter and Keynes were discussing the merits of the English politician David Lloyd George. When Lady Violet asked, "What do you think happens to Mr. Lloyd George when he is alone in a room?" Keynes answered:

> ### When he is alone in a room,
> ### there is nobody there.

★ ★ ★ ★ ★ ★ ★ ★ ★ ★

While serving as president, Abraham Lincoln was given separate hats made by two rival hatmakers. After presenting him with their specially made creations, both men waited expectantly for the president's response. Lincoln examined both hats carefully and announced:

Gentlemen, they mutually excel each other.

★ ★ ★ ★ ★ ★ ★ ★ ★ ★

Shortly after receiving the Nobel Prize in literature in 1929, Thomas Mann was introduced to a rising star on the American literary scene. As the two men shook hands, the American author seemed appropriately humble, saying that he hardly considered himself a writer in the presence of such a legendary figure as Mann. After a few more pleasantries were exchanged, Mann whispered to a friend as they walked away:

He has no right to make himself so modest.
He's not that great.

★ ★ ★ ★ ★ ★ ★ ★ ★ ★

The first Hollywood actor to be officially dubbed a hunk, Victor Mature prominently displayed his beefcake physique in over sixty feature films. He had a humorous, self-deprecating style, once quipping that his acting roles required him to use every muscle in his body except his face. Mature was once denied membership at an exclusive California country club on the grounds that it did not admit actors as members. Mature formally asked the club to reconsider. In his letter to the membership committee, he wrote:

I'm no actor, and I've got 64 pictures to prove it.

✴ ✴ ✴ ✴ ✴ ✴ ✴ ✴ ✴ ✴ ✴

In the 1947 film *Out of the Past,* Robert Mitchum plays a former private eye who is lured out of his prosaic life as a gas station owner by a gangster (Kirk Douglas) who hires him to find his girlfriend (Jane Greer). At one point, as Greer and Mitchum leave a meeting, she is critical of the way he came across, saying, "For a man who's supposed to be clever, you looked like an idiot." Mitchum coolly replies:

> **That's one way to be clever.**
> **Look like an idiot.**

✴ ✴ ✴ ✴ ✴ ✴ ✴ ✴ ✴ ✴ ✴

When once asked why he became a writer, the Hungarian novelist and playwright Ferenc Molnár answered, "In the same way that a woman becomes a prostitute. First I did it to please myself, then I did it to please my friends, and finally I did it for the money." One day, a Budapest theater owner gave Molnár two complimentary tickets to a play. Early in the first act, it was apparent the play was a dud. When Molnár said he'd seen enough, his companion protested, "We can't just walk out. We're guests of management." Molnár shrugged and sat back in his seat. Several agonizing minutes later, he got up from his seat. "Now where are you going?" said the friend. Molnár groused:

> **To the box office to buy two tickets—so we can leave.**

✴ ✴ ✴ ✴ ✴ ✴ ✴ ✴ ✴ ✴ ✴

A revered Columbia University philosophy professor, Sidney Morgenbesser acquired a kibitzing kind of wit as a child on the Lower East Side and used it masterfully in his dialogues with students (when philosopher Robert Nozick described his student days at Columbia, he said, "I majored in Sidney

Morgenbesser"). A few weeks before his death from complications related to ALS, the ailing Morgenbesser was talking with Columbia colleague David Albert about God and human suffering. In response to a comment from Albert, Morgenbesser quipped:

Why is God making me suffer so much?
Just because I don't believe in him?

★ ★ ★ ★ ★ ★ ★ ★ ★ ★ ★

Earlier in Morgenbesser's career as a philosophy professor at Columbia University, an impassioned young Chinese Communist student in one of his classes asked the professor if he disagreed with Chairman Mao's assertion that a proposition could be true and false at the same time. The professor got a huge laugh from the entire class—and even the young ideologue who had asked the question—when he replied:

I do and I don't.

★ ★ ★ ★ ★ ★ ★ ★ ★ ★ ★

At six feet, two inches tall and weighing around 350 pounds, William "The Refrigerator" Perry was huge, but he was also capable of dunking a basketball and running the forty-yard dash in just over five seconds. At defensive nose tackle, he helped the Chicago Bears to victory in Super Bowl XX in 1986. Sometimes inserted as a fullback in short-down situations, he become the heaviest running back in NFL history to score a touchdown. When a sportswriter once asked him "What were you like as a child?" he replied:

Even when I was little, I was big.

★ ★ ★ ★ ★ ★ ★ ★ ★ ★ ★

Soon after Isaac Bashevis Singer emigrated to America from Poland in 1935, he began writing stories—in Yiddish—for the immigrant community in New York City. Within a few years, his engaging stories began to be translated into English and shared with a larger audience. Singer was awarded the Nobel Prize in literature in 1978. When once asked by an interviewer, "Do you believe in free will or predestination?" he said:

> **We have to believe in free will.**
> **We've got no choice.**

★ ★ ★ ★ ★ ★ ★ ★ ★ ★ ★

Actor Rod Steiger said the best advice he ever got was from a psychoanalyst he saw when he was a young man studying at the Actors Studio in Manhattan in the early 1950s. Psychoanalysis was in vogue at the time, and the young actor thought he would give it a try. In his first session, however, he didn't appear to be a good candidate for therapy, saying to his analyst: "Now, look, before we go into this, I have to be free to create. I have to be free to do things. I have to be free to get up when I want, sleep with anyone I want, do what I want to do. I can't be regimented. I have to be free!" These were not exactly the words a psychotherapist wants to hear from a new client, but Steiger's analyst demonstrated maturity and wisdom—and cleverness—when he replied softly:

> **That's fine. Just be careful you don't become a slave to freedom.**

★ ★ ★ ★ ★ ★ ★ ★ ★ ★ ★

A master at political intrigue, French statesman Charles Maurice de Talleyrand was also noted for his quick and clever wit. One day, he and an aide were discussing a beautiful but difficult young courtesan in the king's court. When the aide said to Talleyrand, "Is she not completely intolerable?" he replied:

> **Yes, she is intolerable, but that is her only fault.**

★ ★ ★ ★ ★ ★ ★ ★ ★ ★ ★

At a 1999 prayer breakfast in Washington, DC, President Bill Clinton reported that someone once asked Mother Teresa, "When you pray to God, what do you say?" She replied, "I don't say anything. I listen." The interviewer persisted, "Well, what does God say to you?" She answered:

He doesn't say anything. He listens.

★ ★ ★ ★ ★ ★ ★ ★ ★ ★ ★

One of the legendary Seven Wise Men of Greece, Thales is often described as the first great Western philosopher. He made pioneering efforts in geometry and astronomy, predicting an eclipse of the sun in 585 B.C. If he ever wrote anything down, it has not survived, but stories about him have been told for centuries. When a student asked him why he did not become a father, he gave one of history's first great paradoxical replies:

Because I am fond of children.

★ ★ ★ ★ ★ ★ ★ ★ ★ ★ ★

In the 1933 film *I'm No Angel,* the sultry Mae West plays the role of Tira, an exotic dancer in a traveling circus (the circus barker introduces her as "the girl who discovered you don't have to have feet to be a dancer"). When the circus comes to New York, she meets the handsome millionaire Jack Clayton (a British newcomer named Cary Grant). Even though their developing relationship strains credibility (she's getting older and beginning to put on the pounds; he's very young and very handsome), there are some fabulous scenes featuring the pair. At one point, as he begins to develop feelings for her, he says, "You were wonderful tonight." When she replies saucily, "I'm always wonderful at night," he replies, "Tonight, you were especially good." Grant's straight line allows West to come back with one of her most famous screen replies:

> When I'm good, I'm very good.
> But when I'm bad, I'm better.

inadvertent repartee

Shortly after retiring from political life in 1969, French president Charles de Gaulle and his wife, Yvonne, were lunching with former British prime minister Harold Macmillan and his wife. When Madame de Gaulle was asked, "What are you most looking forward to in the future?" she thought for a moment and said:

> **A penis.**

Her blunt answer startled the Macmillans. For a moment, an uncomfortable cloak of silence descended on the conversation. Finally, her husband broke the silence—and the tension—when he observed:

> **My dear, I don't think the English
> pronounce the word that way.
> They say *'appiness.***

Madame de Gaulle's comment illustrates a fascinating phenomenon in human interaction—some of the most memorable replies have come about by accident and not by design. Her answer is a perfect example of what might be called inadvertent repartee.

Another inadvertent gem comes from one of the most fascinating players in baseball history, Dizzy Dean of the St. Louis Cardinals. In the 1930s, Dean was a dominating pitcher and a special favorite of sports fans because of his zany antics and colorful way of speaking. In 1934, Dean had his best year ever, winning thirty games in the regular season and two in the World Series against the Detroit Tigers (he pitched a shutout in the seventh game to win the series for the Cards). In the fourth game, after being inserted as a pinch runner, he tried to break up a double play by going into second base standing up instead of sliding. As the Tigers' shortstop whipped the ball toward first base, it hit Dean squarely in the middle of the forehead, knocking him out. Dean was taken out of the ball game, and then to a local hospital as a precaution. The next day, when Dean showed up at the ballpark, sportswriters quizzed him about his condition. He assured them he was feeling fine, stating confidently:

The doctors X-rayed my head and found nothing.

Dean wasn't trying to be funny; he was just reporting the facts as he understood them. But overnight, his reply took on a life of its own. Sports pages around the country quoted the remark, and one paper even summarized the development with one of the most famous sports headlines in journalism history: "X-Ray of Dean's Head Reveals Nothing."

Yogi Berra is another major league baseball player who became famous for inadvertent replies (we considered some Yogi-isms in the previous chapter, "Oxymoronic Repartee," and will examine a few more here). Berra, who played for the New York Yankees from the late 1940s to the 1960s, went on to manage both the New York Mets and the Yankees after retiring as a player. During his career, he was a continual source of entertainment to teammates, sportswriters, and fans, who were captivated by his colorful observations. One day, while eating in an Italian restaurant in New York City, he was asked by the waitress if he'd like his pizza cut into four pieces or eight. Yogi thought for a second, and then answered:

**Better make it four.
I don't think I can eat eight.**

As it turns out, the world of sports has been an especially fertile source of inadvertently hilarious replies. Some of the better examples include:

★ When University of Houston wide receiver Torrin Polk was asked by a writer in 1991 why he liked coach John Jenkins, he replied:

He treats us like men. He lets us wear earrings.

★ When Los Angeles Lakers forward Elden Campbell was asked in 1991 if he had earned his degree from Clemson, he replied:

No, but they gave me one anyway.

★ When Seattle Supersonics center Jerome James was asked in 2003 to respond to Coach Nate McMillan's charge that he was selfish, James defended himself by saying:

I don't have the first clue who he is talking about, because all I worry about is Jerome.

★ When San Francisco Giants coach Rocky Bridges was asked in 1985 why he refused to eat snails, he said:

I prefer fast food.

★ When running back George Rogers of the New Orleans Saints was asked about his goals for the upcoming season, he offered:

I want to rush for one thousand or one thousand five hundred yards, whichever comes first.

Another master of the inadvertently clever reply was movie mogul Samuel Goldwyn, who we also featured earlier in the "Oxymoronic Repartee" chapter. The producer of many classic films, including *The Best Years of Our Lives* and *Wuthering Heights,* he was also famous for his fractured English. Whether he actually said most of the things attributed to him is doubtful, but there is no doubt he had a tendency to mangle the language in ways that cracked people up. In one story, Goldwyn backed out of an agreement with someone who then complained, "But we had a verbal contract!" Goldwyn came back with perhaps his most celebrated quote:

A verbal contract isn't worth the paper it's printed on.

We'll examine more replies from Berra and Goldwyn shortly. Before we do, though, it's important to remember that inadvertent replies are not restricted to people with little formal education. Indeed, some of the greatest wordsmiths have made some memorable contributions. One of my favorites involves the noted playwright Tennessee Williams.

Before the 1980s, general knowledge about eating disorders was extremely limited and the technical terms to describe them—now widely known—were used only by a handful of medical specialists. In 1983, the death of pop singer Karen Carpenter helped raise public awareness of both the prevalence and the danger of eating disorders. One day in the 1950s, as Tennessee Williams and actress Sylvia Miles were strolling down a London street, Miles noticed an extremely thin girl approaching. "Look, Tennessee!" Miles whispered discreetly, "Anorexia nervosa." In his distinctive Southern drawl, Williams replied:

Oh, Sylvia, you know everybody.

In another wonderful story about Tennessee Williams, he was once asked why he had stopped seeing his psychoanalyst. According to friends who knew him well, he replied with complete seriousness:

He was meddling too much in my personal life.

Some great inadvertent replies have even been written into the scripts of Hollywood films. In the 1975 suspense classic *Three Days of the Condor*, Robert Redford plays bookish CIA analyst Joe Turner (code-named "Condor"). Turner arrives at his office one day to discover that his entire section has been murdered. Fleeing the scene, he begins to fear that CIA higher-ups are determined to kill him. Abducting photographer Kathy Hale (Faye Dunaway) from the street, Turner seeks safety in her apartment. She is obviously frightened, but a chemistry between the two slowly begins to develop. At one point, he asks her a question, and she angrily replies, "You're not entitled to personal questions! That gun gives you a right to rough me up; it doesn't give you a right to . . ." Finding the notion of violence against a woman abhorrent, Turner interrupts, "Rough you up? Have I roughed you up? Have I . . . have I . . . have I raped you?" In a reply that always brings a snicker from viewers, no matter how many times they've seen the movie, Dunaway's character says:

The night is young.

Examples of *inadvertent repartee* may not be as common as those you'll find elsewhere in these pages, but they're just as interesting, and often even more entertaining. Let's take a look at a few more.

✳ ✳ ✳ ✳ ✳ ✳ ✳ ✳ ✳ ✳

In 1976, the Tampa Bay Buccaneers were the personification of the word *hapless*, losing every single game that season (the only team in NFL history to do so). One day, hoping to turn things around, Coach John McKay gave an emotional locker room lecture on the importance of fundamentals at the line of scrimmage. Again and again, he stressed that football games were "lost in the trenches." In the middle of his lecture, the coach noticed a lineman nodding off in the back of the room. McKay hollered out the athlete's name, rousing him to attention. When

McKay forcefully asked, "Where are most games lost?" the athlete rose and said in his best military manner:

Right here in Tampa, sir!

★ ★ ★ ★ ★ ★ ★ ★ ★ ★ ★

While Yogi Berra was managing the New York Mets in the early 1970s, John Lindsay was the mayor of New York City. Attending a game one day at Shea Stadium, Lindsay and his wife, Mary, chatted with Berra during the team's batting practice. Mrs. Lindsay, who was a fairly hip First Lady, said, "Yogi, you look cool." Berra replied:

Thanks. You don't look so hot yourself.

★ ★ ★ ★ ★ ★ ★ ★ ★ ★ ★

After appearing in a postgame interview with sports announcer Jack Buck, a member of a radio station's production crew handed Yogi Berra a check made out to "Bearer." Upset, Yogi immediately sought out his old friend and said indignantly:

How the hell long have you known me, Jack?
And you still don't know how to spell my name?

★ ★ ★ ★ ★ ★ ★ ★ ★ ★ ★

In 1984, Don Mattingly, the twenty-three-year-old New York Yankees first baseman, had a phenomenal year, batting .343, hitting twenty-three home runs, and knocking in 110 runs. When a sportswriter asked Yogi Berra if he thought Mattingly had exceeded expectations, the former Yankees great observed:

I'd say he's done more than that.

★ ★ ★ ★ ★ ★ ★ ★ ★ ★ ★

In March of 2001, forty-seven Hall of Fame baseball players, including Hank Aaron, Stan Musial, Ernie Banks, and Yogi Berra, lunched with President George W. Bush at the White House. It was a festive occasion and the president made special note of Berra's presence, saying, "Yogi's been an inspiration to me—not only because of his baseball skills, but of course for the enduring mark he left on the English language." And then he got a hearty laugh when he said, "Some of the press corps even think he might be my speechwriter." Berra had been to the White House many times in his career, one early visit resulting in one of his most famous Yogi-isms. When asked by a reporter how he had enjoyed a White House dinner, he answered:

It was hard to have a conversation with anyone, there were so many people talking.

★ ★ ★ ★ ★ ★ ★ ★ ★ ★ ★

Compared to her husband, who often struggled to express himself in the way he desired, Barbara Bush rarely misspoke. However, in the summer of 1992, when a reporter asked the First Lady what she was planning to say in her speech at the upcoming Republican National Convention, she replied:

**My speech is nothing.
I'm just going to remind people
of what George Bush has accomplished.**

★ ★ ★ ★ ★ ★ ★ ★ ★ ★ ★

During the 1970s and '80s, Cesar Cedeno played for four separate clubs. Every time he was traded, he tried hard to keep the same uniform number: 28. After he was dealt from the Houston Astros to the Cincinnati Reds in 1982, Cedeno was greatly relieved to learn that he could keep his old number. When a reporter learned of the news, he asked, "Are you superstitious?" Cedeno answered:

> **No. I've just got too much jewelry
> with the number twenty-eight on it.**

✳ ✳ ✳ ✳ ✳ ✳ ✳ ✳ ✳ ✳ ✳

One of the first female comics to make it big in show business, Phyllis Diller once told a delightful story on herself. Early in her career, she and Tony Randall were guests on a television variety show. Chitchatting in the greenroom before the show, Randall used a word that was completely unfamiliar to Diller: *fellatio*. Not wanting to reveal her lack of sophistication, but well aware of Randall's classical training as an actor, she said:

> **I haven't read much Shakespeare.**

✳ ✳ ✳ ✳ ✳ ✳ ✳ ✳ ✳ ✳ ✳

In 1878, the HMS *Eurydice* capsized in a surprise storm off the Isle of Wight, killing more than three hundred crew and passengers (only two crewmen survived). The frigate was quickly raised and returned to the naval base at Portsmouth. A short while later, Queen Victoria invited a certain Admiral Foley of the Royal Navy to Buckingham Palace to report on the salvage operation. Discussing the project over lunch, the queen decided, after the essential details were quickly provided, to shift to a more pleasant topic. Since the admiral's sister was well known to the queen, she asked, "And how is your sister doing?" After years of wartime service, the admiral suffered from fairly serious hearing loss, and he didn't quite make out the question. Rather than ask for clarification, he decided to forge ahead as best he could. His answer, faithfully recorded by a guest at the table, almost sent the queen and the other luncheon guests into convulsions:

**Well, ma'am, I'm going to have her turned over,
take a good look at her bottom,
and have her well scraped.**

★ ★ ★ ★ ★ ★ ★ ★ ★ ★ ★

In 1967, Joey Bishop tried his luck in the late-night talk show world with *The Joey Bishop Show*. Despite his talent as a comedian, Bishop's show never really caught on and was canceled after only one season. When Arizona senator and Republican presidential candidate Barry Goldwater appeared on the show one evening, Bishop teasingly asked him, "Would you like to become a regular on the show?" Goldwater's answer proved that politicians are sometimes funnier by accident than when trying to be humorous:

**No, thank you.
I'd much rather watch you in bed with my wife.**

★ ★ ★ ★ ★ ★ ★ ★ ★ ★ ★

One day, Samuel Goldwyn and a group of associates were in the MGM conference room discussing a potential movie project when one person sitting at the table said he thought the script was too caustic. Goldwyn erupted:

**Too caustic? To hell with the cost.
Let's do it anyway.**

★ ★ ★ ★ ★ ★ ★ ★ ★ ★ ★

Samuel Goldwyn hit the roof one day when Edmund North, at the time a production assistant, showed him the heavy cost overruns for the 1939 Gary Cooper epic *The Real Glory*. Examining the figures, Goldwyn shouted, "What are you trying to do? You're ruining me!" North countered, "But, Mr. Goldwyn, from the very beginning you said you wanted a spectacle." Goldwyn shouted back:

Yes, but, goddamn it, I wanted an intimate spectacle!

★ ★ ★ ★ ★ ★ ★ ★ ★ ★ ★

Samuel Goldwyn and Louis B. Mayer, who were not exactly the best of friends, got into a shoving match one day in the locker room of the exclusive Hillcrest Country Club (Goldwyn ended up in a laundry hamper). News of the incident soon reached local journalists, who quickly followed up on the story. When Goldwyn was asked by a reporter if the incident would damage the working relationship between the two men, he tried in his own fashion to downplay matters, saying:

What? We're like friends, we're like brothers.
We love each other. We'd do anything for each other.
Why, we'd even cut each other's throats for each other!

★ ★ ★ ★ ★ ★ ★ ★ ★ ★ ★

In 1985, Wales surged from behind to defeat England in a World Cup rugby match. After the game, England's coach, Dick Greenwood, was asked if a costly error by one of his players had demoralized the team. The coach replied:

It didn't demoralize us, but it moralized them.

★ ★ ★ ★ ★ ★ ★ ★ ★ ★ ★

In 1948, with the publication of *Sexual Behavior in the Human Male*, an obscure Indiana University zoology professor named Alfred Kinsey was catapulted to international celebrity status. The 800-page hardcover book, the most detailed study of sexual practice to date, was an immediate sensation and a huge best-seller, even at a pricey $6.50 per copy. When a reporter asked Clara Kinsey, the professor's wife of more than twenty-five years, how her life had changed, she is said to have replied:

> **I don't see much of Alfred anymore
> since he got so interested in sex.**

⋆ ⋆ ⋆ ⋆ ⋆ ⋆ ⋆ ⋆ ⋆ ⋆ ⋆

The author of more than thirty books on the English language, Richard Lederer wrote in his autobiography, *A Man of My Words*, that he greatly enjoyed talking with young students, but often struggled with one of their most predictable questions: "Where do you get the ideas for your books?" After giving the matter considerable thought, he came up with a great idea. The next time the question was asked, he'd answer with a question of his own: "Where does the spider get its web?" A lifelong educator, he reasoned that an analogy like this might be instructive to young minds. After all, asking writers to account for the origin of their ideas was as futile as asking spiders to explain where webs come from. He shortly found himself speaking to a sixth-grade class in Concord, New Hampshire. Sure enough, the question was asked. Prepared for the moment, Lederer posed his question, "Where does the spider get its web?" As it turned out, the class had just finished a lesson plan on spiders, so Lederer's bubble was burst in an instant by a bright-eyed student who eagerly answered:

> **From its butt!**

⋆ ⋆ ⋆ ⋆ ⋆ ⋆ ⋆ ⋆ ⋆ ⋆ ⋆

In the single year of 1966, Muhammad Ali did something that is unthinkable by current standards—he successfully defended his heavyweight boxing title five separate times. On August 6, 1966, he squared off against the British champ, Brian London. It was a one-sided affair, and Ali quickly dispatched the British Bulldog in three rounds. After the fight, London was asked what he thought of Ali's punching ability. London's puzzling reply was reported in every London paper (and a few in America) the very next day:

> **Muhammad Ali isn't a puncher.**
> **He just hit me so many times I didn't know where I was.**

⋆ ⋆ ⋆ ⋆ ⋆ ⋆ ⋆ ⋆ ⋆ ⋆ ⋆

Shaquille O'Neal finally graduated from Louisiana State University in 2000 with a major in general studies and a minor in political science. In 1992, he left LSU after his junior year to become the top pick in the NBA draft, selected by the Orlando Magic. The Rookie of the Year in his first season, he helped the team make their first playoff bid the next year. After the playoffs, he took a break from basketball, making a rap album and vacationing in Greece. On his return, when asked by a reporter if he had visited the Parthenon, he said:

> **I can't really remember the names of the clubs that we went to.**

⋆ ⋆ ⋆ ⋆ ⋆ ⋆ ⋆ ⋆ ⋆ ⋆ ⋆

In 1989, top members of England's Conservative Party met at a London club to mark the retirement of William Stephen Whitelaw. In his long and distinguished career, Whitelaw served in many government posts, including that of home secretary (and close personal and political adviser) of Prime Minister Margaret Thatcher. At the party, many people sang the praises of "Willie," as he was affectionately known. When Mrs. Thatcher was asked to say a few words, she began her remarks by saying:

> **Every prime minister needs a Willie.**

As a ripple of laughter spread through the crowd, Mrs. Thatcher realized the group was snickering because they were thinking about another meaning of the word "willie" (a vernacular expression for *penis*). She immediately added, with an embarrassed smile, "Not a word of this is to go beyond this room." Happily, it did.

★ ★ ★ ★ ★ ★ ★ ★ ★ ★ ★

After *Of Human Bondage* was published in 1915, W. Somerset Maugham was a popular guest at London social gatherings, and rumors that he was a homosexual only added to his mystique among the sophisticated set. One evening, Maugham attended a dinner party at the home of the prominent theatrical figure Sir Herbert Beerbohm Tree. Fairly early in the evening, Maugham rose from the dinner table and said he had to be going home. As he was being escorted to the front door by the disappointed Lady Beerbohm Tree, he explained, "After all, I must look after my youth." Trying to be cosmopolitan, but failing in the attempt, the lady of the house replied:

Next time do bring him.
We *adore* those sort of people.

★ ★ ★ ★ ★ ★ ★ ★ ★ ★ ★

The Australian producer David N. Morton, who has theaters scattered all around the country, once received a telegram from his theater manager in Brisbane, saying:

SHOW STOPPED BY FLYING ANTS.

The intent of the manager was to inform his boss of a serious insect infestation. But that's not how Morton read the telegram. Always on the lookout for show-stopping acts, he gave the telegram the best possible interpretation, wiring back:

BOOK THEM FOR A FURTHER WEEK.

★ ★ ★ ★ ★ ★ ★ ★ ★ ★ ★

One of the most spectacular plays of the 2003 NFL season occurred in a game between the Minnesota Vikings and the Denver Broncos. Just before the end of the first half, Vikings quarterback Daunte Culpepper completed a pass to wide receiver Randy Moss. Moss took the ball forty-four yards and, just before he was about to be tackled, completed a no-look, over-the-shoulder lateral to teammate Moe Williams, who advanced the ball an additional fifteen yards for a touchdown. When one teammate was asked after the game if he had ever seen anything like it, he said, "Only on [Sony] PlayStation!" When Moss was asked about the play after the game, he replied:

> **It's a once-in-a-lifetime thing**
> **that only happens every so often.**

★ ★ ★ ★ ★ ★ ★ ★ ★ ★ ★

In a 1990 World Cup quarterfinal game, the heavily favored England soccer team trailed Cameroon by 2–1 with ten minutes remaining. England tied the score in the final minutes of regulation time and ended up eventually winning 3–2 in overtime. When England manager Bobby Robson was asked if he had underestimated the Cameroon team, he answered:

> **We didn't underestimate them.**
> **They were a lot better than we thought.**

★ ★ ★ ★ ★ ★ ★ ★ ★ ★ ★

The career of Washington Redskins quarterback Joe Theisman came to an abrupt end in 1985 when, sacked by New York Giants linebacker Lawrence Taylor, his leg was snapped like a twig in a nationally televised game. His playing days over,

Theisman became a motivational speaker, a color television analyst, and the author of a book titled *The Complete Idiot's Guide to Understanding Football Like a Pro*. Many felt the book was appropriately titled when Theisman uttered perhaps his best remembered quote. During a 1992 NFL game, someone used the hackneyed expression "a football genius." Theisman, always one to speak his mind, jumped in quickly to observe:

> **The word *genius* isn't applicable in football.**
> **A genius is a guy like Norman Einstein.**

risqué repartee

The *American Heritage Dictionary* defines *risqué* as "suggestive of or bordering on indelicacy or impropriety." Risqué material verges on being obscene, but is not generally regarded as offensive. Unlike X-rated or even R-rated material, risqué stories can be told in a wide range of social situations.

I've been interested in *risqué repartee* since my youth and a number of years ago was delighted to discover a wonderful example in one of the few stories about William Shakespeare that was actually written during his lifetime (most tales about him were penned years—even centuries—after his death).

On March 13, 1602, an English law student named John Manningham recorded in his diary a fascinating story he had just heard from his roommate. A prominent actor named Richard Burbage had recently given a stirring performance as Richard III in a new play by a then-promising writer named William Shakespeare (who was thirty-eight at the time). According to the story, shortly after the performance, Shakespeare observed Burbage talking in hushed tones to a young woman from the audience. Surmising that the couple was arranging a tryst, Shakespeare moved closer and overheard the starstruck young woman earnestly asking Burbage to come to her that evening in the name of Richard III. Sensing a rare opportunity, Shakespeare arrived at the woman's bedroom earlier in the evening, identified himself as the author of the play, and had his way with the young woman. As he was leaving, Shakespeare ran into the startled Burbage, who was just arriving. It was an awkward moment, but as the playwright hurried past the actor, he said with a smile:

William the Conqueror came before Richard the Third.

Another wonderful example of risqué repartee occurred one summer day in the 1920s when President Calvin Coolidge and wife, Grace, visited a Kentucky poultry farm. They were given separate tours, and when Mrs. Coolidge's group came through, the guide said, "The rooster here performs his services up to eight or nine times a day." Mrs. Coolidge got a good laugh when she replied:

**Please see to it that the president
is given that information!**

When the president's group came through a short while later, the guide relayed the First Lady's remark. Coolidge thought for a moment and asked, "Same chicken each time?" "No sir," the guide said, "different chickens each time." The president, who had a terrific sense of humor despite his reputation for being solemn and serious, said:

**Then see to it that Mrs. Coolidge
is given *that* information!**

Coolidge's reply was widely circulated by word of mouth and did much to endear the somewhat somber president to average Americans. It even inspired members of the scientific community. Animal scientists now refer to the phenomenon whereby a male animal is able to achieve extended sexual arousal with a variety of females as the Coolidge Effect.

Stories of risqué repartee continue to be circulated in the Internet era. In January 2000, Monica Lewinsky appeared on CNN's *Larry King Live*. While most viewers tuned in to see what she'd say about the Clinton affair, she had her own agenda. Having recently shed considerable weight on the Jenny Craig diet, she was now a company spokesperson. After her appearance, millions of people (including me) received a forwarded e-mail that quoted her answer to the question: "What have you learned about healthy eating?" She allegedly replied:

> **I've learned not to put things in my mouth**
> **that are bad for me.**

Are the three stories you've just heard true or apocryphal? The Shakespeare story was first recorded in a private diary just after the purported event, and was not discovered until years later. And while there are no witnesses around to confirm the Coolidge story, people who knew the president's capacity for wit believe he could have easily made the remark. So who knows for sure?

The only story that has been proven false is Lewinsky's purported reply to Larry King. A transcript of the show reveals she never said anything of the sort. But it was a great story—and a risqué one to boot—so it was enthusiastically told and retold by countless people all around the world. And, true or not, people loved it because it was an R-rated story that could be told in a G-rated setting.

Risqué repartee has been a staple of stand-up comedy since the early days of vaudeville. One of the early masters of the form was Sophie Tucker, aptly billed as the Last of the Red-Hot Mamas. In a career that spanned six decades (she appeared on stage until just before her death at age eighty-one), she was noted for her racy songs, sultry manner, and salty language. One of her most popular routines used remarks from her boyfriend Ernie as a setup for her risqué rejoinders. There are many examples, but the most popular is the story about when Ernie (now an ex-boyfriend) called her up on his eightieth birthday and said, "Soph! Guess what? I just married a twenty-year-old girl. What do you think of that?" Sophie replied:

> **Well I think I'm gonna marry a twenty-year-old boy.**
> **And let me tell you something, Ernie,**
> **twenty goes into eighty**
> **more than eighty goes into twenty!**

In the rest of the chapter, you'll find many more examples of *risqué repartee*. While many are well documented, some are of doubtful authenticity, and still others are obvious fabrications. But they're all meant to entertain, especially if your taste in humor runs just a little on the wild side. If your taste doesn't run in that direction, you might want to stop reading the chapter right now.

★ ★ ★ ★ ★ ★ ★ ★ ★ ★ ★

The careers of struggling actors Ben Affleck and Matt Damon began to soar soon after the release of their 1997 film *Good Will Hunting*. Against long odds, they wrote the screenplay, arranged the financing, produced the film, and then starred in their own movie. A huge commercial and critical success, the film earned Damon and Affleck the Oscar for Best Original Screenplay (Robin Williams won for Best Supporting Actor). A few weeks later, an interviewer asked Affleck what it was like after the ceremonies. He replied:

> **On the night of the awards,**
> **I just carried the Oscar around waist high.**
> **I never had so many women ask me, "Can I touch it?"**
> **Sadly, they were talking about the statuette.**

★ ★ ★ ★ ★ ★ ★ ★ ★ ★ ★

As the newlyweds were undressing on the first night of their honeymoon, the husband removed his pants and tossed them at his wife, saying, "Here, try these on." She said, "I can't wear these pants; they're much too big for me." "You got it!" he replied smugly. "And don't ever forget who wears the pants in this family." Miffed, the young woman went into the bathroom to regain her composure. She returned a few moments later and tossed her panties at her husband, saying, "Here, try these on." Examining the skimpy piece of apparel, he said, "Forget it! I'll never get into these panties." She replied:

You got it!
And until your attitude changes, you never will!

✶ ✶ ✶ ✶ ✶ ✶ ✶ ✶ ✶ ✶ ✶

A number of years ago, a female journalist interviewed a U.S. Army general about a Boy Scout group that was about to spend a weekend at his army base. When the journalist asked what was planned for the scouts, the general recited a list of activities that included climbing, hiking, canoeing, archery, and shooting. Surprised that firearms were on the agenda, the journalist commented that many might consider weapons training to be irresponsible. When the general assured her the scouts would be carefully supervised, the journalist revealed her antigun bias by saying, "But aren't you equipping them to become killers?" The interview ended abruptly when the general replied:

Well, you're equipped to be a prostitute,
but you're not one, now, are you?

✶ ✶ ✶ ✶ ✶ ✶ ✶ ✶ ✶ ✶ ✶

An American woman visiting Scotland asked a traditionally garbed Scotsman if it was true that men so attired wore nothing under their kilts. The man lifted up his kilt, revealed The Full Monty to the startled tourist, and replied proudly in his Scottish accent, "Wha' da ya think o' that, ma'am?" The woman countered:

Well, it looks like a penis,
only smaller.

✶ ✶ ✶ ✶ ✶ ✶ ✶ ✶ ✶ ✶ ✶

Andy Warhol was famous for outrageous publicity stunts, but one in particular stands out from all the others. In the mid-1970s, Warhol arranged for irreverent New York City artist Neke Carson to do his portrait. Carson, who said he painted in the "rectal realist style," employed one of history's most bizarre painting methods. He did his work in a squatting position, head beneath his knees, with a specially constructed felt-tip pen lodged securely in his rectum. On the day of the sitting—a word normally used to describe the subject of a portrait, not the artist's style of painting—Warhol actually documented the session with a series of photographs. After the portrait was completed, Warhol and his associates gathered around to examine the work of art. The cleverest critique of the day came from a Warhol friend who quipped:

Boy, can that asshole paint!

★ ★ ★ ★ ★ ★ ★ ★ ★ ★

Several years ago, the producer of a local television talk show preinterviewed a one-hundred-year-old woman who was scheduled to appear on the show later in the week. At one point, the producer said, "You look in very good health. Have you ever been bedridden?" The sprightly centenarian replied:

Hundreds of times! And once even in a buggy!
But I probably better not mention that on the air!

★ ★ ★ ★ ★ ★ ★ ★ ★ ★

One of the stage's great classical actors, John Gielgud also produced and directed many plays in his career. While once directing a Shakespearean play in which the male actors all wore leotards, he became concerned that the genitals of the men were a bit too distracting. Meeting with the performers, he said that in the future the men would be required to wear jockstraps under their leotards. One of the bit actors, who sensed an opportunity that was not apparent to the other cast members, innocently asked:

Sir John, does that apply to those of us
who only have small parts?

✳ ✳ ✳ ✳ ✳ ✳ ✳ ✳ ✳ ✳ ✳

In the eighteenth century, Sophie Arnould was one of the leading ladies of pre-Revolutionary France. The lead soprano at the Paris Opéra, she was also a ravishing beauty who took many French noblemen as lovers. As she began to grow a bit older, she was challenged by many young and beautiful rivals. Few, however, could match her legendary wit. One night, a beautiful young actress arrived at a Paris salon on the arm of her wealthy lover. Décolleté dresses were all the rage at the time, and the woman was wearing a long diamond necklace that descended deep into her cleavage. When a friend pointed out the sight, Arnould cattily quipped:

It's just returning to its source.

✳ ✳ ✳ ✳ ✳ ✳ ✳ ✳ ✳ ✳ ✳

Actress Tallulah Bankhead was notorious for her offstage behavior, which included abusing various substances, taking off her clothes in public, and having numerous male and female lovers (she once said, "My father warned me about men and alcohol, but he never said anything about women and cocaine"). When Bette Davis, one of the objects of her affection, was about to open a new play, Bankhead sent her one of the most suggestive telegrams of all time. Since Western Union prohibited profanity or graphic language, the message had to be worded in such a way that it would get past the telegraph operator, but be perfectly clear to the recipient. The telegram read:

KISSES ON YOUR OPENING.

✳ ✳ ✳ ✳ ✳ ✳ ✳ ✳ ✳ ✳ ✳

In England in 1964 for the filming of the horror film *Die! Die! My Darling!*, Tallulah Bankhead wandered into the dressing room of newcomer Donald Sutherland, who had a bit part in the film. As the young actor turned around, he was astonished to see the sixty-something Bankhead standing there stark naked. A few speechless moments passed and all Sutherland could do was stare at the sight before him. Finally, Bankhead said,

**What's the matter, dahling?
Haven't you ever seen a real blonde before?**

★ ★ ★ ★ ★ ★ ★ ★ ★ ★ ★

After a long day of shooting a film in Hollywood, John Barrymore and some fellow actors stopped in at Lucey's, a popular watering hole near Paramount Studios. After one too many drinks, Barrymore excused himself to go to the bathroom. In his slightly inebriated condition, however, he inadvertently chose the ladies' room. As he was relieving himself, a woman entered and was shocked to see a man urinating into one of the toilets. "How dare you!" she exclaimed. "This is for ladies!" The actor turned toward the woman, organ in hand, and resonantly said in full actor's voice:

And so, madam, is this.

★ ★ ★ ★ ★ ★ ★ ★ ★ ★ ★

After a lengthy career that included many bravura Shakespearean performances, John Barrymore was frequently invited to lecture on Shakespeare to students. During one seminar, he was asked, "Did Romeo and Juliet enjoy a full physical relationship?" For a moment, Barrymore seemed deep in thought, looking as if he were about to deliver a major Shakespearean interpretation. Then he replied:

They certainly did in the Chicago company.

✳ ✳ ✳ ✳ ✳ ✳ ✳ ✳ ✳ ✳ ✳

During Sir Thomas Beecham's half-century career as conductor of some of the great orchestras of the world, he developed a reputation as a man with a caustic wit and an acerbic tongue. At a rehearsal of the London Philharmonic one day, Beecham became increasingly frustrated by the subpar performance of the orchestra's female cellist. Finally, in exasperation, he said:

> **Madam, you have between your legs**
> **an instrument capable of giving pleasure to thousands—**
> **and all you can do is scratch it!**

✳ ✳ ✳ ✳ ✳ ✳ ✳ ✳ ✳ ✳ ✳

Even though Augustus Caesar ruled the Roman Empire with an autocratic hand for forty years, he had trouble controlling members of his own family, particularly his rebellious daughter, Julia. During her marriage to her father's top general, Marcus Agrippa, Julia had five children, but Roman society abounded with rumors that she was notoriously unfaithful. Embarrassed and angry, Caesar exiled her for five years to a remote island prison where she was allowed no contact with men. During happier times, one of Julia's friends remarked to her that, despite her many infidelities, all of her children bore an amazing resemblance to her husband. Julia explained:

> **That is because passengers**
> **are never allowed on board**
> **until the hold is full.**

✳ ✳ ✳ ✳ ✳ ✳ ✳ ✳ ✳ ✳ ✳

Winston Churchill and his Conservative Party were often at odds with the postwar reforms of Clement Attlee and his Labour Party. During Attlee's five years as prime minister, England's National Health Service was formed and many industries, including banking, coal, steel, aviation, and railway, were nationalized. One day, Churchill entered a men's room in the House of Commons and noticed Attlee at a urinal. Without saying anything, Churchill chose a urinal at the opposite side of the room. When Attlee took notice of Churchill, he said, "Feeling a bit standoffish today, Winston?" Churchill, who may have been waiting for this moment for years, replied:

> **That's right, Clement.**
> **Every time you see something big,**
> **you want to nationalize it.**

★ ★ ★ ★ ★ ★ ★ ★ ★ ★

Every country has a Great Seal that is used on major official documents, and a number of minor seals as well. After the Great Seal, the next most important seal in England is the Privy Seal. The keeper of the seal is known as the Lord Privy Seal, a position that goes back more than four centuries. A ceremonial position without major responsibilities, the post has been awarded to many well-known English politicians as a sinecure. In a story that has been circulating since the middle of World War II, Winston Churchill was happily ensconced one day in his private bathroom at 10 Downing Street when an aide knocked on the door and said, "Mr. Churchill, the Lord Privy Seal wishes to see you immediately." The keeper of the seal at the time was Clement Attlee, a man Churchill struggled with many times. Churchill barked at the aide from the other side of the door:

> **Tell the Lord Privy Seal that I'm sealed in the privy**
> **and can only deal with one shit at a time.**

★ ★ ★ ★ ★ ★ ★ ★ ★ ★

Noël Coward was once walking down a London street with Laurence Olivier and his daughter Tamsin. The young girl, noticing two dogs copulating on a nearby lawn, interrupted the two adults to eagerly—but innocently—ask, "What are they doing? What are they doing?" Before Olivier could forge an acceptable, age-appropriate answer, Coward jumped in and said:

> **It's like this, dear girl.**
> **The dog in front has gone blind,**
> **and the one behind has very kindly offered**
> **to push him all the way to St. Dunstan's.**

★ ★ ★ ★ ★ ★ ★ ★ ★ ★ ★

Like many actors, Russell Crowe worked as a waiter early in his career. As is often the case with people whose hearts are not really in their work, he occasionally screwed up customers' orders. One day, while working in a restaurant in Sydney, he waited on an American woman who ordered a cup of decaffeinated coffee. A few moments later, after Crowe mistakenly delivered a cup of hot water instead, the irate tourist barked at him, "Waiter! This isn't coffee, it's just boiling water!" Crowe was fired for his rejoinder, but his reply has been passed along by aspiring actors ever since:

> **Lady, when we decaffeinate something in Australia,**
> **we don't fuck around!**

★ ★ ★ ★ ★ ★ ★ ★ ★ ★ ★

In the early decades of the nineteenth century, John Doherty was a rising star in Irish politics, starting off as a Dublin attorney and ending up as Lord Chief Justice of Ireland. A man of wit and wisdom, he once attended a gala social event at Dublin Castle, where many of the female guests were wearing extremely low cut gowns. A male companion, delighted at the abundant décolletage all around the room, exclaimed to Doherty, "Have you ever seen anything like it since you were born?" The Lord Chief Justice replied:

> **I can't say since I was born,**
> **but certainly since I was weaned.**

★ ★ ★ ★ ★ ★ ★ ★ ★ ★

The actress Betsy Drake, who was once married to Cary Grant, was invited to attend a party on the opulent yacht of the Greek shipping tycoon Aristotle Onassis. While sitting at the bar, someone said, "Did you know that the bar stool you are sitting on comes from the skin of a whale's penis?" Ms. Drake jumped up in mock surprise and exclaimed:

Oh my God! Moby's dick!

★ ★ ★ ★ ★ ★ ★ ★ ★ ★

A few years ago, actor David Duchovny posed for a controversial photo shoot. In one series of pictures, the reclining actor appeared totally nude, except for a discreetly placed coffee cup. The cup, which was placed upside down over the genital area, encased the actor's private parts, much like a jockstrap cup would do. Married to actress Téa Leoni, the actor was asked by a reporter what his wife thought about the publicity stunt. He replied, "At first, she thought it was funny. Then she thought I was an idiot for doing it." He paused for a moment and concluded:

And finally, she's vowed
never to drink out of that cup again!

★ ★ ★ ★ ★ ★ ★ ★ ★ ★

In his monologue on NBC's *The Tonight Show with Jay Leno* a few years ago, Jay Leno reported, "A recent study has found that, on average, gay men have substantially larger organs than straight men." After a titter of laughter went through the audience, Leno added with a tone of mock surprise, "Oh my God! Do you know what that means? I'm gay!" The best line of the evening, however, came from Kevin Eubanks, the show's bandleader. Playing on the popular stereotype about African American men, Eubanks quipped:

You think *you're* gay!

✳ ✳ ✳ ✳ ✳ ✳ ✳ ✳ ✳ ✳ ✳

W. C. Fields and other comedians of his era went to great lengths to write risqué material that would get by studio censors but still be obvious to most theater-goers. In the 1933 film *International House*, Fields assembled an all-star cast, including Rudy Vallee, Cab Calloway, Bela Lugosi, George Burns, and Gracie Allen, to produce a wacky farce about a group of American travelers quarantined in a Shanghai hotel. In one scene, a woman exclaims, "I tell you I'm sitting on something! Something's under me! What is it?" Fields reaches under the woman and pulls out a cat, saying:

Ah, a pussy!

✳ ✳ ✳ ✳ ✳ ✳ ✳ ✳ ✳ ✳ ✳

A member of the English literary coterie called the Bloomsbury Group, David Garnett may not have achieved the fame of other members (like Virginia Woolf and E. M. Forster), but he was a prolific and well-regarded writer in the early twentieth century. In an interview a few years before his death in 1981, the aging Garnett was asked, "Have you had homosexual leanings?" He pondered the question for a moment and then replied:

More leaned upon than leaning, I'd have thought.

✳ ✳ ✳ ✳ ✳ ✳ ✳ ✳ ✳ ✳ ✳

In 1995, Los Angeles cops arrested English actor Hugh Grant when they found him seated in his own car, enjoying a familiar streetwalker service provided by an L.A. prostitute named Divine Brown. News of the arrest spread rapidly, and the actor's mug shot was soon being e-mailed around the world. While the news was still on everybody's mind, Grant appeared on *The Tonight Show with Jay Leno*. As soon as Grant sat down, Leno began the interview by asking, "What the hell were you thinking?" Leno's question brought howls of laughter from the audience, who were clearly wondering how the subject would be broached. When the laughter subsided, the exceedingly clever Grant brought the house down when he mumbled softly in reply:

I'm not one to go around blowing my own trumpet.

★ ★ ★ ★ ★ ★ ★ ★ ★ ★

One of the great beauties of the English stage, the turn-of-the-century actress Lillie Langtry was for a time the mistress of Edward, the Prince of Wales (later King Edward VII). Edward, who couldn't have been more different from his strictly principled mother, Queen Victoria, was a fun-loving pleasure seeker who had numerous mistresses (he was dubbed Edward the Caresser by Henry James). During a lovers' quarrel, Edward once groused to Langtry, "I've spent enough on you to buy a battleship!" She retorted:

And you've spent enough *in* me to *float* one!

★ ★ ★ ★ ★ ★ ★ ★ ★ ★

In the early 1990s, an intriguing tale about the young Willie Nelson began making the rounds. A woman had come forward with the astounding claim that she once engaged in sexual intercourse with Nelson for nine consecutive hours. As if that weren't impressive enough, she added that the lovemaking concluded with Nelson doing a full backward somersault, while the two lovers were still completely coupled. When a reporter asked Nelson about the veracity of the report, he replied:

I'm not saying it didn't happen,
but you would've thought I'd remember
at least the last four or five hours.

✩ ✩ ✩ ✩ ✩ ✩ ✩ ✩ ✩ ✩ ✩

Before *The Odd Couple* was a hit movie and successful television sitcom, it was an award-winning Broadway play, directed by Mike Nichols and starring Walter Matthau as Oscar Madison and Art Carney as Felix Unger. In rehearsals for the play one day in 1965, insults filled the air in an acrimonious exchange between Nichols and Matthau. The battle ended abruptly when Nichols delivered a crushing verbal blow. An awkward silence descended on the stage. As the cast and crew squirmed in discomfort, Matthau recovered his composure and did his best to lighten the mood. "Hey, Mike," he said. "Can I have my prick back?" The sense of relief on the stage was immediate. But it was transformed into howls of laughter when Nichols snapped a finger to a stagehand and barked out:

Props!

✩ ✩ ✩ ✩ ✩ ✩ ✩ ✩ ✩ ✩ ✩

In 1926, Dorothy Parker published a book of light verse and humorous sketches titled *Enough Rope*. The book, which contained the oft-quoted poem "Résumé," a darkly comic poem about suicide, became a best-seller, giving Parker the financial wherewithal to seek a replacement for her tiny Manhattan digs. One day, walking out of a luxurious apartment she had just looked at with her realtor, Parker was asked what she thought of the place. Fond of shocking people with off-color remarks, she replied:

Oh, dear, it's much too big.
All I need is enough room to lay a hat—and a few friends.

✩ ✩ ✩ ✩ ✩ ✩ ✩ ✩ ✩ ✩ ✩

At the height of Dorothy Parker's fame, a popular Broadway play featured a character that was based loosely on her life. When a friend asked her why she had not yet seen the play, Parker offered a reply that was so clever that even people normally offended by profanity had to admit they admired it:

**I've been too fucking busy,
and vice versa.**

✶ ✶ ✶ ✶ ✶ ✶ ✶ ✶ ✶ ✶

Dorothy Parker named her pet canary Onan. When people asked, as many did, "Why did you name your canary Onan?" she had a stock answer:

Because he spills his seed upon the ground.

This is a reference to Genesis 38:9. After the death of his eldest son, Judah asked second son Onan to honor an ancient tradition and impregnate his brother's barren widow. Although Onan cohabited with his sister-in-law, he "spilled his seed upon the ground" in an effort to avoid impregnating her. Over the years, "Onanism" became the eponym for masturbation, even though it looks like he technically engaged in "coitus interruptus."

✶ ✶ ✶ ✶ ✶ ✶ ✶ ✶ ✶ ✶

In the middle of the twentieth century, S. J. Perelman was regarded as one of the era's best humorists (William Zinsser described him as "the funniest man alive"). Known for his witty wordplay, his exceptional punning ability even showed up in his personal life. During a trip to the Far East, Perelman was hounded by a group of aggressive prostitutes in Taipei. It took some doing on his part, but Perelman was finally able to shake them. When the disheveled wit finally arrived back at his hotel, a friend asked what had happened. In a clever reversal of the old saying, Perelman replied:

It was a case of the tail dogging the wag.

★ ★ ★ ★ ★ ★ ★ ★ ★ ★ ★

Oliver St. John Gogarty was a Dublin physician who also established a reputation as a pretty fair writer. A friend of James Joyce, William Butler Yeats, George Moore, and George Russell, he wrote a number of highly entertaining memoirs about the Dublin of his youth, including the 1939 book *Tumbling in the Hay*. In one reminiscence, he told of a public meeting that was held to discuss rampant prostitution that was threatening to take over a public park along the banks of Dublin's Liffey River. During the heated meeting, an antiprostitution zealot proposed a radical solution: cutting down all the trees in the park. While many in the meeting were horrified at the suggestion, Gogarty remained calm and won the day for his side when he observed:

Surely the trees are more sinned against than sinning.

★ ★ ★ ★ ★ ★ ★ ★ ★ ★ ★

In an after-dinner discussion with other members of London's Hellfire Club, the eighteenth-century English prelate George Selwyn was told a fascinating story about a father, son, and grandson who had all shared the same mistress, passing her on from generation to generation. While most members of the group considered this quite remarkable, one member of the club, who had heard a similar story years earlier, casually remarked, "There's nothing new under the sun." Selwyn quipped:

Nor under the grandson.

★ ★ ★ ★ ★ ★ ★ ★ ★ ★ ★

In the early 1900s, Lytton Strachey was a prominent member of the Bloomsbury Group. Even though engaged for a time to Virginia Woolf, he was a self-proclaimed homosexual, a rarity at the time. During World War I, Strachey sought exemption from military service as a conscientious objector. Appearing before a military tribunal, he was grilled by members of the board, some of whom were openly hostile to his case. At one point, the head of the tribunal challenged him by asking, "What would you do if you saw a German soldier trying to violate your sister?" Strachey's reply went over the head of his interrogator, but has been celebrated ever since by those who admire the clever use of language. He replied:

I would try to get between them.

★ ★ ★ ★ ★ ★ ★ ★ ★ ★

At a Hollywood gathering in the 1950s, the actor Clifton Webb and the beautiful Sophia Loren were seated next to one another when the buxom Jayne Mansfield—famous for her scene-stealing publicity stunts—sashayed up to the table, leaned in provocatively, and prominently displayed her most obvious physical assets. Mansfield was usually successful in upstaging fellow actors, but this moment went to Webb, who said:

**Please, Miss Mansfield,
we're wine drinkers at this table.**

★ ★ ★ ★ ★ ★ ★ ★ ★ ★

After a film version of Gore Vidal's *Myra Breckinridge* was released in 1970, it was soon being described as one of the worst films of the year. The idea of Rex Reed (as gay film critic Myron Breckinridge) having a sex-change operation and morphing into Raquel Welch (as Myra) strained the credibility of many moviegoers, as did the sight of seventy-five-year-old Mae West playing a sex-starved theatrical agent. In one scene, West is a caricature of her earlier self when she seductively asks a handsome young cowboy how tall he is and he answers, "Well, ma'am, I'm six feet, seven inches." In a line that might have worked three or four decades earlier, she replies:

Let's forget about the six feet and talk about the seven inches.

index